How to Manage Children's Challenging Behaviour

Second edition

"It's easy to see why Bill Rogers is revered by generations of teachers across the world. The stories assembled here are compelling and reflective. They will provide a stimulus and support to teachers 'cutting and chipping themselves into the shape of the key which will have the merit of unlocking the minds and opening the hearts of the pupils they teach'. Bill's overview and commentary will as usual resonate with schools and teachers. It deserves a place along with his other books in the staff library. Any one of the case studies here, along with Bill's observations, could form the basis of any school working group examining the issue of 'behaviour'. It's bound to lead to an improvement among pupils, parents and staff. And it will help teachers at the end of their tether both preserve their sanity and extend the tether!"

Sir Tim Brighouse, Advisor, Hamlyn Foundation and Visiting Professor, Institute of Education, University of London

HOW TO MANAGE CHILDREN'S CHALLENGING BEHAVIOUR

Second edition

Edited by Bill Rogers

Los Angeles | London | New Delhi
Singapore | Washington DC

First published 2004
Reprinted 2004, 2005 and 2006
Second edition published 2009

SAGE Publications Ltd
1 Oliver's Yard
55 City Road
London EC1Y 1SP

SAGE Publications Inc.
2455 Teller Road
Thousand Oaks, California 91320

SAGE Publications India Pvt Ltd
B 1/I 1 Mohan Cooperative Industrial Area
Mathura Road
New Delhi 110 044

SAGE Publications Asia-Pacific Pte Ltd
33 Pekin Street #02–01
Far East Square
Singapore 048763

Library of Congress Control Number: 2009920950

British Library Cataloguing in Publication data

A catalogue record for this book is available from the British Library

ISBN 978–1-84860–684-5
ISBN 978–1-84860–685-2 (pbk)

Typeset by Dorwyn, Wells, Somerset
Printed in Great Britain by T.J. International Ltd, Padstow, Cornwall
Printed on paper from sustainable resources

Contents

Acknowledgements

To all my colleagues who have taken time to share their stories; for their honesty, commitment and patient goodwill recounted here.

This is their book.

These are their children, their students. (We often use the 'possessive' pronoun, don't we, when we talk of 'our' students?)

Having worked in many, many classrooms as a mentor teacher, I want – also – to thank the teachers who have allowed me to teach alongside them and, over endless cups of tea and coffee, try to continue to make 'noticeable and positive sense of it all'.

My thanks to my colleagues at Griffith University, particularly Bette Blanche, Dr Alan Edwards and Professor Neil Russell who have supported this project from the outset.

To my colleagues at SAGE Publications who have encouraged me in this project, particularly Marianne Lagrange and Joyce Lynch. In enabling this second edition, I also wish to thank Jude Bowen and Amy Jarrold, Jeanette Graham and all the team at SAGE Publications (London) for their constant encouragement and support, often at a distance (from the UK to Australia).

I want to thank Sir Tim Brighouse for his generous – and kind – support and feedback to this project.

To Felicia Schmidt for taking on *another* pressured typing task – thanks again.

All royalties from the sale of this book go to World Vision. As editor (with my colleagues), we are greatly encouraged to know that the money raised goes directly to educational programmes in South East Asia.

World Vision have asked me to thank all the contributors for that support.

And to my family – Lora, Elizabeth and Sarah – as ever – many thanks.

Bill Rogers
January 2009

About the Editor

Dr Bill Rogers (editor and contributor) has been an education consultant for the last 20 years and was an adjunct professor (education) at Griffith University, Queensland, Australia, for many years. Bill works in every area of education (primary, post-primary and tertiary) conducting in-service programmes for teachers, lecturing widely at colleges of education and universities, and working with parent groups and students in schools. He is the author of many journal articles and contributions to magazines (in Australia and the UK) and has published a number of books in Australia and the UK. Some of these books have since been translated into other languages (Danish, Polish, Estonian, Chinese and Portugese). He lectures in Australia, the UK and Europe. Dr Rogers is a Fellow of the Australian College of Education (Canberra) and Honorary Life Fellow of Trinity and All Saints College (University of Leeds). He has received awards for Excellence in Education from the Victorian College of Education and the Australian Council for Educational Administration.

   Visit Bill's website – www.billrogers.com.au – for the latest information on where he is lecturing and conducting seminars.

Contributors

Some of the contributors in this book have preferred not to name their school for natural reasons of ethical probity. The names of individual children in each account have been changed for the same reason.

Bette Blance heads up a professional development team (Bette Blance and Associates) in New Zealand. Previously, Bette has been a school principal and was (until recently) Associate Director of the Centre for Professional Development at Griffith University (Australia)

Pamela Curtain is a primary teacher and an education consultant currently supporting schools in Queensland.

Peter D'Angelo is an experienced secondary English teacher. A migrant to Australia, he has always worked in school settings with high multicultural populations. He is also a poet and has had several books of poetry published. Peter's essays are courtesy of *Education Quarterly Australia* (many thanks to Kathy Skelton) and *The Age* newspaper (Melbourne) – and, in particular, thanks to Larry Schwartz for his support.

Ros Daniels is a senior primary school teacher who has worked in schools in southern England. Ros has also been an education consultant to schools in the area of behaviour management and discipline.

Gail Doney is currently deputy principal of a large school near Melbourne and has had many years of experience in primary teaching.

Sharn Donnison has been a practising teacher both in Australia and overseas. At present, Sharn works as an associate lecturer at Griffith University, Queensland. She teaches in the Faculty of Education in the areas of educational psychology, sociology and communication. Her area of interest is concerned with young people's conceptualisations of the future and the cultural realities they appropriate to formulate those visions of the future.

Patsy Finger is a senior primary school teacher currently teaching in Queensland. Patsy has developed a number of initiatives in the area of behaviour support.

Heather Fraser is an experienced primary school teacher. She has taught widely (particularly in country Victoria).

Denise Frost is an experienced primary school teacher currently teaching in Tasmania.

Debbie Hoy is the principal of an infant school near London. Debbie has also had wide experience of consulting to schools in the area of behaviour management and supporting children with special needs.

Karen Kearney is a 'beginning' (mature age) teacher in Queensland. Karen has also been a member of the Australian army and police force. She has worked with young people in Police–Citizens' Youth Clubs and believes sport can be a key tool in educational outcomes.

Jim Gilbert has been a school principal and an educational advisor to many schools in New Zealand for many years.

Elizabeth McPherson (née Rogers) has taught as a primary school teacher in Melbourne. She is currently on leave, mother to three children. She has recently co-authored a book on early years teaching.

Kerrie Miller is an experienced integration teacher currently working in country Victoria. Kerrie works with a wide range of children with special needs.

Alyson Dermody Palmer is deputy head teacher at a Pupil Referral Unit for primary-aged children in London. She has worked with children with special needs for many years.

Carmen Price is a behaviour management psychologist of many years experience and works – widely – with schools in Queensland.

Carmel Ryan is the deputy principal of Labrador State School in Queensland. Carmel and her colleagues have developed a whole-school model for behaviour and learning. Their approach emphasises the concept of a 'peaceable school', emphasising problem-solving, mediation and resolving issues of concern.

Larry Schwartz is a journalist with the *Age* newspaper in Melbourne, Australia.

Ken Sell is an experienced teacher of over 15 years. For the last three years, he has been working as an advisory support teacher for Education Queensland in the Nambour District on the Sunshine Coast. He has designed and implemented many in-service workshops relevant to primary and secondary teachers as well as advising administrators in areas of social equity and the interpersonal dynamics found within schools. Ken is presently finishing a research project relating to his work in schools.

Mara Smart is the deputy principal of Musgrave Hill State School, Queensland. Mara was formerly a behaviour advisory teacher.

Maureen Smyth is a head teacher of a school for students with emotional and behavioural disorders. Maureen has taught in the area of special needs and behaviour disorders for many years in England.

Larry Taylor has, over 30 years, worked in schools as a classroom teacher with Years 2 to 7, as an educational advisor in effective learning and teaching, and as a learning support and learning technology teacher. He has accreditation in the Myers-Briggs personality type indicator and Dr William Glasser's 'Choice Theory'.

Mariette West is a teacher at Musgrave Hill State School, Queensland. Mariette, Pamela and Mara have developed a number of behaviour management plans for children with special needs and behaviour disorders.

Cathy Whalen is the head teacher of a primary school in central England. She has taught for many years in the primary sector in England.

Leanne Wright is an experienced secondary teacher (in Tasmania) currently supporting schools in the area of consultancy in behaviour management, student welfare and discipline.

Note: In the UK, a school principal is called a head teacher.

A teacher's response has crucial consequences ... it creates a climate of compliance or defiance, a mood of contentment or contention, a desire to make amends or to take revenge ...

Teachers have the power to affect a child's life for better or worse. A child becomes what he/she experiences. While parents possess the original key to their offspring's experience, teachers have a spare key.

They, too, can open or close the minds and hearts of children.

Haim Ginott (1971)

In the morning when you rise unwillingly let this thought be present – I am rising to the work of a human being.

Marcus Aurelius (*The Meditations of Marcus Aurelius V*)

All royalties from the sale of this book are donated to the charity *World Vision* for children's health and education programmes in South East Asia.

***World Vision* is a charity that places a special emphasis on ensuring the needs and rights of children are met, because they are often the hardest hit by conflict, disaster and chronic poverty. To provide long-term, ongoing care for children in crisis, World Vision developed its first child sponsorship programme in Korea in 1953. As children began to flourish through sponsorship in Korea, the programme expanded into other Asian countries and eventually into Latin America, Africa, Eastern Europe and the Middle East.**

Introduction

Bill Rogers

This book came about as a result of working directly alongside teachers working with challenging children and children with emotional behaviour disorders. My colleagues and I believed that these accounts deserved a much wider audience. The direct, practical and positive nature of these accounts will immediately resonate with teachers.

These teachers (from Australia and the UK) work with children in mainstream and special education settings. Some I have worked with as a mentor teacher. These accounts range across primary and secondary school settings; from individual children with challenging (and EBD) behaviour through to whole-class settings where challenging and problem behaviour has been effectively addressed by these teachers.

Teachers spend a third of their waking and working day with children. Most teachers in most schools on most days engage students in their learning with effort, energy and goodwill. Many teachers have a passion for making a difference – even a 'deceptively small' difference in children's lives. Their goodwill, energy and patience is sometimes stretched 'to the limit' by some of the children they are called on to teach, 'manage' and support. Some of the children we read of in these accounts are children whose family dynamic does not always support what schools seek to be and do. The 'causative pathology' of some of these children is disturbing, distressing – even dysfunctional – yet these teachers never 're-victimise' a child by saying, 'What can we do with him? What can we expect? Look where he comes from ...!' While these teachers know that there are many factors that affect a child's behaviour (and learning potential), they also know that *behaviour is also developed, and learned, and can be supportively changed in context*. The context of the school can make a significant difference to children's behaviour, self-concept and self-esteem as these accounts testify.

All the teachers who have written here believe that they can, and will, make a difference in the lives of 'their' children. That is why they chose to be teachers.

I am frequently encouraged by the incredible moral energy of the sort demonstrated and lived out by these teachers. In sharing their experiences more widely, I trust you, too, will be encouraged. These teachers have made a difference – a significant difference at times – to the lives of their children. These teachers remind us of what we went into teaching for.

The teachers in this book have shared not just 'accounts' of their children – their teaching and management – they have shared themselves with us. Their honesty, their goodwill, their courage, their passion for what they do (and why) comes across clearly to us. The 'immediacy' of these 'stories' creates that common bond we have with our colleagues.

These narratives are, at times, intensely personal and moving. My colleagues have all indicated that they share these accounts – these 'narratives' – to remind each other of our common struggle yet also to identify our shared journey, shared hopes and to celebrate our profession. I wish these accounts could be read more widely by 'the public' so they – too – could more consciously celebrate our profession. At least the parents of the children recounted here know these teachers made a difference.

All teachers, at every level in a school, face similar issues of behaviour from the typical calling out, butting in, inappropriate loudness (in a very small room) through to the more disturbing issues of bullying, violence and behaviour disorders. Every teacher has also had to address the question of how to meaningfully and realistically support that small percentage of students who present with emotional and behavioural disorders. This 'small' percentage – one to five per cent in most schools (Rogers, 2003) – have the potential to 'eat up' a lot of teacher time and energy, effort and goodwill. These teachers, and the schools in which they were supported, share the realistic and practical measures they took to support these children.

This book addresses the issue of challenging behaviours and behaviour disorders in schools and how teachers – in a supportive collegial team – have made a significant difference to their students. They have made a direct difference in terms of the students' behaviour, attitude, self-esteem and peer acceptance.

Sharn Donnison notes that such narratives can be understood, celebrated and utilised in our professional journey:

> Narratives are active and not just passive retelling of events gone by. They are a way of making meaning out of the experiences of (our) everyday life; of visualising the world, organising the past and explaining the present. They help us identify, create, and justify our place in the world. (2004: 114)

Preface to the second edition

The original project (this book) began while I was an adjunct professor of education at Griffith University in Australia. The purpose of the book was to invite teachers to share their experiences, understandings, ideas and skills of working with children who present with challenging behaviour. This they have done with willingness, candour, realism *and hope*. As they share their accounts, we hear their frustration, stress and pain as well as their professional goodwill, humanity and hope.

In this second edition, we have added a new chapter – 'supporting parents of children with challenging behaviour'. *Some* parents, too, have challenging behaviours arising from stressful and complex life journeys. My colleagues have sought to share how we can support such parents with understanding – remembering, always, that the bond between parent and child is crucial to the child's well-being and development. As you read, where we use the term parent, we mean the parent, guardian or carer of the child.

At all times, my colleagues have been sensitive to the ethical probity involved in such narrative writing. Names of children and parents have been changed, and no school (as such) is identified without the permission of the school and parent/s.

As much as possible, I have tried to let my colleagues share their own stories; to let their voices engage the central learnings we can all draw from these accounts.

In Chapter 6, I have drawn together the key principles of behaviour leadership that clearly emerge from their work with children.

I have been encouraged and supported by these narratives of my colleagues. I hope you, too, will be similarly encouraged to 'make a difference' with your students and colleagues.

Bill Rogers and colleagues, 2009

Opportunities for Reflection

There are many texts that address the issues, practices and skills of behaviour management and discipline; this is not primarily that kind of text. The reviews of the first edition were uniformly positive – we are thankful for that. One teacher reviewer said it would be helpful to add some 'tools of the trade' (as it were) – a kind of 'box of tricks', to help with the management of challenging children's behaviour. I am reminded of the old saying, 'Don't learn the "tricks of the trade" – learn the trade'. There are no 'tricks of the trade' here. We manage – if at all well – *because of the kind of teacher we choose to be*. Those choices (over our years of teaching) are clearly based in skills and approaches to management that seek to build relationships with children that enable trust, confidence and hope.

These skills and approaches (I resist the word 'techniques') are not easy to delineate in a text like this. Wherever possible (and appropriate), I have added editorial reflection, comment and postscript that I trust will help. Most of all though, I ask you to read the teachers here and let our profession speak, through observing the kind of teachers who work with challenging children.

These essays are designed to engage a collegial discussion – in print. It is an opportunity for colleagues *to share their direct experiences*, and from that sharing engage our thinking about children and challenging behaviours. As we read our colleagues' accounts, I would encourage you to reflect on:

- How would we address the issues, situations and concerns shared here?
- How would we address the sorts of challenging behaviours we read of here? What would we say or do?
- When confronted by extreme behaviours (and those that arise from trauma); when confronted with angry and aggressive children and even hostile and angry parents, what would we say or do?
- And, most of all, why? As we read these intensely personal – and challenging – accounts of children, teachers and parents, we will (no doubt) be reminded of similar situations we have had to face. It is important to ask, *what would we do*? But crucially we also need to ask why. Utility is no proof of good practice; any humanity in our practice must be grounded in our values (the *why* we do what we do). In all aspects of our leadership, we need to remember the relational dynamic without which any skill or practice can become mere 'technique'.

As we make our personal and collegial response to these accounts, I encourage you to raise and explore such questions.

Note

This text does not detail clinical aspects of behaviour disorders or research on medication-assisted therapies for children with behaviour disorders. Colleagues are directed to the excellent text, *Handbook of Emotional and Behavioural Difficulties* (2005) by Clough et al.

Further reading

Kyriacou, C. (1992) *Effective Teaching in Schools*, second edition. Cheltenham: Nelson Thornes.

Robertson, J. (1996) *Effective Classroom Control*, third edition. London: Hodder & Stoughton.

Rogers, B. (2003) *Behaviour Recovery*, second edition. Melbourne: Australian Council for Educational Research. (In the UK, London: Sage Publications.)

Rogers, B. (2006) *Classroom Behaviour*, second edition. London: Sage Publications.

Rogers, B. (2006) *Behaviour Management: A Whole-School Approach*, second edition. Sydney: Scholastic Publications. (In the UK, London: Sage Publications.)

Chapter 1

Challenging Behaviour:
Our Thinking, Attitudes and Strategy

We cannot predict where our students may end up

Bill Rogers

Some teachers get into a habit of predicting what will happen to 'their charges' – where they'll probably 'end up'. 'He'll never get anywhere, he's lazy, slow, doesn't concentrate, doesn't apply himself ... '; 'He's so stupid ...' 'He'll never amount to anything; 'He'll probably end up in jail ...' . I had a few teachers who told me I'd 'never amount to anything'.

When we struggle to make sense of children's behaviour – in a school context – it can be tempting to make easy judgements about their future. I have done it myself as a teacher. In reflecting on the many challenging students I've worked with, I've sometimes predicted and been proved wrong. The issue is not whether we are 'right' or 'wrong' in our predictions, but that predicting – as such – is unhelpful. Like the well-known 'expectancy effect' (Rosenthal and Jacobson, 1986), it can unwittingly affect our relationship and our directed beliefs about how effectively we can work with the student in their learning and behaviour.

These four essays address how teachers reflect on such predictive teacher behaviour and the effect it can have on their students' learning and behaviour.

I had some strange teachers in the 1950s in post-war Britain. It was a different time, a different society with different hierarchies and social structure. The authority and power of teachers – particularly at school – was rarely questioned (at least by most 'pupils'). If I 'chatted' in class or spoke while the teacher was teaching, I had chalk thrown at me, was verbally chastised many times, got a 'thick ear' (a smack across the ear, or ear pulling – ouch!!) or had to do detention. (I had many detentions while at school – mostly for what teachers today would regard as minor 'infractions'.) Talking while the teacher was talking was considered a serious disruptive behaviour by some teachers. On one such occasion (when I was 14), a teacher strode over to my desk and jabbed my shoulder with a vigorous, kinaesthetic finger, demanding to know if I was 'brought up or dragged up' (in reference to my chatting quietly to my mate during 'class instruction'). I can still hear the words. It was the only occasion when I physically stood up to a teacher, standing – facing him – and said, 'It's none of your bloody business!' No teacher was going to have a go at my parents! I walked out of the classroom to a stunned silence – my heart thumping. Some of my classmates at the back of the classroom gave me a surreptitious thumbs up and wry smiles as I walked past them. I was a kind of 'Trojan horse' for the class group. Even then (1960), I think this teacher realised he'd gone too far.

I 'answered teachers back' on other occasions – mostly I got detentions; on other occasions I got the cane. I once got caned (hands and back of leg) by the headmaster for breaking a pencil which a student had initially snatched from me. The principal (supervising our class) had only seen me; he miscued, mistargetted and I had 'argued' and 'answered back' to him and was consequently 'rude'. I got the cane. No right of reply in those days. This same principal once pulled at my ear so badly he scored a nail print that drew blood at the back of my ear – another ouch! It was the only occasion my mother went to the school in my 'defence' – she was magnificent as she told him what she would do if he *ever* laid his hands on me again. He apologised (reluctantly), becoming annoyingly sycophantic the following day. I had little respect already for this head teacher; I lost any after this episode.

It is interesting – in forgiving retrospect – to wonder what I would do as a teacher in similar situations to those of my teachers in the '50s and early '60s. I know what I would not do. I wouldn't make a student move briskly up and down three flights of stairs as a punishment for not paying attention in science class and 'being *stupid*' with weights and pulleys – 'a little unthinking perhaps, hardly stupid, Mr Siddons' – 'Don't answer back, Rogers. Take those 4 lb weights' (one in each hand, they had rings on their semi-pyramidal structures) 'and walk briskly up and down' (three flights of stairs) 'and then report straight back here to me!' All of this (of course) in front of fellow students who – in part – grinned and who – in part – were glad it wasn't them!

Once outside the classroom, I went and sat at the bottom of the stairs for five minutes or so. I came back into the class feigning breathlessness. (Was he *really* so stupid in thinking I'd actually carry two 4 lb weights up three flights of stairs?! Apparently, he believed I was that 'biddable'.) 'Now will you learn?! Let that be a lesson to you.' He berated me in front of my peers. I gave a suitable – demure – 'I-have-learned' look and went back to the entrails of my weights and pulleys experiment. My fellow students and I believed this kind of teacher behaviour was 'par for the course'. The way that some teachers spoke to, treated and managed children in sarcastic, petty and punitive ways was enculturated. That never makes it right; it does make it harder to challenge and change.

My 'challenging behaviour'

Two days before I left high school in 1961 (summer term in Great Britain), I went to school half an hour earlier than normal; secreted under my jumper was a very large painting on oil paper. I had painted a portrait of my science teacher surrounded by several other luminaries (portraits of teachers I didn't like). It was painted after the manner of Salvador Dali, the Spanish surrealist painter. Dali was (apparently) inspired by Freudian theories of the unconscious. I didn't know this at the time but I had read of his work (at the library) and been inspired by Dali's 'melting', dreamlike surrealist imagery. It took me a few weeks to get the painting 'right'. I'm colour blind so the colours must have looked interesting.

On the day in question, I arrived early at school, complete with sturdy drawing pins and, alone, I pinned it on the large notice board just inside the double doors (the main entrance) – at least I thought I was alone. A prefect had espied me. In those days, some prefects were like quasi police. He reported me.

At morning form assembly, Mr Siddons (my form master and the discipline master – his title) held up my unsigned picture. 'This is yours, is it not, Rogers?' I didn't deny it – I was rather proud of it, only I hadn't planned *this* kind of exposure. 'You know what's going to happen to you, don't you?' Suitably mollified, I said 'Yes'. 'Lunchtime – my office.' I sighed – the cane again, and just two days before the end of term. As he dismissed us, I saw him take the rolled-up painting into his office, close the door and walk off. I quietly and carefully sneaked in after he had gone, retrieved my property and waited for a suitable moment before period 1 to put it back on the notice board. I then hot-footed it up to Level 3 to the double classroom to watch a black and white film, *Otters in Canada* (or something similar). It was an end of term 'filler', taken – no doubt – by a teacher dreaming of his summer holidays and partial freedom (as I would many years later when I became a teacher).

Mr Siddons, of course, found out all too soon about this dastardly, anarchic act. He was – apparently – livid. He sent a prefect around the school to ferret me out. I was sitting with the Form 4 students in the darkened double classroom while the 16 mm film reels clicked on ... A loud knock on the classroom door, a narrow band of light fell across the darkened room and a voice squeaked out, 'Is Billy Rogers, 4C, here?' 'Who?' The teacher sounded barely interested. The student went on – 'Mr Siddons wants to see him immediately.' Maybe the student messenger didn't sound urgent enough – the supervising teacher said 'I'll send him as soon as the film's finished, don't worry.'

Back in the darkness, with distracting otters (or was it beavers?), I quickly planned my getaway. I whispered to my mate, 'I'm off – don't tell them I've gone.' I sneaked out, arms feeling for the wall; I inched my back along the wall towards the door and found freedom. I had seen many black and white films of military men in *Stalag 17*, *The Wooden Horse* and *The Colditz Story*. I often imagined myself as the head of the 'escape committee' at school. I was now 'on the run'. I raced downstairs on tip-toe (not easy), grabbed bag, gear and coat and made my way out the rear entrance of the school to avoid capture. I ran home. Later that day, I told my mum and dad. My dad wisely – and helpfully – asked me what I wanted to do about 'it all'. I told him that I didn't want to go back to *that* school. We were not on the phone at home so the school could not reach us quickly. We got the statutory letter some days later, 'We are extremely disappointed ...' (etc.) *'Please report to the head-master's office with your parents before the start of the school year!'* I didn't; I went to another school for almost 12 months and then we emigrated to Australia – as a family – for the princely sum of ten English pounds. It was well worth it.

Teachers who believed in me

There were – thankfully – kind, generous, caring, motivational teachers at that school. I remember my art teacher with flowing cape, ambiguous perfume (from under the cape), flowing chestnut locks (the Lady of Shallot?). We were entranced by Mrs Hart, then highly respectful of this talented and motivational teacher. She enrolled me in a national art exam. I complained I couldn't do it because I was badly colour blind. She believed in me, however, and encouraged me and supported me to 'go for it'. I did a painting of 'Men Trawling in the North Sea' (a set topic choice). I had painted men straining at nets, on a bucking trawler in a rough sea. I had apparently painted the men with green hair, and strangely coloured Anglo-Saxon skin (puce?). I think I got the sou'westers an acceptable yellow or orangey colour. I received no final placing in the exam but I got a beautiful, embossed (national) certificate; I was so proud. My confidence in drawing and art owes much to Mrs Hart.

I had a few other teachers who believed in me, like Mr Randall, my English teacher, who was most supportive of my writing, particularly my essays on the novels of Charles Dickens. He always treated me with courtesy and respect, and addressed the 'emergent adult' in me. I remember these teachers with affection – some teachers make a difference in your life.

So; I left school at 15, a migrant to Australia with mixed memories of school. I worked on building sites in Queensland. I had a brief stint in the army (National Service. I was called up. A conscript. Artillery.) I became a teacher later in life (as a mature-age learner), having also been a carpenter, an architectural draughtsman, a young parish minister (seven years) and then a teacher, consultant, university lecturer, professor and roving lecturer (back in my old country ...).

The moral of the story

We cannot predict (nor is it worth predicting) what will happen to our students. We are better served working with, encouraging and supporting our students for the short time they are with us.

It is also worth remembering that learning is lifelong; it doesn't begin, or end, with formal schooling. Some of my teachers taught me how *not* to teach and how *not* to manage and discipline students. Others gave me sufficient messages of hope, confidence and encouragement to make the choices that have helped form my ongoing educational journey. I wish I could share that with Mrs Hart and Mr Randall.

Teach; encourage a student's potential and hopeful tomorrow. Don't predict.

The 'Pygmalion effect': where expectancy can lead

Bill Rogers

There is a story in classical Greek mythology where Pygmalion, King of Cyprus and part-time sculptor, spends his days on the island creating a beautiful female statue. The myth doesn't say he was dimwitted, it simply records that he 'fell in love' with it and earnestly prayed to Aphrodite (Venus) to bring the statue to life. He married the former statue ... love bore fruit ... (sounds like a bad American soap, doesn't it?). George Bernard Shaw took the myth much further.

In 1914, George Bernard Shaw's play **Pygmalion** *was performed in London. Among other things, his story demonstrated that what one believes, attributes and communicates to another person can have a profound effect in terms of self-belief and behaviour change of that person. In the play, the professor of linguistics has a bet with a friend (the Colonel) that given sufficient time he can train a 'mere' cockney flower girl to pass for a 'real lady'. Eliza the flower girl is treated quite differently by the professor of linguistics and the Colonel. Eliza says:*

> *... the difference between a lady and a flower girl is not how she behaves, but how she's treated. I shall always be a flower girl to Professor Higgins, because he always treats me as a flower girl, and always will; but I know I can be a lady to you, because you always treat me as a lady, and always will. (Shaw, 1913)*

Perhaps the message of the play is that our expectations may determine more than we realise. It may not always be the other person who is 'the problem'.

Back in 1963, the psychologist Robert Rosenthal and his colleagues set up experiments to test what is sometimes called the 'expectancy effect' or 'self-fulfilling prophecy'. Randomly assigned rats were divided into two groups termed 'maze-bright' and 'maze-dull'. College undergraduates who tested the rats on maze trials only knew their rat sample as either 'bright' or 'dull'. Ten trials later (over five consecutive days), the results indicated that the 'bright' rats' scores were nearly double the 'dull' rats' scores in maze performances. Rosenthal concluded that rather than any real 'intelligence' differences increasing the score of the 'bright' rats, it was the expectations of the experimenters communicated via tactile and kinetic cues that had a differential effect on rat performance.

This 'expectancy effect' has been widely studied with child and teacher relationships in classroom settings. Would randomly assigned children – identified only as 'dull' or 'bright' – exhibit similar differences? That 'painful and dull grade'; those 'swines' in grade 6, contrasted with the really 'bright grade'; 'You're a lucky so and so, they're the best lot in our school ...'; 'I had that group and they're marvellous ....' 'That group in grade 5, they're very bright, you know ....' Would such labelled associations present a similar picture, and outcome, to the tests of Rosenthal? If an experiment was designed (and conducted) that allocated classes of students to teachers as either 'dull' or 'bright', would it have similar effects? Evidently yes. Rosenthal and Jacobson wrote about their research in schools and entitled their work *Pygmalion in the Classroom (1986)*.[1]

If we *characteristically* think of a particular grade (or group of students) as a 'pain', 'hopeless' or 'never-amount-to-anything'; if we assign them to a mental slag heap; if we expect them (or particular individuals) to fail, to always or *only* be a pest or *always* 'drive us up the wall'; if we expect them to perform to the badinage of staff room gossip ... we might find our expectations working as a self-fulfilling prophecy. I have worked with colleagues who have described, even defined, a group of students as 'them' in contrast to 'us': 'I've got to win here; I've got to

---

1. Of course, these days, social research does not utilise experimental constructs that allow adults to believe that their classes are 'actually' what the researchers have labelled. This does not delimit the significant outcomes that Rosenthal and Jacobson's research have demonstrated. Rosenthal (1973) made the observation that teachers who believe (or are led to believe) that their students are 'good' students who are likely to perform well *then tend to communicate with those students in particular ways:*

   • they create, and sustain, a more positive, 'warmer' socio-emotional manner in communication
   • they give more feedback and encouragement (particularly positive feedback)
   • they also give more opportunities to those students to question (and respond)
   • they challenge and extend those students.

   These 'teacher expectations' are, of course, one side of the 'relational coin' as it were.
   McInerney and McInerney (1998) note that the sources for teachers' erroneous expectations are: socio-economic status; social class; sex differences (i.e. girls are 'less interested in Maths than boys' and 'girls are better behaved than boys'); physical appearance ('good looking' children are perceived as more motivated than 'unattractive' children); racial grouping (Asian students are more studious ...) and previous negative teachers' reporting influence the next teacher (particularly in student profiles) (pp. 198–9).
   Confirmation (or disconfirmation) of one's beliefs and attitudes about children and their behaviour,

prove that I'm the boss.' I've even heard teachers describe a class (with admittedly challenging students) as 'the enemy'. It is not even a contest, let alone a 'war'. There are teachers who will communicate their expectations through consequent behaviour as if students are the 'enemy' – a recipe for tension and conflict.

Of course, student behaviour can be extremely difficult, challenging and stressful at times. What my colleagues and I have learned is that colleague support is crucial in helping one to cope, understand, address and manage such behaviours. Importantly, our colleagues are a critical resource for the development of schoolwide strategies, plans and programmes, necessary when managing and supporting challenging student behaviours. When teachers lapse into such frequent negative descriptors, it is – mostly – out of intense (often unrelieved) frustration. If teachers are not given necessary colleague support, then that stress will only compound self-doubt, and negative ways of thinking about themselves or their students.

In classes in the more 'challenging schools' (as they are often described in 'teacher shorthand'), 60 or 70 per cent of students are basically co-operative, considerate, responsible and mostly amenable to positive, respectful and confident teacher leadership. Between 15 and 20 per cent (broad by distributive percentages) are those students who tend to behave in attentional and distracting ways. Some behave in more challenging ways that exhibit a miscue of 'power' ('I can do what I want and no one can really stop me!') These students will often exhibit such behaviours in the first meetings over the first few weeks. Often, many of these students can be supportively encouraged, within confident teacher leadership, to work with shared – and fair – rights and responsibilities (see later, Ch. 4). A much smaller percentage (one to five per cent) present with emotional and behavioural disorders.

However, the more we *characteristically* expect (think, believe, attribute) that particular students, or even a whole class, will be difficult – even impossible – to teach or manage, the more we may unintentionally communicate negative behaviour traits to Johnny, or to his class group. Our 'prophecy' may seem as if it is fulfilled. 'I knew

---

and aptitude, are only likely to have a deleterious, and pervasive, effect, 'when the teacher holds them consistently and implements practices in line with these expectations which are not challenged by changes in student behaviour or other environmental factors' (McInerney and McInerney 1998: 199; see also Brophy, 1983 and 1985 and Brophy and Good, 1986).

Eleanor Leacock's seminal research (in the late '60s, early '70s), based on classroom observations of teachers and students, showed that teachers' expectations about student behaviour and aptitude did vary particularly along class and race lines. The degree, and extent, of teacher interactions also varied when teachers 'expected' 'poorer', 'lower-class' children not to do very well. Teachers tended to show less interest, less engaged motivation and to be more critical of students' work and behaviour (in Sprinthall and Sprinthall, 1974: p. 406).

Cummings (1989) also notes that teachers smile more often and nod their heads more if they perceive a student to be 'bright', giving the student more encouraging non-verbal feedback *and* more opportunity to respond. Conversely, when teachers respond to 'low-achieving' students, their perception affects the students obversely (see also Rogers, *Classroom Behaviour*, 2006b).

Fortunately (as all researchers note), *teachers can learn to be aware of their own expectations, challenge, modify and even change them ...*

he'd bomb out – he *always* does ...!'; 'I knew they'd upset me, they *always* upset me.'

Listening to staff room gossip and badinage – 'Oh no! I've got those b......s in 9C again!'; 'He's a real little sh-t'; '8D are such a pack of animals!' – one wonders how much some teachers telegraph the attribute of 'sh-tness' to the children, or class, they teach.

Did your parents ever say, 'You're *just* like your father ... he *always* leaves his clothes around'; 'Lazy ... *just* like your brother'; 'You *never* do what I ask'; 'You *always* whine'; 'Why don't you *ever* concentrate?!'; '*How many times* have I told you!?'; 'Don't you *ever* listen?'; 'Look!! You *should* be able to do that maths *by now*!'. If children hear this kind of language frequently, it will have an effect, but it may not be the 'wake-up' effect some adults expect. It may only reinforce the very behaviours the parent is hoping they can change in their children. Even if our global attributions are partly true, stating them frequently will unnecessarily reinforce the self-defeating expectations.

Martin Seligman has noted in his research on *learned helplessness* (1970, 1975) and *learned optimism* (1991) that our 'characteristic explanatory style' has a direct relationship to how we feel and cope in stressful contexts and also how effectively we behave and relate when under stress.

If we frequently make demands about social reality that are not realised, the beliefs that form those demands can create as much stress as the social reality itself. When we work with, and seek to teach, children with challenging behaviours, some teachers will get quite annoyed, even angry, when a student is rude, arrogant or sarcastic in their manner. Not that such behaviour is not annoying – of course it is. However, when we find ourselves insistently saying, '... but children *should* not be rude ...' (some are!) '... *should* not answer back ...' (some do!); 'children *must not* swear (even under their breath) ...' (some bleedin' well do!); 'children *must* respect their teachers ...' (some do not!) – such a 'loaded' explanatory style is *itself* stressful, let alone the student's actual behaviour. When we 'explain' stressful situations in absolutistic imperatives ('*never* ...', '*always* ...', *must /mustn't/should* ...) and then find a mismatch between the reality of the situation and our *characteristic* explanatory style, we are doubly stressed! (Rogers, 2006b).

Countless times I have seen different teachers manage the *same* difficult class, the *same* challenging student, with significantly differing outcomes for students and teachers.

For example, when we ask a student to do something 'really difficult' like go back to his seat to do his classwork (he has been walkabout in the classroom), and he goes – adding the whining, 'Alright, alright! I was *just* getting a pen from my mate!' It is not just what the student says, it is the extended, accentuated sigh; it is the rolling of the eyes skyward; it is the snort of the nostrils, it is his *gait* ...

It is not merely the 'primary' behaviour ('wandering' and task-avoidance), it is the 'secondary behaviours' (the sigh, the muted whine, the eyes, the exaggerated shuffle back to the seat, the grin, the gait ...).

Some teachers will over-focus on these aspects of the student's behaviour –

'Look, why can't you just do as I say without making a blasted drama of it all? Why do you have to make it such a big deal!?' An argument soon ensues – 'You're *always* picking on me ...!'

The teacher then argues back, 'Well, I wouldn't if you just did as you're told!' Ad frustratum!

Some teachers' anger is not merely fuelled by those 'secondary behaviours'; the teacher also processes the situation in terms of an 'explanatory style' that says, 'Children *must* respect their teachers ...'; 'Children *should* not be rude or answer back ...'; 'Good teachers *must* be in control at all times ...'.

Other teachers will get irritated, annoyed and (at times) angry about children's behaviour but be less stressed and more effective in managing challenging students because their 'explanatory style' is not unrealistically demanding, or pessimistic (e.g. 'I'll *never* reach him'; 'I'll *never* be able to connect with that class'; 'It's *all* my fault ...'; 'It will *always* be this way ...'). As Seligman (1991) notes, a typical 'pessimistic explanatory' style 'consists of certain kinds of explanations for bad events: personal ("It's my fault"), permanent ("It's always going to be like this"), and pervasive ("It's going to undermine every aspect of my life"). If you explain a failure permanently and pervasively, you project your present failure into the future and into all new situations' (p. 76).

This is not an issue about standards of behaviour, nor is it about accepting, or excusing, unacceptable or bad behaviour. It is about how we *characteristically* explain our daily stressful (even bad) events to ourselves and others. Teachers who have learned to interpret aspects of challenging behaviours as annoying, unpleasant, frustrating rather than, '*I can't stand it!*'; '*And kids shouldn't be like this*!', are still stressed but not *as* stressed, *as* often, *as* long. They have learned to hold a more realistic 'explanatory style'. They have learned to recognise when they start 'absolutising' about daily social reality; they have learned to dispute unrealistic, demanding, thinking patterns and reframe how they think and interpret and manage stressful reality. This is more than merely saying positive things to oneself, it is a conscious activity that seeks to address failure and bad events (in our daily living) as difficult – yes – but *temporary*. The skills of disputing absolutistic and negative thinking need some practice to become characteristic and realistically useful – it is worth the effort. Martin Seligman's (1991) book *Learned Optimism* is highly recommended, so too is Michael Bernard's (1990) book *Taking the Stress Out Of Teaching* (see also the appendix in Rogers (2002a) and see Rogers (1996)). They have also developed skills of management that minimise unnecessary confrontation and argument with more challenging children (see Chapter 6 in this text).

The 'Pygmalion effect' thrives on hyperbole and the global misconception that says behaviour and person are equivalent – or that things, people, relationships have an inevitable 'mustness' about them. 'This kid *must* be difficult because his mother is ..., his father has just "shot through" and he lives in those awful flats

... and there's substance abuse and ...' or 'We *can't* expect much more from him because of his home life ...'. Further, such negative expectancy may significantly affect the realistic support we can give, and the difference we can make in our schools – even as an individual teacher – to students whose home lives and circumstances are disturbing and dysfunctional (Rogers, 2003).

We can communicate expectation in a variety of ways, and we know, from our experiences in our own childhood, adolescence and adulthood, when somebody is telegraphing inadequacy, failure, incompetence or easy judgement. We have also felt the effect of those expectations and – hopefully – moved beyond them.

Case example (Ted)

Ted was 'dumped' in my class because the other grade 6 teacher couldn't cope (sorry, he was 'placed' in my class. Other colleagues had used the word 'dumped'.) I was told he was 'totally disruptive', 'dirty', 'unreliable', 'never listens', 'grossly untidy work', etc. Outwardly, Ted looked like the young children sometimes displayed on Salvation Army posters. He boldly asserted that he was 'tough' and the first day was overly disruptive (attention-seeking, loud, verbally rude and knew how to skilfully drop a swear word). Any work he handed in looked like it had been used as a breakfast serviette.

After what seemed a slow month, things began to change. No magic formulas. I accepted his work as it was (he especially enjoyed maths) and commented clearly, and specifically, only on correct work, and his attempts at achieving his best. 'Good on you, Ted; the way you worked those fractions out was spot-on; different from the way we set it out on the board and easier too'. I ignored the scribble over his decimal fractions and the many dirty thumbprints (he learned, later, to wash his hands).

Whenever he evidenced co-operative behaviour, I affirmed his efforts; specifically and often quietly (and one-to-one) so as not to unnecessarily embarrass him. 'Thanks, Ted for helping Maria and sharing your ideas ...'; 'You were co-operative when ...'. When he was disruptive, affecting other students' rights, I sought to address his behaviour as calmly and consistently as possible. The times I snapped at him, I always apologised. I remember it did not happen often (the 'snapping') but Ted always said things like, 'Well, that's OK. It's OK, Mr Rogers.' At times I addressed his more extreme attentional and provocative behaviour firmly. I always followed up one-to-one with Ted later to enable ongoing repairing and rebuilding. Most of his provocation and swearing was not directed at me personally – he was, at times, quite a frustrated lad. After a while, I sensed his bad days at the very beginning of the day and would quietly tune in and acknowledge what I had sensed. It helped. I continued to *expect* Ted to develop positive learning and behaviour. It wasn't easy. Day by day, I saw small changes in Ted's attitude to learning, his overall behaviour and his relations with other students and the way he was relating to me as his teacher. The early attentional 'showing off' and 'alpha maleness' transmuted into a more relaxed confidence with a touch of the 'knowing class clown'. His class peers began to respond much more positively to him; he was clearly enjoying school.

Near to the close of that term (and close to the upcoming parent–teacher night), he came up, crooked his arm around my neck and said, 'You're OK.' 'Thanks Ted,' I replied (nursing my neck), 'so are you.'

His mother, who had missed other parent–teacher nights (who wants to listen to bad news all the time?) actually came along on this night. The first thing I did was to ask her if she'd like a cup of tea. Well, she was a bit hostile and just sat upright, frowning, crisply refused the tea and waited for the regular reportage. I said, 'Mrs ____, thanks for coming, it's been a pleasure to have Ted here this term. His maths work has always been completed with effort and skill' (I didn't tell her about the early dirty thumb prints) 'and he really gets on well with other children in the class' (I didn't tell her about the first four weeks). I showed her examples of Ted's work, describing his effort, his energy, his growing confidence. Her eyes nearly fell out and she said, 'That's the first time I've ever heard Ted spoken about like that ... that's why I came up. He said the teacher (I mean you) said how pleased he was with his maths and that and I couldn't believe it.' She left with a big smile, a hearty thanks and added as a quiet aside, 'Oh, Mr Rogers, he's washing a lot now ...'.

Ted left a few weeks before Christmas (before the rest of the class). He was moving to another part of Australia. He came up to me the day before he left school, drew me aside and quietly asked me if I liked lobster. 'Love it!' (I was a bit surprised by the question.) He turned up the day before he left, combed hair (same jeans and jumper), twinkle in his eye and handed me a dampish bundle wrapped in Christmas paper. It was a lobster. I thanked him (I do like lobster). However, when I cracked it open, later at home, well ... it sort of smelt. I gave it to our cat. Ted, if you read this, no offence mate, I probably left it too long in the sun. (Ted would be nearly 30 now.)

'Dear Luke': what I saw at the outset and how children's behaviour challenges us in positive ways

Elizabeth McPherson

Elizabeth McPherson (née Rogers) was in her first year of teaching when she wrote this letter. As a primary school teacher, she has come across the widest range of behaviour, needs and backgrounds in her students. In this account,

Elizabeth shares a letter she wrote to one of her students at the close of that first year. Luke is a little boy who made a significant impact on her life (as she did in his). She has asked his mother to pass this letter on to Luke when he starts high school. Luke's mother really appreciated the letter.

This account clearly illustrates how a child's first perceptions of school can affect their behaviour and the difference a teacher's perception, beliefs and commitment can have on how challenging behaviour can be positively addressed.

This article was first published in Classroom Magazine: Scholastic Australia *(May, 2002).*

Dear Luke,

When I first met you – day one – you were clinging to your mother's skirt; I had never seen a five-year-old so small. You must have been only 70 centimetres high, how big the school must have seemed.

When your mother finally summoned the courage to leave you on that first day, you hid under the tables. Despite my best efforts I couldn't persuade you to come out and join the rest of our grade. When I still hadn't coaxed you out two days later, I approached your mum. 'What should I do, he won't join in with anything?' I asked. 'Shall I leave him till he's ready or try to 'force' him to join in?' Your mum began to cry, she said she just wanted everything to be perfect for you. You're very fortunate that she loves you so much; some of the other children in our class aren't so lucky. I wanted everything to be perfect too and already in my first week of teaching, I felt like I was failing two people.

It took your mum and dad a few days to decide what they wanted me to do, and in the end they asked me to leave you until you were ready to join in with the rest of the grade. I asked the other children not to fuss over you when you were hiding under the classroom furniture, funnily enough they were happy just to let you be. Plenty of them were probably feeling scared too; maybe they wished that they'd thought of your approach to school. Some recesses I didn't get a break, I didn't want to leave you alone in the classroom, but then most of the time you would come out to playground duty with me and follow at a little distance.

It must have been difficult for you, not knowing what to do at school; sometimes it was a bit difficult and scary for me too. Like your mum, I wanted my whole class to have a perfect start to school life. But I guess with people there's no such thing as perfection.

On the day of our first assembly, we lined up and rushed over to the hall. You were really scared, this was new for you, and I'd forgotten to explain to you what was going on; I was cross at myself. You taught me my first and most valuable rule when teaching grade preps [infants] – explain every detail and role-play new situations!

When we started going to specialist classes, you got very nervous. You told me you hated the library teacher, the art and music teacher and the Italian teacher, you said you wanted to stay with me. A light bulb suddenly switched on in the cavernous recesses of my mind – you were scared of everyone – except me. I began to realise that I was special to you and you were special to me.

I remember, only too well, the day one of our 'more challenging' class members nearly cut your finger off with some scissors. I was helping someone on a computer and when I turned around, I saw you clutching your hand and you were dripping with blood. It's funny the way people react in situations like that. All I could think of, Luke, was making it all right for you ... I scooped you up and carried you to the sick bay, while the principal minded the rest of our grade. You were sobbing and I had blood dripping down my arms and legs and smeared on my face – we must have looked a sight. You were so brave, even when the school secretary called your mum you decided to stick it out until the end of the day. I remember you asked me 'Why do we have to have naughty boys in our class?' I didn't know what to say, my heart was breaking for you. How could I explain that I didn't want the 'naughty' boys to be there any more than you did?

I don't remember when you started joining in with the rest of us, I suppose it happened gradually, but it didn't take too long. I do, however, remember your first entry in your writing book ... you picked up your grey lead in your fist and scribbled all over your page. Do you know that your mum told me that you had hardly picked up a pencil before you started school? I wondered how I was going to teach you, I knew you were clever and full of life, but I didn't know how to break through to you.

In term two we started an integrated unit on farming. Do you remember how you all got a toy animal to choose and you had to make a shelter for them and discover what they liked to eat and drink? I wanted you to choose first, so you could have the animal you most wanted; I wanted to fan any spark of interest I could detect, however small. You chose a turkey to take home as your project. So, that night I went shopping; I bought a stamp of a turkey with a snow dome on top and turkeys inside it, something to encourage you, I thought. Then one day you drew a picture of a turkey – it was amazing, I couldn't believe that this picture had come from someone who didn't even like to use pencils. Boy did I praise you over that; I was nearly moved to tears when I showed your mum. I was so proud of you.

By third term you were continually amazing me. You were reading above the class average and writing your own sentences. As I slipped writing samples into your file, I looked at the first entry in your writing book and then at what you were writing now. I showed the two pages to the other teachers and to the principal: 'Look at how far my Luke has come this year, isn't he amazing?' I think that anyone you meet in your life will have to admit that – yes, you are amazing.

In fourth term, a week or two before the end of term, I lost one of my cats in a terrible accident. On a Thursday night I was at the animal hospital most of the night and came to school only having had three hours sleep. Before school I had been crying again, but by the time the class started to arrive at school I had dried the tears and made myself look presentable.

It was a Friday, so you had art for the first hour and I was using the time before school to correct work. I was kneeling on the floor with books spread out around me. You walked in and came up to me and we were the same height. You put your hand on my back and rubbed it, you looked down into my face and said in the tenderest of voices, 'Are you all right? You look really tired.' Later that day I was still correcting books, you came up and stroked my back again and said, 'You look so beautiful today, just so beautiful.' You stroked the pale blue scarf in my hair and now I'll never forget what I was wearing that day. Throughout that day you cuddled my legs as I walked around the classroom. It made walking difficult, but I was glad to have you around.

As strange as it sounds, I feel like we have a bond. I guess it's like the bond between a mother and a child, but it's not quite that.

At university, in one of our less useless subjects, we brainstormed the various roles of a teacher, things like: mediator, mentor, first aid administrator, secretary, wiper of tears, detective, finder of spare hats ... bringing up the rear. In all these brainstorms was the role of educator. The academic aspect of teaching can only fill so much of a year, the rest involves those human interactions, which we are not taught about at university. While learning about how to extend your 'zone of proximal development' did come in handy, it's children like you, Luke, who teach us the things we really need to know.

I often say to people, 'Teaching is such a weird job. What other profession is there where you are responsible (in so many ways) for the social, emotional and educational needs of so many people? You spend all day every day with them for a year, sometimes they drive you crazy, but then you learn to love them. Then all of a sudden they get taken away from you and it starts all over again.'

As I read over this letter to you, Luke, I realise that there are about 15 alternative letters that I could have written about children who have touched my life this year and helped me grow as a teacher. But you are the one who stands out the most; we have tested each other's boundaries and stretched each other's limits. A year later we are both better people for having shared each other's lives.

If I have the good fortune to touch the life of a child like you each year, I will consider myself a fortunate teacher. If you are the only child I will come across like this in my whole teaching career, it has already been worth it. We have taught each other this year and we have grown together. I consider myself to have been blessed to know you, Luke, and I hope that you will never forget me, because I will always remember you.

Your teacher,

Elizabeth

My global classroom

Peter D'Angelo

Empathy is one of a good teacher's most important assets. Many bring it with them to the classroom and inculcate it in their students – thankfully! Poet and teacher, Peter D'Angelo, who migrated to Australia as a child, takes us into his global classroom where empathy and language learning have always gone hand in hand. Peter is a senior teacher at Noble Park Secondary College, Victoria, Australia. He has had several books of poetry published.

Here Peter reflects on how perception, positive expectation, reflection and empathy affect his teaching and his students.

Peter D'Angelo's article 'My Global Classroom' first appeared in EQ Australia, *Issue Four, Summer 2000, 'Australian Education: How are we doing?'* EQ Australia *is a quarterly magazine published by Curriculum Corporation. www.curriculum.edu.au/eq.*

I still vividly remember my first teaching day in 1979 when, fresh out of university and with fixed ideas on education, I found myself face to face with newly arrived Vietnamese and Cambodian refugee students sitting stone silent in a rundown classroom of the Noble Park Language Centre, near Melbourne.

It was my brief to teach them intensive English for six months, after which they would move on to regular schooling, to be replaced by another group who would then receive the same course.

It all sounded straightforward and achievable, but, as I discovered ten minutes into the lesson, a degree proudly hanging on a study wall was no guarantee that, as a result of the process of teaching, learning was automatically going to occur.

First lesson

I began somewhat shakily with the standard introduction: 'Good morning, class. My name is Mr D'Angelo and I will be your new English teacher this semester. I hope that we will have a very positive and productive time together.'

I waited expectantly for the usual student outburst, but nothing came – just an eerie silence of a kind that I have never encountered in any of the boisterous class-rooms that had been part of my teaching rounds.

Once again I tried, hoping at least for a few mumbled voices. But, as before, nothing came. There was no hint from any of them that this was a classroom and I was their teacher and it was normal for them to put me through a 'baptism of fire'.

For one petrifying moment, I felt completely lost, my mind scrambling back through all the lectures and tutorials, hoping to find something that I could grab hold of in order to break this surreal deadlock.

Instinctively, I turned away from the group towards the blackboard and began to slowly print my name in large capital letters. Turning back to the class, I pointed at myself and said desperately, 'My name is Mr D'Angelo. MR D'ANGELO.'

But it was still the same unnerving silence and the vacant stare of expression-less eyes which seemed to be lost somewhere else in time. Feeling light-headed and as though I might collapse at any minute, I turned back to the board and printed my first name, hoping that its two syllables would be easier for the students to pronounce. 'Mr Peter. I am Mr Peter.'

I could feel the sweat trickling down my spine. Then it came, the first sound of a trembling voice from a boy sitting in the front row. 'M ... Mita Pita.' He tried again. 'Mita Pita.'

'Yes, that's right. Yes, I am Mister Peter. Who are you?' I was pleading for a reply.

Slowly he looked up and I could see him desperately trying to form the words. 'You Trung,' he said. 'You Trung,' he repeated, gaining confidence.

'Yes, that's right!' I almost screamed because, finally, I had broken through the wall of silence and it didn't matter that the pronoun was 'wrong'. Communication had just begun and I could hardly hide my joy. 'Yes, you are Trung and I am Mister Peter. Hello Trung, how are you today?'

In the excitement, the others quickly sensed that something was going on and soon they were all telling me their names, which I feverishly wrote on the board.

This in itself was a learning experience as it was my first contact with the exotic sounds of Sokha Sun, Nguyen Thi Tuyet, Phuoc My Lan and, of course, Huyn Duc Trung. I was having as much difficulty pronouncing their names as they orig-inally had pronouncing mine and I quickly realised something that had been unheard of in teachers' college – in this class, education was going to be an interactive journey involving everyone.

Trung's story

And so, we continued as we had started, day after day, week after week, my students soaking up the new language at an astonishing rate and me becoming more and more aware of their backgrounds and situations as their English proficiency increased.

Often, we would gather around the tattered map of the world whose borders seemed to be changing daily and talk about how it felt to leave behind your country of birth and to start life again in a strange new land.

These conversations, although often tinged with sadness and longing, always had a certain spark of hope. It was this positive element that I would focus on to get my students to write about themselves and it was during one of these sessions that Trung quietly left his chair and walked up to my desk.

'Mita Pita. I want to tell you something Vietnam. I want to tell you saddest day of my life.'

He went on to detail how he, his mother and three younger sisters were forced to leave the family home under cover of darkness and how they walked for three days and nights through jungle to board an overcrowded fishing boat in the hope it would take them to Australia.

'We sleep on top each other, eat nothing five days. One night the pirate come and take six girl, kill two men. Lucky not my sister. Father can do nothing, gun at head. Mother scream and cry but nobody can fight the pirate.'

Trung stopped talking for a while, then looked at me again. 'Mita Pita, my English still not good, but you teach and help me a lot. You help me for my future, so I tell you this.'

I sat there in silence, humbled by his experience. I'd read accounts of people escaping war and persecution but to hear it so honestly first-hand was to have a lasting effect on both my teaching career and my life.

... and other lessons

Inevitably, the time came for this first class of mine to move on. I remember sitting alone in my classroom on the last day of term, sifting through the stories and poems that the students had given me as souvenirs. I knew that I had been a part of something special and, as it turned out, it proved to be something that I would experience over and over again.

In the 1980s, my class was home to Poles, Afghans, Romanians, Turks, Russians, Armenians, El Salvadorians, Chileans, Peruvians, Mauritians, Samoans and Chinese. They were followed in the '90s by students from the former Yugoslavia, East Timorese, Eritreans, Somalians, Iraqis, Iranians, Palestinians and a host of other displaced and often traumatised students.

Sometimes their accounts of personal tragedy were so overwhelming that I began to question every value and belief I held. Yet, every time I was in danger of 'losing the plot', my students' reaffirmation of hope for themselves, their families and the future renewed my commitment to them and their education.

In the mid-1990s, I moved from the language centre to Noble Park Secondary College, a school that had taken many of my ex-pupils over the years. The move was fuelled by a series of organisational changes over time to the language centre and to education policy, which had left me disillusioned. I knew that it was time to move on and re-establish myself professionally and spiritually.

Reunion

The change proved to be just what I needed and teaching my former students once again proved as rewarding as it had the first time. They were still as eager and polite as they'd been in those early days and by the end of the first year in my new position, I'd become totally recharged professionally, especially knowing that I had reconnected with these students at another critical stage of their lives.

I have now been at the school for five years, during which time I have seen many students move on to tertiary education and the next stages of their lives.

Often, they come back to visit and inevitably the conversation turns to those first weeks at the language centre. As always, I'm reminded of just how privileged I am to have been a part of their new lives in Australia.

I am also reminded of my own experience of migration when I was five years old, suddenly finding myself on a ship leaving Italy, crying and waving goodbye to my grandfather and not understanding why we were being separated.

On my first day at school in Australia, there was the strange sound of a language I had never heard before. I felt completely isolated and afraid as the other kids in the class sneered, using words that were meaningless to my ears yet were still able to make me shrivel to nothing inside.

It wasn't long before the teacher took me aside and, in a calm voice, began slowly to teach me the alphabet. In what seemed a very short time, the sounds around me became words, then sentences and stories, and soon I was able to understand and make sense of my new world.

This was the gift my first teacher gave to me. It is a gift I have always tried to give back to my students, hoping to revive in them the same sense of dignity and worth instilled in me so long ago.

I sometimes go back to the empty spot where the language centre once stood (it was physically moved to another site) and as I walk around, the past comes flooding back. Every feature of this area has its own special significance – its own memory and meaning – because it was here that I really came to understand that no matter what we've been through, we can all come together and begin to live in peace with ourselves, each other and the changing world.

I have learnt this from all of my students over 20 years. It has forged within me an unshakeable belief that, in essence, we are one family, united on common ground, no matter how far apart we might once have been.

William

Jim Gilbert

In this account Jim (a principal in a small rural school) describes his meeting with a very 'interesting' new student, and the effect on other students. This is familiar to all of us but the setting and context with young William and his dad illustrates the strange and unusual issues we have to face at times as teachers with challenging students. Jim also recounts the natural tensions and stresses we face with such children, and their parents, in situations where there is significant stress and trauma.

The little 'sole charge school' where I was the teaching principal was in a township that had seen much better days. There were a number of very dilapidated houses that some locals would have preferred to see bulldozed because of the people who would come to live in them. We lived in the schoolhouse just adjacent to the school and across the road from us was such a house. It looked like it had been abandoned for years with rotting timbers and grass growing from the rusting guttering. The 'garden' was a jungle of long grass and shrubs that seemed impenetrable.

One Sunday we came back after dark from an out-of-town trip. There was an old car parked across the road from the schoolhouse and a faint glow of light from a side window of the old house.

Next day, a gruff, unshaven, roughly dressed man in his thirties walked in to the school with a 'hard-case looking' boy of about ten years standing with him. 'Jim McGuigan,' he said, and stuck his calloused hand out at me for a handshake. 'This is William. He's in Standard 4. We are going to be living here for a while so he better go to school.'

William made an immediate impact on the other 15 reserved and well-behaved pupils at the school. The scar on his forehead was a subject of intense speculation as to what had caused it.

The swagger in William's walk was just too flashy for any of them to replicate and nobody could spit with anything like the noise, distance, or accuracy of William. He settled quite quickly into the class finding that with nobody to challenge him – as the toughest – he could afford to 'relax'.

I didn't feel able to relax though. His dad was rumoured to be very difficult to deal with and prone to moodiness and violence. Local word was that he was hiding away from some trouble he had got into. What bothered me was his obvious distrust of me as a teacher when he brought William in to enrol. Often, we would be outside doing a physical education lesson, or it would simply be a break time, and I would look across the road and see Jim standing outside his house with a pair of binoculars trained on me, or on William and the pupils he was with. It was unnerving to say the least.

William soon began to show a good-natured mischievous sense of humour that delighted his peers and which I tended to encourage. We had our own small bus at the school which I often drove. Once a week, we would drive a few kilometres to a neighbouring small school where we'd pool pupils and teachers for sport.

About two weeks after William started with us, we were in the bus driving to the school down the road. The usual excited chatter suddenly ceased. There was a bit of whispering then silence. I looked in the mirror and scanned all of the heads. They all seemed to be turned towards William. William had his head tipped forward and seemed to be working at the side of his face with one hand.

'William!' I called over my shoulder. 'William, what's going on back there?'

'Nothing much,' William said. 'Just having some trouble with my eye!' Then he lifted his head and looked straight at the mirror with his teeth bared in a cheesy grin.

His right eyelid was rolled back up over the eyebrow and the blood vessels were raised and stood out dark red against the pink flesh of the eyelid. The eyeball itself was left exposed and seemed to be hanging unsupported from the socket.

Startled, and not a little concerned, I braked sharply to a halt. Lots of the pupils were covering their eyes with their hands, a couple looked quite queasy and some were giggling and full of, 'Did you see the look on the teacher's face?' statements. William just continued to grin and when the noise all died right down, he slowly and deliberately turned his eyes to the right and then back to the left.

The effect of the unsupported eye below the inverted eyelid rotating from side to side was quite macabre. 'Put your face back together now, William,' I said, as calmly as I could. 'Better warn me if you're going to surprise like that again while I'm driving or I'm likely to drive off the road.'

William was now famous in two schools and seemed to coast along, secure in the legend of the day that he terrified the teacher with his eyeball trick. His dad seemed to relax and the binoculars were no longer in use.

Then one morning, William, clowning on a tower in the mini adventure play-ground, slipped and fell several metres onto the ground, knocking himself out briefly and opening a deep cut on his head. Our teacher's aide and my wife were both on site and they tended to William with first aid. It was apparent that he would have to be taken to Casualty, over an hour away in the nearest city. The teacher's aide, my wife or even myself could take William to get the medical atten-tion he needed but I was worried about taking him anywhere without parental consent – given the unusual, even suspicious behaviour his dad had displayed up to now.

In fact, I was worried full-stop! Jim's car was outside the house. Leaving my wife in charge of the site, I rushed over to the house and went around to the back door and knocked loudly. No response. 'Jim, Jim!' I called out and waited.

Nothing. Unsure of what to do next, I remembered that two houses down the street was a drinking mate of Jim's. Perhaps it would be better to raise him and tell him what had happened?

I ran down to this place and breathlessly explained what was happening.

'Sh-t!' said his mate. 'He was really full last night. He'll be sleeping it off. No way I'm going to wake him though. Bastard sleeps with a machete under the pillow!'

I ran back to school. The consensus was that we shouldn't waste too much time. One more go at raising Jim and if we couldn't wake him, I'd take William to Casualty myself and cope with the consequences later.

So again I approached the back door, knocked loudly and called Jim's name. No response. Reluctantly, I opened the door and stepped into the roughly furnished and untidy kitchen. There was a door into a hallway. I knocked on that and again called out. Still nothing.

Carefully opening this passage door, I stepped into the dim, cobwebbed hallway. There was a deep snoring coming from the open door to one side of the hallway.

'Jim, Jim. It's me … William's teacher from school! I need you to wake up! Jim!' Nothing! Taking a deep breath I slowly looked around the door into the dim, dingy, musty bedroom. Jim's wild-looking, unshaven head was tipped back across the pillow. I could see the handle of the machete to the right of his head. His hands were well away from the handle.

'Well, I've come this far!' I thought and stepped across to the bedside and shook Jim's shoulder. Then I leapt back to the doorway and stood out in the hall.

'What? Who the hell is that? What bloody time is it?' Jim began to stumble around in the bedroom and I began to back towards the kitchen door as I called back. 'William has hurt himself, Jim. You need to get dressed and help us get him to hospital.'

I needn't have been concerned. Jim was actually very calm as it turned out. Within minutes, he was dressed and had his car outside the closest gate to where William was being watched over. He gently carried him to the car and thanked us, saying they would be okay now.

Late that day, the old car pulled up across the road and William came to the house to show off the damage. He had some mild concussion and several stitches in the cut. He would have another scar but this one was above the hairline so it wouldn't show.

A couple of days later, William arrived at the back door of the schoolhouse after school was over for the day. 'Dad said to give you this!' he said, thrusting a big ice-cream container at my wife. It was full of whitebait! More whitebait in one container than we had ever seen before.

Several weeks later, the McGuigans moved away as suddenly as they had arrived. More than 25 years have passed since then, but if I close my eyes I can still see in my mind the macabre sight of William's eyeball trick reflected in the interior mirror of the school bus! I can still hear the stunned silence of his peers as he slowly rotated his gaze to the right and then to the left.

Editor's postscript
Jim got whitebait; I got a lobster (p. 11).

- You cannot predict.
- You can teach, care and *be there*.
- And – in a crisis – we do our best to stay calm and focused on what matters!

Muddling through

Jim Gilbert

Teaching is such a very personal way to make your living. Reading, Writing and Arithmetic are among the easiest aspects of the task to manage. The hardest things can often be dealing with the ripples from events which happen outside of the classroom. In particular, the trauma in the families of pupils and teachers impacts heavily on the tone of the classroom or indeed the whole school.

There was a period of several years where the dreadful deficiencies of teacher training in respect of preparing me for real issues were only too apparent. In fact, it was in my first four years of teaching.

I had been four years in and around a teachers' college and university. The diploma I was awarded had the word Distinction emblazoned on it. I soon found though that I was hopelessly ill-prepared for the events that really matter when as a teacher you deal with the impact of family trauma in your pupils' lives.

The first time I realised how suddenly these things can come up was one morning close to the end of my first year of teaching. Just before class began at 9.00 a.m., my principal visited my room and beckoned me outside. 'I have some sad news. You know little Doreen?' – he looked at me with a concerned expression. I nodded. Doreen was a very slim and frail-seeming girl in the sea of six-year-old faces in my room. 'Last night her mother died. Drowned! She took her own life! She's gone! Doreen will be away for a couple of days but you need to be ready, and get your class ready, for when she comes back.'

I was stunned. I had no idea what to do to prepare myself to be most appropriately helpful for Doreen, and what her classmates might say, or how they might respond. I had no idea whether or not to contact her dad. Should I make a point of telling the whole class and if so what should I tell them? Nobody had any really useful answers for me. Basically we 'muddled through' the next few days and weeks.

Next, I found myself in a small country school, with two teaching colleagues. Just weeks into that teaching position, the mother of one of the senior boys died suddenly. An inexperienced young woman was acting in the principal role and I was the only male staff member. Again, we 'muddled through'.

As well as teaching, I was also supplementing the lowish income of that time with a job driving the school bus. On one of the early morning pick-ups, we stopped at a place where three kids got on. Two were in my class and one in the senior room. Sometimes they would be accompanied to the bus stop by their mum. An attractive, tall woman, she was a skilled horsewoman. Her daughters both looked like her and shared her interest in horses.

One evening I met the lady, at school interviews. She was quiet and reserved. She asked a number of questions about her children that later events put in a light that gave me a great deal of reason for reflection.

The next morning, there was no one at the bus stop at this family's place. After waiting a couple of minutes, I drove away.

When I eventually got to school and the pupils were all headed for their rooms, the principal gathered the staff up and took us into the tiny office. In shocked tones, he told us that the mum I have described had late the previous night taken her own life. Her husband found her, gassed, in her car, in a shed behind the barn.

The principal and I had both talked to her at the interviews the previous afternoon. When we compared notes, we realised that she had asked us both questions about the independence and resilience of her children. As the realisation dawned that we had both given very positive and affirmative answers to these questions, we looked at each other and then both looked away. There were questions in our heads that would not go away. There were three classes waiting that had to be taught. We 'muddled through'.

Surely now this period would be behind me? The old saw is that bad luck comes in threes. If only!

Relationships are close in small communities. Teachers become friends with school parents. Work and social life boundaries blur. About a year after the third family death, I arrived at school one morning to find the principal absent. That meant that I was in charge and needed to organise a bus driver and then a teacher for his room.

The principal's wife tearfully told me that he was in the intensive care unit at Dunedin Hospital supporting members of one of our school families. Last night he had been at a social gathering with a school dad. The dad had a new motorcycle for the farm – one that was big enough to be quite brisk on the road too. He rode the bike to the gathering that night.

On the way back home, he ran off the road and his helmet smashed against a strainer post. His friend, my colleague, saw his headlights vanish somewhere behind him, had to search the roadside for his friend and had to do what he could afterwards.

Several days later, a subdued principal was back at school. The prognosis for his friend was not good. A family meeting was being held that morning with medical staff at the hospital.

At the end of lunch break, my colleague took a phone call. The machines had been switched off. A man every person in this little school knew as the father of two of their classmates was dead.

My colleague physically and emotionally collapsed in front of my eyes. I had a school to manage for the rest of the day, probably for several. There were decisions to make, but first my colleague had to be got to a safe place. I half carried, half dragged him to the schoolhouse and left him with an equally distressed wife. Then, along with my third colleague on site, we got on with muddling through.

The ripples from this tragedy were widespread and lasting. During the aftermath, I learned a great deal about the precariously balanced nature of relationships in tightly knit communities.

Fortunately for me, that was the last such school family trauma for quite some time. Many years have passed since that time and schools have policies and procedures written for helping pupils dealing with grief, loss and change. Managing school trauma is also recognised as something to think about before a crisis hits.

Many of the academics who specialise in education, many politicians, many of those who review the performance of schools, consider that education can be seen as an empirical exercise. These inputs, mixed 'just so', equal these outputs. Like a sausage recipe! They all hopelessly underestimate the effect of school family issues on the school in action.

For all of the plans and policies we put in place, there is a reality which experienced educators acknowledge. Things happen! Things happen in this intensely human profession and when they do, we just have to 'muddle through'.

Editor's postscript

Jim and his colleagues underrate – even underplay – what they describe as 'muddling through'.

- They were *available*: to listen; to care; to support the children and the parents (if they expressed such need). Mostly, the surviving parents knew that *the school was there for their children* – that one safe, secure, stable, sane place.
- In family trauma, we can never be fully prepared as teachers. As Jim notes, our teacher training does not prepare us (perhaps it never can) for traumatic incidents, particularly when a child loses a parent to suicide.
- Teachers, like Jim, will – in time – consider sensitively how to broach the topic of death, loss and grief with their children.
- It is also crucial we support each other *in our support of others*. This, Jim and his colleagues clearly did. The terrible trauma and suffering and grief of others always has its human cost, well beyond the children and their families. We too, as teachers, carry some of that suffering. That too is a part of our humanity.

Parents: The difficult chat

Bill Rogers

In this short essay I've tried to outline how difficult it can be – at times – to communicate with parents, particularly over issues concerning the behaviour of their children. In this case example the difficulty was further accentuated by my concerns about the mother's behaviour.

I was speaking with a parent about her son's behaviour; it was not her first visit to address issues of Sean's behaviour. We were standing in an alcove, near the principal's office. She had come to the school – at our invitation. I was about to ask her to come into the office and discuss the positive progress Sean had been making on his behaviour 'plan' and she said, 'The little sh-t's always getting into trouble and I've got to come and sort it out! He's a pain in the arse – always getting into trouble.' Sean (aged seven) was standing near his mother – how could he not be listening?

I beckoned Mrs Smith to the office and asked Sean if he would like to read some of the books in the alcove area. (I wanted Sean to be distracted – for a while – while I spoke to his mother.) Now – with Sean out of our hearing – I beckoned Mrs Smith to take a seat and quietly said, 'Mrs Smith, I've asked Sean to sit outside, away from us, for a while. I don't know if you were aware of what you said in Sean's hearing just now. I was concerned ...' Before I could finish, she said, 'What?! What are you talking about – *what* did I say?' No doubt she could hear, and sense, the quiet concern in my voice. 'I'm concerned you called Sean a little sh-t and a pain in the arse while he was standing right next to us.'

She looked genuinely surprised, and then annoyed – but more surprised at my 'observation' and the seeming importance my manner had – now – placed on what she had said. Obviously I did not use the tone of voice or inflection she had used in speaking about her son. I did – however – want to alert her to my concern that she had spoken *about* her son in such a degrading way. I am sure she did not mean to; well, I hope she did not mean to. I am also sure that Sean's behaviour (at home) would have been at times challenging and a frequent source of frustration. Not having a supportive partner, and other children to parent, would have all compounded her stress and (naturally) her frustration.

There have been many times I have heard parents say appalling things to their child in school contexts – in playgrounds or (as in this example) while the child is in direct hearing in a parent–teacher meeting. The example above is (in a sense) one of the more 'mild' I have chosen to share. I have often thought that if parents speak to (or of) their children like that in 'public' (at school) or in an 'interview' context, what in heaven's name do they say in the privacy of their homes? Most of us have been witness to some extremely offensive, even disgusting, language on home visits. It is not easy keeping a sense of calmness while at the same time *registering appropriate concern, without sounding overly judgemental or 'prudish'*.

On the occasion I have noted here (with Sean's mother), I wanted to quickly, quietly and 'privately' make her aware that I was concerned – for Sean; I was concerned about *the effect on him* of being spoken about or described in that way.

As in the earlier essay addressing the expectancy effect, this 'effect' has its genesis in the way parents speak about their children (p. 8f). It is not easy for a child (in his self-concept) to work against frequent negative descriptions from the most significant person in his life. (His father was in prison …) If you are frequently told you are 'useless', 'will *never* be any good at …', 'are *always* (a 'sh-t' or a pain in the …!)', it is highly likely that you may end up believing – and conceiving – of yourself within those descriptors. That is – in part – how we form a conception of our self (self-concept). Further, the value we place on that concept (self-esteem) is also significantly affected. As Aristotle notes, '[one must be] a perfect fool who is unaware that people's characters take their bias from the steady direction of their activities …' (Aristotle, 1969: 91).

As noted in Chapter 7, when we are in the position of having to work with, speak with, an angry parent, *our calmness* is a crucial factor. Our non-judgemental attitude is also an important factor in our ability to enable any meaningful connection and support. It is my belief – however – that we do not (however) merely excuse what the parent says about their child (in our hearing) because we might too easily 'offend' them and affect any workable trust and communication.

My concern – at this point – is for the child. I had a brief chat with Sean's mother about the effect of our language on how children *think* and *feel* about themselves and moved (fairly quickly) from my concern about what she had said to what we were trying to focus on with Sean in his 'behaviour plan' *now at school* (see Chapter 3). I encouraged her – then – to invite Sean back in the office so he could share with her about how he was going with his behaviour plan at school.

This shift seemed to enable a more positive (and more hopeful) tone to our conversation. In the course of Sean sharing his plan, we also discussed how we were encouraging him. I was hoping this – too – would signal to the mother the importance of encouragement to Sean's behaviour *and* his self-esteem. She nodded and said, 'That's good …', 'That's OK'. A couple of times, she looked at Sean frowning and with (fortunately) some smiling and said, 'Well you're improving yourself then, aren't you?' He raised his eyes and very nearly grinned! It was a positive start (see Chapter 7).

Chapter 2

Understanding Challenging Children and Children with Emotional and Behavioural Disorder

Understanding emotional and behavioural disorders in mainstream schools

Bill Rogers

All the teachers writing in this book have realised, early in their careers, that there are many factors in a child's life that affect their behaviour at school; we have little control over those factors:

- *disturbing patterns of family dysfunction*
- *disruptive parenting patterns*
- *substance abuse*
- *structural and generational poverty*
- *long-term unemployment*
- *a significant lack of positive male role-modelling in children (particularly – perhaps – in male children)*
- *the characteristic diet of the child*
- *the role, extent and kind of TV characteristically watched by the child*
- *the kind of internet usage (by some children).*
  (Howell, 1993; Rogers, 2003; Rutter et al., 1979)

Factors such as how race, ethnicity, gender and even religion are typically communicated (in negative and stereotypical ways) in family dynamics can affect children's behaviour in self-defeating ways in a community like a school.

What all these teachers have done is to 'de-victimise' the child and not 're-victimise' him in the school setting. While many of the factors – noted above – can significantly affect a child's behaviour and self-perception (self-concept and self-esteem), they do not automatically bind him to dysfunctional self-coping, poor peer relationships and failure at school and beyond.

> *These teachers – unfailingly – enable these children to believe in them-*
> *selves and to value learning. They also encourage the child to find a positive*
> *sense of peer acceptance.*

Even if a child is 'at risk' (from family circumstances, special needs considerations or poor or dysfunctional behaviour at school), it is likely that they will be attending school on a more or less regular basis – particularly so at primary level. It is here, at school, that teachers (supporting each other) can make a difference. Children spend a third of their waking day at school. School can, and does, awaken a child's potential to *learn*; not just to learn literacy and numeracy skills (crucial as they are) but to learn that life has many possibilities – and that better, more positive choices can be made in life. A third of their waking day in a school – that's a hefty (legally required) slice of their life and development. Most children enjoy school, and cope well with the formal and informal demands of schooling and education. That small percentage of children who are frequently challenging, or emotionally behaviourally disordered, need some extra level (and kind) of support while they are with us.

Every teacher (one hopes) considers the special needs that some children have in areas of literacy and numeracy. Schools allocate teaching personnel and time for such students. Programmes are developed, plans are made and implemented. The teachers in this book apply the same sense of 'need' to children with behaviour concerns and behaviour disorders. These children, too, need support as well as necessary and appropriate discipline. This support will need to include a teaching component related to the students' 'academic' and 'social survival skills' (Rogers, 2003). This is discussed at some length in Chapter 3.

Schools are a *crucial* factor in the total social mix. As Elizabeth McPherson notes in her essay, at early years level, the teacher may be, for some children, the most secure person in their day-to-day lives. In understanding challenging behaviours (and emotional and behavioural disorders), we need to understand that we work with, we relate to, a child – a person – not merely a difficult or challenging student.

- These essays affirm how teachers perceive challenging behaviour in their students. They note, frankly, how they sought *to understand* the disruptive and even bizarre behaviours exhibited by this (thankfully) small percentage of 'their children'.
- These teachers do not 're-victimise' a child because of where they are from, or their unfortunate family background. They find ways to connect with – and then support – the child.
- Communication – these teachers seek to gain a *common* bridge between child and teacher; no mean feat. They share how they found ways to connect and build positive, workable, relationships.

- Each of these teachers honestly acknowledges the struggle, the frustrations and stress that working with challenging behaviour can occasion. They also *reflect on*, and learn from, that struggle.
- They acknowledge – and value greatly – the support of their colleagues in meeting the challenge of working with these children. This is a crucial factor in all that we do to enable, and work with, challenging children and their families.
- 'Separating behaviour from the person' is difficult when a child's behaviour is lazy, rude, arrogant, mean-spirited, selfish, hostile and aggressive. While on the one hand these teachers advocate appropriate discipline (and consequences for disruptive or wrong behaviour), they do not hold grudges; they repair, rebuild and move on with the child; the teachers work with the child within.
- They provide supportive 'structures', 'programmes' or 'plans' to teach the child the *behaviour skills* they need, particularly the skills they will need at school (see Chapter 3).

At the end of the day, however, it is not the programmes we provide (essential as they are to a child's learning), it is *the kind of teacher* who uses whatever teaching practice, strategy and content, that enables the positive connections in these children's lives.

Measurement of difference or meaning (when working with challenging children)

Ken Sell

Ken is an experienced teacher of over 15 years. For the last three years, he has been working as an advisory support teacher for Education Queensland in the Nambour District on the Sunshine Coast. He has designed and implemented many in-service workshops relevant to primary and secondary teachers as well as advising administrators in areas of social equity and the interpersonal dynamics found within schools. Ken is presently finishing a research project relating to his work in schools. In this account, Ken weaves the threads of three stories about children, which span over 15 years. These stories illustrate how, as teachers, we often significantly impact on the lives of our students. They illustrate how teachers demonstrate care and compassion through their role as a teacher. It is difficult, if not impossible, to 'measure' (with any accuracy) the effect of these many interactions we engage in as teachers. The meaning, however, can be demonstrated in the telling of the stories.

'He's dead.'

'How?'

'Car accident.'

'Is his father OK?'

'Yes, he wasn't in the car. He was running away.'

The look in the eyes suggested all was not right. Those around knew little of Michael, perhaps cared little for Michael. What could I do? I'm a teacher not a social worker. I'm not trained for this. Michael needed something, someone to connect with, to trust, to love. These were subjects not taught at university.

He was 11 when he died, hitch-hiking. Metal, blood, screams, silence.

Even in death, when a cold calmness surrounds the noises of sirens and the living, there is time for onlookers to make assumptions. Families torn apart in seconds. The mother, the father, the brothers and sisters – how do they feel? The officer by the roadside can see his own family. Visions of faces smiling, angry, laughing, talking, playing, working, sleeping. How this would tear his family apart!

Michael's family was torn apart well before the crunching metal took hold.

His mother had left him; gone to the big city, problems in the mind. She ran.

His father was running but going nowhere. He ran to the pub.

Now it was Michael's turn to run. He ran head on.

What was he thinking as he stood by the roadside, thumb out, rain dripping, waiting for a stranger to become his friend, to drive him away? He was 11 years old. What was he running from?

Michael had started the marathon long ago. Long before I'd met him. He'd been hurt, emptied of trust. Lost. His smile gave a different impression. One of hope – there's a chance; I'm not a bad kid. The smile hid the confusion. He was confused and so was I. His smile carried all the emotion attached to someone crying for love; his face looked for peace, but his body was angry. He couldn't connect, he didn't know how. His eyes were saying, 'Please look after me', but his voice was saying, 'Get f___ed. You can't make me do it! What's happening? I don't want to go home. Can I go with you? It isn't my fault. Don't get too close to me. Shit, I need help. Will you help?'

He's dead.

He can't be, he's only 11. A child, 11 years old, leaving home, in a stranger's car about to crash on the highway. Met head on by the loneliness of life, the noise of silence, the loneliness of death.

Did his father weep or was he too pissed? Did his mother weep? She may have – but for the overdose. People went to the funeral. It was a long time ago now. He'd be 26 all going well. Now I wonder who remembers the boy of 11.

Clinging to the cliffs, through the tunnels as black as the stockpiled coal on the sidings, the train made its way down the coast. Like that night of death, there was a coldness about the air from the south as it shot up the escarpment. I was leaving one kind of work behind, apprehensive as to what to expect as the train pulled into the platform that is a university.

I know I could not have stopped Michael's death, but my training as a teacher left me ill-equipped to recognise the problems with Michael, to cope with Michael's emotional disturbances or to teach Michael about himself. The years of further education in an institution that pays scant attention to social justice in terms other than theoretical was never going to prepare me for Michael.

Like the officer at the roadside, I made assumptions. I thought those at the cutting edge would have an educated memory. It wasn't as I thought.

When I walked into the university, I was clear in my thoughts about education. I had vision, compassion and intent. When I walked out a qualified teacher, I suffered from fragmentation of thought and mixed messages about pedagogy, unable to declare with any confidence what education is all about.

Teaching, like parenting, doesn't come with a ready-made formula. Both Michael's parents and I made many mistakes. I'm lucky enough to have been able to learn from mine. I cried for Michael but I didn't know why.

Much later I found out.

Gee, you're a good bloke!

Years later, my aunt told me that regardless of what's happened, *leaving the door open* is the most important thing when working with people.

But sometimes finding the spare key to my house is difficult enough, let alone the key to the minds of students so that they realise they have unconditional access into our classroom. Even though sometimes when I do find the 'key' and open the door some students won't come in, this doesn't mean we should be selective in our invitations to enter; far from it. I firmly believe we do make a difference to the lives of all students we come in contact with.

It is the *type* of difference that is important.

This first story is a simple and uncomplicated one about the influence we have on children both young and adolescent. Recently on the Australian Broadcasting Commission's programme, *Radio National*, I heard someone talking about resilience. The point he was making is that although a group of children can grow up in very similar circumstances (namely structural poverty), some end up contributing positively to society while others are a cost to it. The man speaking on the radio believes the difference is partly due to the *quality* rather than quantity of childcare given to the child that makes the difference.

Teacher *quantity* of care is easily 'measurable' by those outside the relationship. However, it is a far more difficult task to measure the quality of the care we give students, because of the subjective nature of quality relationships and the fact that the results are not always immediate.

Listening to these ideas about resilience and the difference we as teachers make reminded me of the time I was given a nice bottle of red wine some five years after I had taught a child in Year 2. Unbeknown to me, this child was miserable and hated Year 1, and he was finding it difficult to come to school each morning. When I was leaving the school, the parent of this child gave me the bottle of wine in recognition of the work I had done in 'turning her son around' all those years ago.

'Thanks, but what did I do?' I asked the parent of a child heading down the path of school refusal.

She told me that she remembered the day her son came home and said that now he liked going to school. When she asked him why, he said, 'Mr Sell said, "Gee, you're a good bloke".'

Five words of encouragement to the boy. At the time, I thought nothing of it. However, five years later, I was told of it and nearly a further five years later, I began to understand what quality really is. So now when the economic rationalists come to measure my performance I say to them – when they look miserable and don't really want to be at work – 'Gee, you're a good bloke'.

Terry

Like the first story, this one is also about a boy who lived in structural poverty and despair. The previous year, Terry nearly succeeded in providing a very well organised and experienced Year 1 teacher with an opportunity to have a 'nervous breakdown'. She refused but did suffer a great deal in the meantime and was exhausted by the end of the year. I wasn't going to become his second victim.

But how could I prevent this from happening? I worked on two things. First, I gathered as much information as possible about past teacher experiences and became determined to avoid those situations that lead to conflict. Not an easy task given Terry's need to be the 'boss of everything'. Second, I decided that Terry needed a trusting relationship if he was to develop the social skills expected and that this relationship would not be created through coercion. All that aside, I still had to deal with a boy whose life picture was less than happy. After two weeks of bloody hard work, I decided that this child needed only one rule to follow.

The rule was that *he was not to infringe others' rights*.

Nothing else. Pretty simple.

What does it mean?

Good question and one I worked on throughout the year. In his language, the rule became: *he has to get along with others*.

This meant he didn't have to do his school work, line up, sit on the carpet, join in group work or anything if he didn't want to; *however*, when he was interacting with others (which he really wanted to do), he simply had to get along with them. Of course, to teach the boy the skills he needed to get along with others, I needed help. This was a problem too big for me alone. Realising it was a shared problem, I enlisted the other students in the class to help and help they did. Before we made our plans, it was important to know what we were all talking about and what the problem was. As a group with a shared problem, we informed each other by being quite transparent about the problem. We then mapped the boy's misbehaviour so we could all recognise it as it happened and then we had a plan to do something about it.

We agreed the problem was that: *usually when Terry doesn't get his own way he throws a tantrum.*

Then we used a very transparent mapping process which the whole class – with the student – helps to construct. It is a very interesting process and one I've since used repeatedly with varying degrees of success.

I wrote on the board:

1 Terry wants to be the Boss. (He replied, 'Do not', and rubbed it off the board.)
2 Terry becomes verbally aggressive. ('F___in' don't', as he rubbed it off the board.)
3 Terry becomes physically aggressive. ('Bullsh_t!', as he kicks the furniture around the room and rubs it off the board.)
4 I have to 'remove' Terry from the room. ('Can't do that. I know my rights', as he is 'removed' kicking and screaming.)
5 Terry in a calm manner wants to return after about five minutes (and he does).

All through this, Terry 'did not want to know'. This was a very big room full of 'mirrors' for this student and I feel he didn't like what he saw. In his discussion, he proceeded to rub out each part as I wrote it up. The next day, I wrote the same thing on a piece of paper with a felt pen and this time he accepted it.

By doing this, we gave Terry a very good idea about his own behaviour and how his peers saw his behaviour at times. It also provided an 'instrument' for me – as his teacher – and the other students to identify what was coming next. It was a positive experience to watch them say to Terry, 'You're up to number 2. Do you really want to do this?'

Of course, there was far more to it than I've described. But we were confronting the reality as we saw it and we found agreement to that reality and the belief that it could move forward in a learning context rather than one of mere containment or management.

I firmly believe that if we put behaviour in the context of education, we can look at new and creative ways of developing teaching practice based on learning theory. With Terry, we spent a lot of time giving him an opportunity to recognise his current inappropriate behaviour and then learn the skills to change the misbehaviour. We had an open door policy for Terry, despite his misbehaviours, and we helped him change the picture in his own mind of schools and people in authority.

His peers rallied to the cause like neighbours can rally together when faced with disaster that could destroy their community. They, too, learnt new skills about dealing with difficult people.

Before he left, just prior to the end of the year, he was still occasionally telling someone where to go, doing next to no school work set by me (he was already very good at 'readin', writing and the other thing') and generally misbehaving. I asked him what he had learnt in Year 2 at this school.

He replied, 'Mr Sell, I've learned to get on with people.'

Try measuring that.

Changing perceptions of challenging behaviour: Tom and his teacher

Larry Taylor

Larry was transferred to a new and rapidly growing school a few weeks before the end of term three and given a 2/4 class. The children were drawn from eight different classes. The school was growing so fast that the classroom was a temporarily partitioned off section of the school library which had been partitioned once already and currently was home to a Year 6 class.

The children, without exception, were feeling unwanted and uncared for, having been uprooted from their existing classes so far into the year. They were less than impressed by their 'new' home and more than a little unsure of their 'new' teacher. He had to deal with tears and anger as he helped them move, and cope with the angst from parents as well.

Larry shares the 'strategies' that connected with his challenging students, noting that there are no 'formulas' for building the sorts of relationships that encourage positive change in a child's perception and behaviour.

In my year 4 class, I noticed a young boy – Tom – looking sullen and discontented, already. Unhappy with his new lot, he dealt with this situation with an approach that some might call 'creative disobedience'. When the group lined up after breaks, Tom would be in the vicinity of the line leaning against a post. When asked to join the line properly, he would do so but stretch out his hand to the post and lean slightly towards it. When the line moved, he would wait until the last moment to release contact with the post. He looked at me at each stage with a look that dared me to say something. When I made the 'mistake' of doing so, the immediate response was along the lines of 'What? I'm in line.'

This type of scenario was also regularly played out in class. Tom would speak when silence was required, speak louder than necessary when quiet talk was asked for, be last to sit down when quickness was needed and so on. These actions, however, were always accompanied by a well-thought-out, if somewhat manufactured, 'good reason'. I'm sure all of this was Tom's way of letting me know that he was not happy about being moved from his previous class. Instead of simply telling him that what he was doing was inappropriate – 'Tom, keep your voice down, thank you' – I found that asking a question – such as, 'Are you doing what everyone else is doing?' – was the more effective strategy (because Tom always had a 'reasonable' answer).

There were several other students in the group posing problems of their own, as well as Tom, and I took every opportunity to build a relationship with them as well. I did this by asking questions to find out what they were interested in and what they did in their spare time. With Tom, it was like pulling teeth initially; there was a great reluctance on his part to give me more than monosyllabic responses. As I showed more interest, however, he grudgingly gave more information. I made numerous attempts to hook into these interests, with little success, and I was becoming frustrated by the whole experience. The rest of the class were beginning to adjust to their new circumstances, but problems with Tom continued. I decided that whenever I needed to speak to Tom about some problem, I would call him over and speak to him quietly one-on-one so that less attention was drawn to the problem, but Tom frequently countered this by loudly saying, 'I didn't do anything!', or something similar, as he approached me.

There were times when juggling razor sharp knives in busy traffic seemed a more attractive proposition than going to work. I spent many days and nights pondering how best to deal with this – and I should add that we had regular class meetings from day one, where we all talked about what we were thinking and feeling about the changes we had been subject to. We also did 'getting to know you' and team-building activities, mixed in with a healthy dose of fun, but Tom steadfastly refused to buy into any of this. Then one day, unexpectedly, in a matter of minutes, everything changed forever. I had not thought through the particular strategy that I ended up using. When the breakthrough came, it did so from a seeming spur of the moment action on my part.

Without waiting for a problem to occur, I once again called Tom out to speak to me. My request was greeted by the now predictable loud voice, saying, 'What did I do now?', to which I quietly replied, 'You're not in trouble.' His demeanour changed instantly. I then sat on the carpet in front of a whiteboard divider and invited Tom to do the same. I picked up a whiteboard marker pen, drew a circle on the board and wrote Tom's name in it. I then said, 'This is what I know about you.' I drew a line out from the circle and at the end wrote 'likes' and then began saying and listing the things Tom had been telling me he liked. Then I drew a second line and at the end wrote 'friends' and then spoke and wrote down the friends he had talked about. I continued with 'good at', 'groups', 'music', 'TV shows', 'movies', 'books' and anything that I remembered that he had told me. I resisted the temptation to write anything that he might perceive as 'negative' and focused only on the 'positives'.

Tom mostly sat quietly and listened, occasionally correcting, clarifying or adding to some piece of information I was listing. I acknowledged these additions by amending what I had written and discussing some points with him. We were having a 'real' conversation for the first time and it was a pleasant experience. What happened next took me completely by surprise. Tom asked for the whiteboard marker, and then drew a circle on the board and wrote my name in it. He drew a line from the circle and then wrote 'likes' and began listing things like 'sketching' and 'computers'. As he went on listing things like 'good at science and maths', I became more and more amazed at how much he had learnt about me. But the last two things he wrote surprised me most of all. He wrote that I was 'friendly' and 'cared about kids'. If anyone had asked me how Tom perceived me, those two items would probably have been the last two things I would have ever considered. From that moment on, Tom and I got on really well. There was a new-found respect that altered all our perceptions and interactions from that moment on. Tom left the school, and that district, at the end of the year. Two years later, he returned to pay me a visit and the mutual respect was still there. I was interested in being updated on how he was getting on and what he was currently doing. He seemed to be equally interested in how I was going as I answered his similar questions about me.

When I look back on those early months with Tom, I think that the strategy I had spontaneously used allowed Tom to see that my overall perception of him was favourable. I had included words like 'friendly' too, because he was, towards everyone else. It also gave Tom some control, in that he was able to update or amend my perceptions of him as we went, something he would not normally have been able to do – at least, not usually in a positive way. Although I didn't think of the other half of this strategy, the half that Tom used, I now realise that I could have invited him to take the pen and list what he knew about me, having already modelled the process using him as the example. A possibly risky venture, granted, but nevertheless informative. The value in doing so was, firstly, that Tom was now in control of the interaction, something he often tried to be anyway, although this was a different and more positive type of control. Secondly, it gave me an insight into how Tom perceived me. This was something that I often attempted to influence by my actions, but – prior to Tom's revelations – I had judged my actions to be unsuccessful and Tom's perception of me to be unfavourable. Obviously, I could not have been more wrong. Clearly, Tom had been unwilling to share anything favourable he had learnt about me, until after I had first shared – in an 'organised' way – the favourable impressions I had formed of him.

Finding a connection point for change in behaviour: Alex 'wins a race'

Karen Kearney

Karen shares her journey with a 12-year-old and how she helped him to 'belong'.

A Year 6 student (whom we shall call Alex) had a one per cent attendance record and read at 'beginner' level. Alex had difficulty completing tasks and was assigned a peer tutor. When he did attend school, he spent a great deal of time with teachers from the Special Education Unit. Alex lacked social skills and often behaved aggressively toward other students. Not surprisingly, he spent most of his lunch and recess time under administrative supervision.

In this short essay, Karen shows how she was able to find a connection point for a change in the student's sense of belonging at school.

During the first lesson for which I took the class (as a student teacher), I attempted to establish a rapport with Alex, but he responded by covering his work and placing his head on the desk. Alex stated that he 'knew what to do' and that his peer tutor would help him if he had any problems. I subsequently actively observed Alex's activities and noted that half way through the lesson, he had not attempted the task.

Later, I discretely asked Alex why he had not started the activity and he replied that he was 'not interested'. In an effort to identify motivators that could be adapted to aid Alex's education, I asked what did interest him and he replied 'running and sport'. I therefore suggested to Alex that if he finished his work, I would take the class for a run in preparation for the upcoming athletics carnival.

Alex immediately commenced to put some effort into the task – although he did rush, was initially reluctant to accept assistance and demonstrated a short concentration span. During the next 20 minutes, Alex sought immediate progression to the sports activity by constantly claiming to have finished the task. On each occasion, I acknowledged his efforts and encouraged him to continue. When Alex did eventually complete the task, his personal satisfaction was quite evident.

I adjourned the class to the oval soon afterwards. Alex was very enthusiastic and difficult to quieten. I informed the students that we would 'run the first lap as a slow jog to warm up' and then do some stretching. The race was to be then run with a requirement that runners stay within the marked lanes. As an incentive, I informed the students that anyone who obeyed the rules and completed the race before I did would receive a prize.

Alex and a few other children immediately raced around the oval during the warm-up lap. Alex then approached me and stated that he had won. I asked him what my instructions were for the first lap, but he did not reply. I restated my instructions and then commenced some stretching exercises. I asked Alex if he knew of any stretches; he did and *ably demonstrated an exercise to the class.* Alex's turn (possibly first ever) at peer tutoring appeared to help him over his earlier disappointment and he enthusiastically completed all the stretching exercises.

We then conducted the race and at the finish, Alex informed me that he had won and wanted his prize. However, Alex had not stayed in the 'lanes' and I advised him that he was disqualified from receiving the prize because he had not complied with the rules. Two boys who completed the race correctly were awarded prizes.

As we returned to class, Alex told me that he knew he was the fastest and that next time he would win. I replied that if he completed his work tomorrow, we would go out and race again.

The next day, Alex completed his work and won an important race.

Choosing to teach: choosing to make a difference

Elizabeth McPherson

'When I chose to be a teacher people said that it would be difficult, but I certainly didn't think it would be like this...'

Elizabeth scans the students in her class group of infants and reflects on the wide range of emotional and behavioural disorders present in a number of her students. Aware that many of the 'reasons' for such behaviour lie outside her control, she nonetheless asks how a teacher can still make a difference.

When I was completing my BA and about to start my Bachelor of teaching, that's when all of our friends began, in earnest, their full scale attempts to dissuade me from the profession of teaching. Surely, I thought, what could be a more honourable, rewarding and fulfilling career than teaching? One year down the track and now I see what some of them meant. In my first year of teaching, I have been exposed to more diseases than a third world tourist, had less sleep than an emergency room doctor and been exposed to more unusual, strange, even bizarre people than an American talk show host.

At university, the proverbial 'they' enjoyed using analogies such as 'a child is like a flower, that when nurtured, will blossom into a thing of beauty'. Within the first week of knowing my more challenging students, I was tempted to use the analogy 'some children are like weeds that take over the garden'. In a perfect world and even on a good day in the classroom, the first analogy is true, yet easy to forget. This year, I have often needed to remind myself that my children are 'flowers', not 'weeds'.

On teaching rounds, I felt a connection with the children with whom I worked, I felt close to them. But in my first year on the job, I would have to say that I have (for the most part) felt like a mother with post-natal depression, longing to feel a connection to her child, but often feeling frustration and resentment. I found the first few months of teaching frustrating and heartbreaking at times. Most of my children came from dysfunctional, violent or underprivileged homes and my classroom, despite my best efforts, was not the educational 'utopia' that I had hoped it would be.

Then, one day, I heard a startling statistic at a professional development session: that children hear 100 negative comments to every one piece of encouragement they receive. The next day, I walked into my classroom determined to focus on the positives. As the year has progressed, I have learnt to become closer to my children and have come to accept them for who, and what, they are. One of my achievements this year has been developing a close relationship with a particular child who used to hide under tables and refuse to come out. This particular child refused to join the rest of the class or do anything, was petrified of the playground, of specialist classes, of theme days or anything out of the ordinary. Just recently at the school concert, not only did he go out on the stage, but he even led his line on; I was so proud. He still climbs up onto my lap whenever he is in need of 'sanctuary', but he has certainly blossomed.

Another one of my 'flowers' is the child of parents with heroin addiction. He was so violent that the assistant principal asked him to remain indoors at play times so as not to jeopardise the safety of others. This child has had a lot of trouble sitting still or focusing on his learning tasks and is extremely impulsive. I have always said to my own mum and dad, 'In what other job do you see potential doctors, teachers, parents; the person who will cure cancer, car thieves, murderers, prime ministers?' I looked at this beautiful little boy and thought, 'What will become of you, what chance do you have, what horrors do you go home to at night?' I have worked hard *while he is with us at school* to help make this child feel important. He sometimes sits on my chair and chooses people who are 'sitting beautifully' to go and get their play lunch, and he is now the one who tries to have the 'hardest working table'. At one level, I see myself reflected in him. When he is playing, he pretends to be me, and I know I am doing a good job when I like what I see.

I went to the birthday party of one girl in my class as a surprise guest, organised by her parents. While I was there, I was amazed to see that I was the one they all came to for conflict resolution, encouragement, opinions … I discovered that teachers are never 'off duty'. After the party, I drove another one of my students and her mother home. On the way home, she brought to my attention that we, the teachers, are the ones who spend the most time with their children. In *some* cases, we know the children better than their parents and may be the only really stable and positive influence in their lives. This is perhaps the first thing that made me want to become a teacher.

Teaching is definitely not a job you go into for the fame and glory; you do it to make a difference.

These days, there is an ever-increasing push towards globalisation. As a result, there has been an increased push towards technology in the classroom in addition to the traditional three Rs. As teachers become evermore accountable for the performance of their students, the academic side of schooling is pushed to the forefront of classroom planning while childhoods may be at risk of being marginalised.

I too – at times – have been guilty of pushing my students too hard and have needed to remind myself that they are only five years old. Talking to one of my parent helpers, I commented on one of my student's writing – 'Can you remember writing like this at this age?' – to which she replied, 'I can't even remember learning to write in grade prep' (infants). We are putting more and more weight on little shoulders and I, for one, think that we should allow space for 'developmental play' in our work programmes.

During the lead up to the school concert, I was reminded of the importance of play in the lives of my students. We were heading off to an unscheduled rehearsal when one of my boys began to show obvious signs of distress. 'What about free time?' he said. 'Why are they making us do our dance again? We know how to do it ...' As I thought about getting him a paper bag to breathe into, I was reminded, yet again, of the desperate need for play in children's overall development. I recall seeing a child from my mother's school who developed 'environmental autism' from having no stimulation as an infant. From birth, he was left to lie in his cot for hours on end and as he grew he was never allowed to play with paints, play-dough, puzzles ... anything that 'messed up the house'. As a result, he was placed in a special school when he turned five. Although I make no claim to be an expert on this topic, I do claim to be genuinely scared by this story.

Some of the highlights of this year – as a teacher – have been:

- The time Corey cut the tip of Luke's finger off, and – carrying a hysterical Luke – I found myself drenched in blood.
- The time Lachlan told the Italian teacher that he was going to 'rip her f___ing arms off' and the numerous occasions on which he threatened to 'burn the f___ing school down'. (He didn't – thankfully.) Later, he would come over to me, hold me and seek reassurance that 'I was going to stay, wasn't I? Don't leave, Elizabeth!' I didn't.
- The period of several weeks in which Luke refused to come out from under the table (see p. 12f).
- The candid revelation of Nick's mother that she was a heroin addict (that helped explain why Nick was often late and why she often forgot to pick him up at the end of the school day and ...).
- Finding out that some of my students are confusingly related through various torrid 'affairs' of their parents.
- The day that Damien's auntie got him in a head lock and practically ripped his

ear off during a sports lesson I was conducting.

- Having dirt thrown in my eyes, and being kicked, punched and sworn at by a student on yard duty (playground supervision).
- Another teacher finding one of the students soaked to the bone (rolling in a puddle) because, in her words, she had decided to 'fall' repeatedly into a puddle.
- Seeing nits for the first time and many, many times since.

Every recess or lunchtime, I wait for the inevitable knock on the staff room door announcing that one of my children needs an ice pack because they have been punched or kicked or are covered in some new strain of violent rash. All I could say to the other teachers (with a wry smile) was that I didn't give birth to them – *but I am their teacher*.

We live in a society where some of our children present as 'damaged goods' in school.

It is not their fault.

At the end of my first year of teaching, I am left with one thin, elusive but crucial strand of idealism: if I can make a difference in one child's life, if one child finds some self-worth in my class, if one child makes something of themselves, then I have done my job.

I am a teacher.

Chapter 3

Teaching Children with Emotional and Behavioural Disorder

Introduction

Bill Rogers

This is the longest chapter in the book; it is devoted to several accounts of how teachers have developed individual support programmes and plans for children with challenging behaviours and for children with emotional behavioural disorders.

As noted earlier (p. 27), while home background, parenting styles, family dysfunction and structural poverty can significantly affect a child's behaviour at school, such 'causal pathology' is not merely inevitable or immutable with regard to a child's future. Behaviour – like 'intelligence' – is not fixed.

Behaviour is learned as well as conditioned. And it is *learned and conditioned* in *varying contexts*. If we accept that 'conditioning' leads to challenging behaviour, that behaviour has been learnt – even if the genesis of that learning is forgotten by the child. Those who work effectively with children with significant behaviour needs create new, structured and positive learning contexts for the child in the one place that as teachers we can make a difference – *the third of the day he is with us at school*.

This chapter addresses a common theme, noted by all the teachers, that notwithstanding any 'causal pathology' contributing to behaviour and predisposition, a child always has the potential for *un*-learning, and developing *new* learning – providing they have adequate ongoing support.

Sound principles of learning underlie this assumption. Even where a child has a behaviour disorder such as attention deficit hyperactivity disorder (ADHD), teachers will emphasise academic and social survival skills when they work with the child within the schooling context. Children with Autism Spectrum Behaviours and Tourette's syndrome, have very often benefited from the concepts and strategies noted in this chapter.

Where a child has 'learnt' poor, inadequate, inappropriate or dysfunctional patterns of behaviour, teachers work with the child to directly teach new, appropriate self-coping behaviours that will strengthen a positive sense of self and learning and relationships at school.

All children want to belong; it is a central – social – need (Dreikurs et al., 1982; Erickson, 1970; Maslow, 1970). The children described in these accounts often seek to belong in attentional or power-seeking ways, with adverse, or even self-destructive patterns of attention- and power-seeking.

These teachers do not easily get sidetracked by those factors – in the child's behaviour patterns – over which they have no control. They focus on what they can do, *at school*, while the child is with them.

When addressing patterns of distracting, disruptive or dysfunctional behaviour, they ask:

- How *frequent* is the calling-out; the 'clownish' behaviour; the butting in; the pushing in line; the inappropriate loudness; the task avoidance; the challenging or oppositional behaviour, etc.?
- How *durable* is such attentional or power-seeking behaviour? Is such behaviour more than 'bad-day syndrome'? Many children have a 'bad day' (or weeks!) affected by a wide range of issues, concerns and relationships. The children we are writing about here express challenging behaviour with a high frequency and durability (many times in a given lesson; almost every lesson; almost every day ...).
- How *generally* is such behaviour observed? Is such behaviour frequent and durable in the grade/subject class or is such behaviour frequent and durable across all teachers (and support staff) who work with this child? If a child significantly changes his behaviour pattern across several teachers/classes, he can hardly be termed emotionally/behaviourally disordered. He may well be *selectively disruptive*; in this case, it is often a teacher personality/subject issue. In such cases, it will always help if a supportive senior colleague can work on a plan *between* the child and that teacher. For such a plan (in such a context) to have any success, the teacher will need to be empathetic to the issues that signal a significant variance of behaviour by the child *when in their class*.
- How *intensely* is such behaviour displayed? There's a big difference (in teacher tolerance) between a child calling out and *loud* calling out, between a six-year-old quietly rolling on the mat, and loud, kinaesthetic rolling, or wandering or pushing or shoving ...

When any *pattern* of behaviour (as above) is observed, these teachers – with their colleagues – have developed a *whole-school plan* to give some structural and educational support to the child to learn new patterns of behaviour (Rogers, 2003). When children are supported by developing academic and social *skills,* their self-esteem and self-concept is strengthened.

One, two, three, four, out the door – or STOP (Straight To the Office Please)

Bette Blance

The day starts out well. The trip to school is uneventful, even though the long trip each day from home to school sometimes brings its own pressures. At least there is time to think about the class and Bert. His behaviour is getting worse and Bette has spent so much of her waking time thinking about him lately. What is she going to do?

Bette shares how she – with her colleagues – helped Bert to develop his own plan for his own behaviour.

These thoughts are common, with many anxious teachers wondering what to do about those children who choose behaviours that do not help their learning and disrupt the learning of others. Very often, as these behaviours are recalled, they crowd out any thoughts about the rest of the class and their learning. This adds feelings of guilt to the feeling of inadequacy as a teacher.

Much has been written about how to work with these students and teachers continue to try to solve the problems with a variety of approaches.

Out of sheer frustration and not knowing what else to do, some teachers send the child to the office with a note. They vainly hope the child will be 'fixed up' and sent back to try again for another day. While it does still happen, teachers today are less likely to want the child to come back fearful and remorseful. Whatever the motive the teacher has in sending the child out of the classroom, some students spend an inordinate amount of time on 'the pathway' between the classroom and the office.

What messages are conveyed to the student who is sent to the office by the teacher? What kind of thoughts do students have as they set off for yet another interaction with one of the administrators?

Is it thoughts of 'Yeah! I've won again.'
Or 'I couldn't do the work anyway. This school sucks!!!'
Or 'What will my parents say this time?'
Or 'I knew I was a rotten kid, I've done it again! Why can't I be like the others?'
Or 'It wasn't my fault, I'll get that Jason when I get back to class, it's all his fault.'
Or even 'I haven't taken my tablet this morning.'

Whatever the thinking that accompanies the student as they go to the office, as teachers we need to ask ourselves, 'Has what I have just done (sending the child to the office) brought us closer together or has it pushed us further apart?'

Dr William Glasser, in his book *The Quality School* (1992), has written extensively about a 'lead management' approach in the classroom. He proposes that teachers need to provide a warm and caring environment and encourage responsibility by teaching the students to become self-managing.

If we do send children to the office for particular disruptive behaviours or because they have reached a certain 'level' on our school behaviour plan, are we then enhancing or damaging the relationship that we really need to establish and maintain with the child?

In his book *Behaviour Recovery* (1994, revised 2003), Bill Rogers proposes an approach in which the child is not simply sent to the office but where 'the office' comes to the classroom so that the teacher remains involved; involved *and supportive.*

In 1999, as school administrator, I used this process with the six Year 3 classes for which I had responsibility. I encouraged the teachers to become involved in a trial of the process that would enable them to put the process in action. I asked them to act sooner rather than later so that behaviours did not escalate, creating even greater concern.

My initial actions were to conduct professional development sessions with the teachers so that they could take over the process as outlined in *Behaviour Recovery.* I discussed the importance of maintaining involvement in helping the children to make better choices. As the grade teachers, they were the ones who could be with the child consistently to encourage him or her to stick to a plan. The whole process itself would enhance the relationship with the child.

During our professional development, we discussed the process and agreed to follow these procedures:

1 The teacher and the student *clarify the behaviour* and discuss why it was (or is) inappropriate (they would do this one-to-one with the child and at a time when they could do so *supportively*).

2 The teacher *mirrors* the inappropriate behaviour so that the student can see what it looks like. 'Mirroring' involves the teacher showing the student what it is – specifically – about his behaviour that is inappropriate/unacceptable/wrong. All 'mirroring' is always conducted one-to-one *away from any other students.* The teacher will always ask the student's 'permission' before 'mirroring' their *typical* distracting or disruptive behaviour, e.g. 'Do you mind if I …?' or 'I'd like to show you what it looks like when you call out lots of times in class …'. This 'display' of their behaviour is brief and the teacher will physically step away a pace, to indicate she is out of 'student role'. The 'mirroring' gives the student a more concrete reflection of their behaviour, as it were.

3 Together, the teacher and the student *draw pictures*, to further acknowledge the 'target behaviour'. These pictures can be in simple 'stick-figure' form. They would illustrate (for example) a child putting his hand up without calling out (and not waiting his turn) (see Figure 3.1). These kinds of drawings are

extremely helpful for children in early years, though we have used a wide range of picture cues even at secondary level.

This is the part of the plan the student keeps as an *aide memoire*. *(Editor)*

NB: Many teachers (and teaching assistants) at early years level will use basic 'stick figure' drawings for such plans. Some teachers will use photos of the child behaving 'within his plan' (as it were). If photos are used there needs to be parent/carer persmission (Editor).

Figure 3.1

4 The discussion around the pictures (drawn) would be about the *impact of the behaviour* on the other children in the class.

Editor's note: Many teachers, for example, will have a small drawing of the teacher looking upset, and the other children looking upset, as a child repeatedly calls out in class and interrupts. A second picture illustrates the child remembering his plan with the teacher and classmates looking 'happy'. This links the concepts of peer affirmation with the child's positive behaviours (see Figure 3.1).

5 The student *rehearses better behaviour choices* in a second role play.

6 The teacher and the child *identify strengths* that will help the child to keep to the plan.

7 The teacher *encourages* better choices of behaviour in the classroom and *facilitates self-evaluation* by the child.

We developed a planning sheet (see Figure 3.2) that would be used in the discussion with the child and all agreed to try the process.

What have I been doing that is stopping my learning?	What will I be doing to help my learning?

My plan is to do more of ... _____

My plan is to do less of ... _____

Student signature _____

Teacher signature _____

Parent signature _____

Figure 3.2

My role was to respond to a note from the teacher when I was to take over the class while the class teacher used the *Behaviour Recovery* process. I also designed a self-evaluation book (see Figure 3.3) to enable the child to monitor their own behaviour and to let me know periodically how their plan was going. This was set out with a page for each day.

Following the professional development, we were ready to begin. The first message arrived. Bert had continued to talk after several warnings while the teacher was teaching the class. The teacher would like to try *Behaviour Recovery*. I went to the classroom to find that the children were engrossed in their own work and so I was able to support the teacher as she implemented the process.

We became involved in a role play where Bert became 'the teacher'. His jaw dropped as his teacher acted out the typical (and frequent) nudging and talking behind his hand to his friend. His amusement at his teacher and the deputy principal taking on the roles could hardly be contained. He laughed aloud at our antics. Now, some teachers would believe that managing students is a serious business and that laughter was inappropriate. We believe that learning and fun are closely linked. We also believe that memory is enhanced by the fun and enjoyment that was inherent in this process. Bert also tried some of the managing techniques that the teacher had used in her classroom. This gave her information about her own style of managing students.

Following the role plays, the teacher set aside some one-to-one time to work with the child to formulate a plan for change. The plan included the self-evaluation book, which was used each session and verified by the teacher. A small notebook with a 'thumbs-up' sign on the front (found in most supermarkets) is the

Is this how I want school to be?

I made thoughtful and helpful choices all session   ☐   ☐   ☐

I made more good choices   ☐   ☐   ☐

I didn't make good choices but I can do better next session ☐   ☐   ☐

Is what I am doing helping or hurting?

Figure 3.3

ideal size. A copy of the self-evaluation tool in Figure 3.3 was pasted on several pages of this notebook.

Bert was given control of how long he wanted to use the self-evaluation book. Inside the cover, I had written the following information:

> *When you think that you no longer need this book and you can manage your own behaviour, please bring it to Mrs Blance for a surprise.*

After about three weeks, when Bert brought the book back to me, he stated that he would no longer need the book, as he was now 'self-managing'. I asked if he would like a certificate or to play a game. Surprise, surprise, he chose a game. We proceeded to the courtyard outside the office and with some string I tied a balloon to my leg. His task was to try to pop the balloon and mine was to try to keep the balloon out of his way (without running away). There was great hilarity as he tried to stand on the balloon. Thankfully, he was able to do it before I ran out of steam.

To heighten the experience, and add to Bert's need for 'power' and fun, I asked Bert if he would like to teach the game to his class. We went back to the classroom, where I asked the class about how Bert had been choosing to behave in class lately. (I checked with Bert – beforehand – if this was OK for him.) They affirmed that he was now making much better behaviour choices. Bert then invited the class outside. He had the children line up, giving half the class a balloon to tie on to one foot with the other half of the class the task of popping it. In this way, Bert was able to receive positive recognition from his classmates for the changes he had made in the way he was choosing to behave. The teacher reported ongoing improvements in his behaviour.

The *Behaviour Recovery* process enables the teacher to maintain their contact with the student and be fully involved in the *recovery* from the behaviours that hinder learning. Some teachers think that children need to be sorry for their behaviour. They think that by choosing language that implies guilt, the child will change. Such teacher behaviours are destructive to the relationship between the child and the teacher. If a child is laughing and looking forward to putting the plan into action or making better choices, they are working from a position of strength rather than a position of weakness.

The position of weakness may result from a number of responses. Children may choose the fight or flight response. They may back-chat or argue or they may withdraw. They may blame others and self-talk adds to their feeling of inadequacy. If we want to work from a position of strength, *Behaviour Recovery* is an excellent teaching model to use.

I did have some amusement from a note I received during my last days at that school (see later). While I was not involved in the process, I often wondered how the role play went for this incident (particularly how one might use 'mirroring'!):

> *This student has been looking up rude words in the dictionary and showing his underwear to students who were lining up for school.*

There is always a way back: an individual behaviour management plan

Mara Smart, Mariette West and Pamela Curtain

Nick, a grade 6 student, was frequently in trouble for distracting and disruptive behaviour; frequent loud noises; hitting and touching others' belongings; task refusal; at times throwing things around the room; and non-compliant behaviour. His behaviour was also creating peer alienation.

Mara, Mariette and Pamela share how 'negotiated boundaries' and a consistent plan helped Nick change his attitude and behaviour and improve peer acceptance.

Most schools have a downward vertical model for their school behaviour management plan. While school communities might discuss choice and negotiation, most expect students to conform to guidelines that begin with a warning and end with exclusion. Students then choose to behave or not to behave in the appropriate manner. If they continuously opt for the latter, they can convince themselves that they're 'bad' and accept the downward spiral. Students can feel disempowered with no control and think it is futile to change their behaviour. Here, we propose an alternative approach and present a case study of a student where this approach is working effectively.

'There is always a way back' is a programme that encourages school communities to revisualise the behaviour management structure as circular rather than vertical (see Appendix, p. 178f). This model encourages the student to think about where they are, where they would like to be and how they can get what they want in fair and co-operative ways. The plan is negotiated by the teacher, the deputy principal, the student and the parent, who all sign an agreement. The student draws a line from each marker back to the start and discusses ways to repair and rebuild relationships with their teacher and the class. The teacher is provided with a 'scripted plan' to give some guided structure to enable them to remain calm and consistent when informing the student about their choices and consequences. When the teacher calmly places negotiated boundaries around the student, the student feels 'safe' – negative emotion is minimised, escalation is avoided and successful outcomes are facilitated. This is illustrated in the student's comment below:

> I'm on marker one, I've made a mistake but I know there is always a way back. If I follow my plan and I make the right choices I can get back where I want to be. Even if I'm on marker two or marker three or marker four there's always a way back. The teachers here want to help me, it's up to me to find my way back just like when I drew the lines from each marker back to where I want to be on my plan.
>
> (See plan in Appendix p.178f)

Proactive relationship-building strategies are articulated in the plan; this is essential. Connections are made and sustained between the student and key players in the school. The adults are encouraged to ask themselves – regularly – if the ways in which they relate to, and lead and manage, the student will bring them closer to the student or push them further apart. Ways to acknowledge the student's achievement of his goals that are student-valued, immediate, frequent and regular are also negotiated. Parental support is gained so that significant family members (like Nick's grandmother) are included.

Whole-school support is organised so that the teacher is sustained by their colleagues. In the case of Nick (see Appendix), a behaviour management plan has been developed to incorporate a sense of supportive community and positive relationship building. Each morning, Nick makes breakfast for himself and the deputy principal, and therefore appreciates the administrator's open door policy as a comfort zone and a place to settle down before the school day begins. He is able to ring his grandmother when he needs the connection with family for added reassurance. A team case conference, early in the year, involved Nick's mother, his previous class and current class teachers, the senior guidance officer, a behaviour management support colleague, the principal and deputy principal and the support teacher for learning difficulties. A specific plan was developed to include roles and strategies as mentioned above and within the classroom and whole-school community. See below:

Deputy principal:
- mentoring of the student and an open-door policy
- co-developing an individual behaviour management plan and modified programme with the class teacher and trialling and modifying them (collaboratively)

- responding immediately to the teacher's phone calls (this is crucial for time-out situations when a student is *repeatedly* disruptive and not responding to the class teacher; or when there is any significant safety issue. All time-out options need to have been canvassed and a 'staged' time-out plan developed) (see Chapter 6).
- facilitating a whole-class exit from the room, when necessary, and staying in the empty room with the student until he is calm again. In a crisis situation, where a student's behaviour is *repeatedly* disruptive or dangerous, and where they refuse a calm, supported time-out from the classroom, and are – in effect – 'holding the class to ransom'. The class teacher calmly exits the whole class and leaves the disruptive student in the time-out care of a senior colleague. This form of 'crisis time-out' needs to be well planned – it involves being able to phone for a senior (nominated) colleague who is able to come to the class and stay with the disruptive student while the class teacher exits the whole class. In effect, if we cannot enable the student to exit the room for necessary time-out, we need to enable the peer audience to be away from the disruptive student.
- organising for the school counsellor/chaplain, a male mentor for Nick, to train in Freerk Ykema's 'Rock and Water' programme and lead the students through it. (This is a self-esteem development programme for students.)

    There are many such programmes in schools where mentors from outside the school facilitate programmes to support students in school.

Support teacher for learning difficulties and guidance officer:
- liaising with the team so that Nick's academic needs are determined and provided for.

Mariette (Nick's class teacher) speaks of her experiences:

> My name is Mariette West. I teach Year 6/7 at Musgrave Hill State School where we have a school-wide behaviour management plan. Before coming to Australia, I taught in a school in Canada for one year. Recently, however, it became obvious that the behaviour strategies I had used in the past don't work for all students and in particular not with one of the students in my class.
>
> I was asked, a week into the new year, if I would take into my class a student who wasn't functioning in his previous class. The combination of students in his previous class was such that with Nick in the room as well, very little effective learning was happening for anyone in the room.
>
> Nick's arrival into the classroom wasn't welcomed by those students who had been his classmates in the previous year. Nick's negative, attention-seeking behaviours became evident very quickly and these included:
>
> - making continuous loud noises
> - refusing to complete any work
> - throwing things around the room.
> - hitting and touching others' belongings as he went past their desks

After a month of trial and error dealing with Nick's behaviour, it became clear that I had to put into place a programme that was suited specifically to him. I begged for help. After meetings with his mother, previous teachers, the school psychologist who had worked with him in the past, and the administration team at our school, we began to get an idea of where we had to go with Nick.

As a result of the meetings, Mara Smart and I began developing an individual behaviour management plan. Nick was given four goals to focus on (e.g. work quietly, use computer only when allowed, hands and feet to himself and follow teacher's instructions).

Editor's note

The concept of 'work quietly' was *specifically* conceptualised.

This was best developed by 'mirroring' typical loud voice usage and then *modelling* and *rehearsing* what we mean by 'work quietly'. Without the specific *identifying*, *modelling* and *rehearsing*, children may be unclear about a general behaviour concept such as 'work quietly'.

In a sense, if we (as teacher) cannot *specifically* identify/target necessary behaviour/s and then model and rehearse them, the child may be unclear about what we actually mean when we say 'work quietly' or 'sit properly on the mat'. It is crucial, when working with children whose behaviour presents within the autism spectrum, that we are able to *specifically* connect with the child's understanding and experience.

Each time Nick achieves a goal, he is acknowledged. If he doesn't, then I have a specific four-marker plan to follow.

I have been following the plan for a week and a half. Nick seems to like the structure and most times does the right thing, but when he doesn't, I know the steps to take. It takes the guesswork out of it. I am optimistic that Nick will show improvement as long as I consistently follow the plan.

Mariette's optimism – backed by colleague support – was rewarded.

In discussing behaviour management, the idea of a long, torturous visit to the dentist comes to mind. The prying, poking and prodding is like the intervention we put in place for some students and their families, who sometimes see us as interfering 'do-gooders'. It hurts. It touches nerves. It gets too close. The intervention places stresses and pressures on everybody in the student's 'system'. Often, the situation seems to worsen before it improves. We have witnessed the pain of parents coming to grips with the consequences of their child's aggressive and, sometimes, violent, interactions with fellow students and staff. Often, they inflict their anger on those intervening. Like dentists, perhaps, we need to hang in there for as long as it takes; to build trust, to send calm, positive messages to ourselves and everyone involved, to reassure and to keep them all informed, so they know in advance that some things will work and others might not.

In their book *The School for Quality Learning* (1993), Crawford, Bodine and Hoglund write that all individuals are driven by genetically transmitted needs that serve as instructions for attempting to live their lives. They are the need to *survive*, the need to *belong*, the need to gain *personal power*, the need to have *fun* and the need to be *free*. Influenced by past experiences, everyone adds to their needs differently. We all have our own memories of need-satisfying behaviours specific to our own unique life experiences. These pleasurable memories make up our *quality world* and become the most important part of our life. For most of us, this 'quality world' is composed of pictures (or perceptions) representing what we enjoy in life. These perceptions become the standard for behavioural choices. When what is happening in our lives matches our *quality world pictures*, we feel in control. When what is happening in our lives does not match our quality world pictures, the mismatch is often a source of stress.

We all have a 'quality world picture' of the teacher we want to be, of the classroom environment we want to develop. We all have a quality world picture of what we want our students to be like. We make behavioural choices to match our pictures. When we think, feel or act in a way that does not match our picture of the teacher we want to be, or when children act in a way that does not match our picture of the students we want to teach, we can choose frustration and anger.

When a school and its teachers seek to engage the quality world of students, they are more likely to make behavioural choices that can help them get what they need. Individual behaviour management plans can help us restructure students' school days so that school is part of their quality world.

At Musgrave Hill State School, we believe that 'there is always a way back' for our students. We intervene with team case-conferences, individual behaviour management plans and modified weekly programmes which all involve a wide range of people in the student's 'system'. The modified programme means that Nick's day is varied so that his 'multiple intelligences' are harnessed, his basic needs can be added to and the responsibility for teaching him is collegially shared across several staff members (see Appendix).

Extensive collegial support structures underpin all our strategies. These structures include time-out partners across the school, an appropriate behaviour classroom at break times, a behaviour management teacher on-site, a male chaplain/counsellor, a formal mentoring programme with mentors trained by Griffith University (Gold Coast) and an Establishing Teachers Network which is co-ordinated by four Musgrave Hill teachers across the local area. Students designated *at risk* are a whole-school shared challenge and with this supportive environment, individual weekly programmes can help shift the school into their 'quality world'. Students can then recognise that survival, belonging, personal power, freedom and fun are accessible and that with effort and understanding from all concerned, 'there is always a way back'.

Helping a child change his behaviour and his short attention span

Kerrie Miller

Kerrie works with young children with special needs in learning and behaviour. She shares an account of how a behaviour recovery plan helped a young student refocus his attention and learning in class. This plan helped change the focus from discipline and correction to learning support.

I work with a wonderful young man called Matt who has Downs syndrome. He has a very short concentration span and was constantly interrupting the class learning time by rolling on the floor and playing with his shoelaces. Constant verbal reminding was not working for him, in fact it was actually contributing to the class disruption – it was affecting other students' attention and learning.

Using the *Behaviour Recovery* model (Rogers, 1994 revised 2003), I decided to try picture cues to help in our behavioural modification task. I drew Matt rolling on the floor and emphasised the sad faces of his friends and teacher. (On discussion, Matt didn't like the picture.) I also drew another picture (some simple 'stick figure' drawings) – Matt sitting up and listening intently. The faces of his peers were happy and his teacher's face was relaxed and happy. (Matt loved this picture and wanted to show everyone.) These pictures (the picture cues) became Matt's personal behaviour plan. These pictures were used in the one-to-one behaviour-teaching sessions as a basis for *clear* awareness of required behaviour and as a basis for discussion and *behaviour* rehearsal.

During class time, the picture cues became his reminder cards; I often used them to remind and encourage Matt. Initially during classroom time – particularly during whole-class teaching time when the students sit on the carpet at the front of the room – I would very briefly draw Matt's attention to the cards and he would correct his behaviour immediately. I gradually reduced my interaction – to tapping the card and non-verbal contribution – until all I had to do was use Makaton cues (sign-language) to direct his attention to the cards. (See also p. 46).

The overall result of this programme was that Matt's behaviour improved rapidly, as did the behaviour of the rest of the class (this was an unintended bonus!). The non-verbal instruction (and reminder cues) allowed the learning time for the whole class not to be interrupted.

I now use picture cues, and behaviour rehearsal skills, as part of my behaviour support, to modify specific behaviours of other students and have had great success.

AD/HD and teaching academic survival behaviours

Bill Rogers

A number of the children who present with emotional behavioural disorder have been diagnosed with AD/HD – attention deficit/hyperactivity disorder. Further, many of these children take medication for this 'disorder' such as Ritalin or Dexamphetamine (both amphetamine by-products, 'stimulants' that can assist concentration and attentiveness).

When an older student says, 'I can't help what I do because I've got ADD', we respond with a supportive wink, 'Well, we'll have to teach you then'.

I was chatting with a nine-year-old lad (one-to-one) about his 'behaviour problems' (as he called them). 'Do you know what my problem is?', he frowned then raised his eyebrows as if to say to me 'listen carefully, Mr Rogers'. 'No, I don't know what your problem is, Craig.'

'Well,' he said, 'I've got ADD.'

'Have you – what do you do about it?' I asked.

'I take some tablets.'

'Ritalin?' I asked.

'Yes.' He went quiet; a little serious.

'Do these tablets help you to come into class without pushing or shoving other students?' I asked.

He seemed puzzled but then said, 'No,' with a slight frown.

'Does the Ritalin help you to go to your desk area without decking your mates on the way?' As I asked this, I added a slight smile. (*Note*: 'decking' in this context is Australian slang for 'playful' – testosteronic – punching.)

This time, he smiled back as he said, 'Nope.'

I asked one more question. 'Do the tablets help you to put your hand up without calling out, and to get organised with your class work?'

He was grinning now.

I whispered, 'So why do you take the tablets?' I paused; 'It's not my job to tell you not to take the tablets. I'm a teacher, I'm not a doctor. But I can teach you how to …'

We then had a discussion about how we work together on a *behaviour plan* that could help him to focus on the skills that would help him with his learning and his behaviour.

A copy of Craig's visual reminder plan is noted in Figure 3.4, p. 58.

My colleagues and I are not unsympathetic to behaviour disorders such as AD/HD, or autistic spectrum behaviour such as Asperger's syndrome; we have learned that children with special needs and behavioural disorders have a genuine learning need (see Cooper, 1997; O'Brien, 1998; Rogers, 2003). This knowledge is – at times – held in creative tension with the stress of working with children with emotional and behavioural disorders. In mainstream schools, the degree and extent of support is not always available for the development of behaviour support programmes.

We are also aware that many children with behavioural disorders take pre-scribed medication for such behaviour disorders.[1] However, if a child is on medication, they will still need some form of behaviour plan to assist them *while at school*. Medication can affect, significantly affect (at times), brain chemistry and aspects of physiological behaviour. Medication cannot – obviously – teach a child what to do with any increased concentration and attentiveness that might arise from prescription medication for AD/HD.

All the teachers who have shared their journey in this book have emphasised how they spent *time* with a child (with challenging behaviour or emotional behav-ioural disorder) *teaching* alternative patterns of behaviour.

For example, take an older child (diagnosed with ADD) at primary or secondary level who finds it very difficult to get settled or focused during 'on-task' learning time: their desk is overly cluttered, they can't find the right book for that activity, they've got a pencil case that needs a crane to get it on the desk. One young lad called me over in a Year 8 class; he hadn't started his classwork. Some five minutes had gone by … I chatted with him to help get some focus and I commented on how large his pencil case was; he looked up and said, 'You know what, Mr Rogers? I can fit my head in here.' I said I believed him. 'I'll show you!' I replied, 'It's OK, I believe you, Craig.' He then stuck his head into the pencil case to prove the point. 'What have you got in there, Craig?' I should not have asked. He emptied it out: a broken watch, football cards, broken biros, dried out felt-tipped pens, a can of soft drink, a screwed up sandwich, a mobile phone … He had the tiniest space left on the table to actually do any 'work'. In many cases, the 'busy pencil case' is another task-avoiding strategy. Some students would rather be seen as a distracting student than a student who is unable to do the class work. The pencil case is a kind of 'mask' for their insecurity (as well as a bit of attentional fun!)

In such cases, many teachers now develop a personal plan for the student (developed out of class time). This plan focuses on deceptively basic 'academic survival skills' (Rogers, 2003) and is centred in a supportive one-to-one pro-gramme emphasising positive role play, behaviour rehearsal, cueing and feedback.

---

1. Such medications include Dexamphetamine and Ritalin (these are amphetamine-based medications – stimulants). There are also non-stimulant medications used for some types of ADD (see also Clough et al., 2005).

The aim is always to increase the child's behaviour self-awareness and lead them to self-monitoring and self-regulating behaviour. In the example of increasing a student's on-task skill, the plan focuses on:

- **Teaching** the student how to have an organised and uncluttered desk.
- **Colour-coding** workbooks so they know – quickly – what subject books they need to have on their desk. Only *that* book on the table at *that* time.
- 'Garaging' the big pencil case (that crowds the desk and is a time/visual distractor) and having a much smaller, and accessible, **table pencil case** on the desk, with only a red and a blue pen (checked once a week for viability), pencil (no sharpener), ruler and eraser. Some students will spend several or more minutes playing with little toys – or other special paraphernalia – in that large pencil case. Often, too, they do not have a pen that actually works.
- Discussing with the student about *reading carefully.* This is a significant challenge. Many of the male students with learning needs are embarrassed about their struggles with reading and comprehension. As part of the *individual management plan,* we offer to the students the option of working with a reading partner (RP). This is a fellow student with high social intelligence – someone the student is likely to be willing to sit with who can quietly assist with reading (of board, book or worksheet task) – in a way that will not embarrass their classmate or 'do all the work for them'. It will help to offer two or three names of potential reading partners to the student. Sometimes the students are willing to let the teacher act as a reading partner. The essential issue, though, is to give the student reading *support* (in class time) in a way that minimises any embarrassment. Many of these children are also on supporting, parallel reading programmes.
- Teaching the student through **one-to-one role play** how to: approach a learning task, asking themself questions such as '*What* am I asked to think about/do right now?' (whether 'board'/book/worksheet or group task) and then begin the task (bit by bit) with date, margin, etc. This is all practised with the student in one-to-one behaviour recovery sessions (Rogers, 2003). Such practice always occurs away from the audience of his peers, normally in 'non-classroom' times.
- Each three to five minutes, the class teacher will come to the child's table to **check** and to *briefly* **encourage** them in their plan. A small reminder card stays on the child's desk (if they want) as a visual *aide memoire* with the key reminder points of their plan (see Figure 3.4), p. 58.
- The message is clearly communicated (in the one-to-one sessions) that 'If you need teacher help this is *how* you get it ...' We never assume; always **explain clearly *how* to fairly gain teacher assistance.** This is to counteract easy calling out or 'wandering'. Even such behaviour as seeking teacher assistance can be practised.

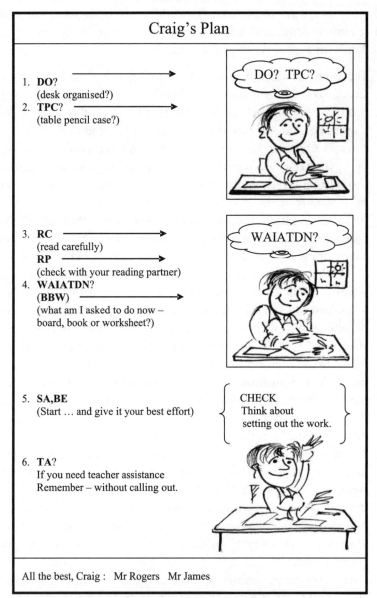

Figure 3.4

The teacher will frequently encourage the child – during classwork time – by giving brief, positive, quiet, 'private' and *descriptive* feedback, e.g. 'You started quickly. You got your table pencil case out ...' The teacher will come back again briefly – to quietly give more descriptive feedback. 'You've written half a page,

Craig ... and you remembered to use all the words we brainwaved about ... I notice you've added a few more of your own.'

Encouragement

As with all encouragement, we avoid overly public encouragement in the sense of broadcasting to other students. At upper primary and secondary level, students tend to be easily embarrassed by public encouragement (such as mentioning or showing an individual's work to the whole class – something we should never do without their permission). By 'private' encouragement, I mean the quiet word (as we move around the room during on-task learning time): the quiet, often brief, positive descriptive aside or comment.

Some children with challenging behaviours do not respond positively to the sorts of glowing praise that some teachers give, such as, 'That's great work, Sean!' Some students will respond with, 'No, it's not, it's rubbish!' Conversely, some students may only believe a teacher is valuing them (and their work) if they are *frequently* praised in glowing terms such as 'brilliant', 'fantastic', 'marvellous', 'wonderful', 'great' ... We are on safer, fairer, surer ground when we *describe* (rather than evaluate); avoiding non-specific words like 'fantastic' and 'brilliant'.

While not ignoring a student's mistakes or errors in their classwork (these can obviously be supportively acknowledged), it is not helpful to *disclaim*, or judgementally *qualify*, a student's effort in work or behaviour. Easy qualifiers such as 'Why?', 'But' and 'If only' will often mean the child focuses on the last part of the feedback, e.g. 'You've remembered many times, today, to put your hand up without calling out (the positive feedback for the behaviour plan) – *if only you would do that all the time, we would have a much happier class, wouldn't we?*'; 'You've done half a page of maths so far, *why can't you do that all the time?*'; 'You've completed the exercises *but there are too many mistakes. You need to be careful, don't you?*'

Teachers who give such *qualified* feedback I'm sure mean well. But I wonder how we (as adults) in a similar situation might feel and how such feedback might affect our ongoing motivation and effort.

When addressing a student's errors (in 'academic' learning and in behaviour), our tone and manner are as important as our words. The simplest corrective is to acknowledge and affirm the student's effort and *supportively note the area for correction*, fine-tuning or change. For example:

You have been very careful in using all the terms for sea mammals and how they breathe. I couldn't quite understand what this part here means ... When you read it through you'll see what I mean. Check the spelling of porpoise and dolphin. You've explained, clearly and helpfully, how they are different ...

I'm glad you managed to answer all the topic questions – some of them were not so easy, were they? Well done! Remember to put the date on and the topic heading.

Descriptive feedback (and encouragement) always takes a little longer but is more constructive than a grading (8 out of 10 or 'B') with a 'well done' or 'good effort'. These terms don't carry any information about *what* was 'well done' or 'good' about a student's work or behaviour (see also pp. 130f).

Children within the Attention Deficit Disorder spectrum do sometimes miscue and rush their work and they will need support to become more thoughtful and paced learners. Behaviour plans noted in this and other essays give students a structure for that skill development.

A tall order: a challenging student on day one and after

Patsy Finger

Patsy Finger describes the 'tall order' of balancing rights and responsibilities with 11-year-olds. She shares how she developed an individual and whole-class focus for responsible student behaviour.

Patsy recalls her first day back at school after a relaxing, refreshing Christmas holiday. Enthusiastic and looking forward to the new year, she was feeling very positive. The Year 6 children were welcomed warmly to the class-room ...

First encounters

Unexpectedly, a noisy Year 6 boy caught my attention as he reluctantly entered the classroom with a parent first day back. As he approached, he declared that he wasn't staying. In fact, he insisted that he was leaving. I was bewildered because he claimed to have no books or any other belongings to put into his desk. He had his 'rights' he said. He then blasted at me and stubbornly refused to unpack the contents of his school bag. When he sat down, he put his feet up on the desk and folded his arms. Needless to say, his parent had (by this time) disappeared. He ordered me not to touch his school bag because it was his property. I must admit that the day had already taken a sharp dip downhill, and things were not looking good. All my good cheer was falling on deaf ears. A further confrontation with him seemed pointless. Power struggle? I had the awful feeling that he had the upper hand!

At this stage, the bell signalled the commencement of class and I did, after all, have a new group of children to attend to. I spoke positively to the children as they listened attentively, with keen enthusiasm etched on their faces. They all looked so refreshed after their holiday. But my challenging young lad wanted to make his presence known. He achieved this by interrupting the class discussion, by badgering me – and other class members – and frequently calling out. It was jarring to say the least! My apprehension was further exacerbated by his flat refusal to do anything he was asked.

He claimed to have the right to do exactly as he wished.

Pressing buttons

Calming myself, I decided that I was definitely sending out negative vibrations. How could he possibly be so antagonistic and fired up *already*? After all, it was only 9.15 a.m. on day one! I even began to think that maybe I was wearing the wrong deodorant. Was I wearing red? Something was aggravating him! He was certainly trying to 'press my buttons' and test my patience. Was I pressing his?

Whatever the reason, I had to find a way of ensuring he could not repeatedly continue to disrupt us in this manner. Standing close to him, making direct eye contact, speaking quietly but firmly, I asked him to take out his pencil and a book. He barked back at me that he had none and firmly held his desk closed with his knees, and ordered me not to touch his desk. I offered him a piece of paper and a pencil which he repeatedly threw away, but added that I could sharpen the pencil. I repeated my directions firmly and indicated that his behaviour was unacceptable, but he declared that he had had enough and he was leaving.

The search

Since I had a whole class of children to attend to, I decided that it was time to contact the principal of the school, who had talked with me about our young lad earlier. When the lad realised that the principal was approaching the classroom, he bolted.

People searched for him all day in vain until, at 2.50 p.m., he boldly waltzed into the classroom, soaking wet. He announced to all that he had only come back to collect his bag. What a wonderful day he had experienced. While we were at school and people had been searching for him, he had spent the day jumping off the Chevron Island Bridge into the cool waters below!

The slow change process

I knew I needed to work with my colleagues if I was going to reach this young lad.

My colleagues supported me in developing an approach based on team work: setting goals with the child (one-to-one, away from the pressure of the 'peer audience') and taking time to talk with him and learn what interests he had. It took some time for trust to develop between us but I 'persisted'. Building trust takes time and there is some natural risk with trust. I also took time to consider his preferred learning style (we do this with all our students). I frequently looked for ways to encourage him and help him build success in his learning.

Above all, I had to learn to be patient and kind to myself, realising I couldn't change him – *but I could change how I related to and worked with him.*

Principles for behaviour management, growth and understanding

Team work

- Gain support from the behaviour management team.
- Work in collaboration with the parents.
- Gain support from other teachers and administration.
- Seek advice and support, with the consent of parents, from Juvenile Aid Bureau (in extreme cases).
- Gain assistance from the school counsellor.

Goal setting

- Set firm, clear expectations for behaviour.

Editor's note

These expectations are set around three non-negotiable fundamentals:

- We all have a right to feel safe at school (this means not just physical safety but how we feel at school).
- We all have a right to basic respect (this means we show manners and thoughtfulness to one another).
- We all have the right to learn (which means we do not interfere with others' learning, and we support each other as learners).

The implications of these expectations are discussed with the whole class but also in more detail with respect to *individual behaviour plans*.

- Provide rewards and appropriate consequences within fair discipline. That discipline was based in class-wide, school-wide rights, responsibilities, fair rules and consequences (see Chapter 6).
- Set small, *attainable*, work goals suited to ability. In this case, programmes needed to be modified and the student worked on an *individual* programme.

- Plant the seeds of success – nothing succeeds like success. That success, though, was not accidental; it came from a collegially supported process and planning.

Understanding the learner

- Remember that the crucial 'first step' is consciously taking a positive, and willing, interest in the child. This involves taking time to listen to the child in order to *build trust*.
- Apply the principles of multiple intelligences.
- Encourage the child to learn using his preferred learning style.
- Be flexible – where possible – with learning experiences and modes of assessment.

Self-esteem

- Offer encouragement; look for the positives, small though they may seem at first.
- Be enthusiastic in what you say and do – it is contagious and raises the morale of those around you.
- Success breeds success like a rolling stone gathering momentum – leading to more and more success.

Your own needs

- Allow yourself to have some fun.
- Be kind and patient with yourself.

Editor's note

Teachers are – normally – very caring people. We can also – at times – be quite self-critical. Many of the issues surrounding a child's challenging behaviour are outside of our control. It is important we do not easily 'blame' ourselves for a child's progress while they are with us. It is important we do our best, with our colleagues' support. There will be 'bad days'; there will be days when we do not seem to 'connect' with the child – who knows what has happened with that student prior to coming to school on any given day?

Being patient with oneself means that we remind ourselves that while we could always 'do more', teaching is a profession that could easily take more than we could ever realistically give. We do our best; we do it with collegial assurance and as much goodwill as we can muster. And we remember that we – too – have a life and a family and we need to affirm that balance (p. 176).

Graduation (in time!)

My friend completed his year upon the stormy seas. Progress at first was slow and steady, with moderate changes in behaviour. I believe that he actually began to enjoy many aspects of school life. A great deal of his learning involved 'hands on': constructing, designing, computer work, games, cooking, art and craft and sport. A more thoughtful *structure* in assisting with his reading, writing and mathematics proved to be successful. His behaviour remained quite rebellious, particularly with new people, but his anger management did improve.

Outside of school, he achieved success in Scouts and managed the responsibility of a paper-run before school. These also helped to build his self-esteem. Within the school setting, he also accepted monitor positions readily.

Reflection

The experience was certainly a challenge, but it is important to acknowledge, as a final thought, the valuable growth that took place within the child and myself, both professionally and personally, as a result of our struggles.

Editor's postscript
When we consciously seek to find supportive *and creative* ways to work with the child, his parents and our colleagues, the struggle is often worth it.

Individual behaviour management plans and group support with infant-age children: Troy's story

Debbie Hoy

Debbie is currently head teacher of an infant school in a London suburb. Here, Debbie details her journey with a child presenting with 'emotional–behavioural disorder' and how she (with the understanding of her class group) helped Troy. Although these were infant children, Debbie was able to engage whole-class (peer) support for this very challenging child. It was this whole-class support, a personal behaviour plan, clear and firm guidelines and unfailing teacher encouragement that helped this young boy change his behaviour. A crucial feature of Debbie's experience with Troy was the unfailing colleague support she received.

Troy's background

Troy came into my class at nearly six years old for his second year at school. He was a very angry little boy with particularly low self-esteem. He comes from quite a dysfunctional family even though both parents are living in the home. His father cannot effectively read or write and has spent time in prison (fairly regularly) for drug offences. His mum is young and loves Troy in her own way, but finds it difficult to deal with his behaviours, and has trouble disciplining him. She is usually late bringing him to school and he often misses the first session of the day. He also has a sister who is two years younger than him.

I chose to take Troy into my class, knowing that he was challenging in his behaviour and making little progress academically, but also seeing a very sad little boy who had potential.

Making a start

The first six weeks of the school year were very challenging. Troy displayed a lot of different types of behaviours, and on some days tested me and the school behaviour policy to the limits. Some days he was quite withdrawn, refusing to do anything much in terms of the curriculum. He would say 'I can't …!' or 'I'm no good at anything!' Most days, he would display highly attention-seeking behaviours, trying to make other children laugh at him or notice him. These were the days that were hardest to deal with. He would climb under tables, onto tables, dance around the room instead of lining up, use a very loud voice for almost all conversation, walk 'through' the other children in such a way as to knock into them (to get a reaction, not hurt them), insist on wearing his cap indoors, or on not putting his toys away. During 'carpet time', he would call out, distract others or play with anything he could touch … The behaviours were many and varied in their frequency and intensity.

> **Editor's note**
>
> Rudolf Dreikurs (1968; Dreikurs et al., 1982) has noted that when children come into a social setting (like school), their primary *social need* is to belong. Often, a child's disruptive behaviour is a way in which the child seeks this 'goal' of belonging. The child may not be consciously aware that his attentional behaviours are his social goal; his 'private' logic – however – does see the connection between attentional behaviours and teacher and peer response. That response may be negative *but it is still attention.* Where a child does not believe or 'feel' he can get a sense of 'belonging' in co-operative ways, he knows how to get an attentional sense of belonging.
>
> The challenge is to help the child to change his *means* of achieving a desirable personal and social goal. (See also pp. 121, 122)

I went through the normal pattern of 'establishing' with the class as a whole: setting up the rules to support the shared rights, and helping children to take responsibility for their behaviour through a system of choices and consequences (within the rules and routines). Troy tested 'the system' to see if it was consistent time after time. Some days, he responded fairly well to the choices and consequences given to him and would co-operate. On other occasions, he would run out of the school, or would become very angry with me and would shout and scream and hit out. At these times, I would sometimes take Troy to another place for cool-off time (time-out) so that the other children could carry on with their activities. Sometimes it was better to take out the whole of the rest of the class for something special (stickers from the head teacher, an extra playtime, etc.). This obviously had implications for the curriculum for the other children, and also on staffing. Fortunately, I had a full-time teaching assistant in my room who was able to deal with either Troy, or the rest of the class. Sometimes we had to restrain Troy physically. We had a policy on when and how this should be done. It was always carried out with another adult in the room, sometimes in the classroom and sometimes in another room. At first, the other children were worried and concerned about his anger and resulting behaviour and we had several class meetings (without Troy present) where they could talk about their fears and we role-played different situations so that they felt safe. They quickly learned when to give him appropriate attention and when to 'ignore' his behaviour.

Making progress

Gradually, Troy's behaviour began to improve. We worked very hard at increasing his self-esteem by talking about what he was good at and giving him lots of praise and attention for everything we possibly could. This was very time-consuming but we could see the pay-off in Troy. His whole manner changed from being a very sullen-looking boy to being a much happier and often more smiling child. He learned how to talk to others positively and with a quiet voice, how to sit on the carpet and listen, how to put his hand up without calling out, how to line up quietly and without touching anyone else, how to calm himself down when he felt angry inside, etc. We had observed that he found it hard on the days when he was brought to school late. We were conscious to help and encourage him to come in quietly and settle into the group which had already got going without him. As adults, we often find it hard to walk into a room full of people when we are late. So we helped him by giving him strategies. One of the highlights of the school year was in January when Troy became the 'star of the week' for our class and received his star at assembly.

He wasn't perfect by any means but Troy became a child who enjoyed coming to school, and he began to fit into the expected 'normal' patterns of behaviour that we get in any classroom. His behaviour continued to improve with the help of these behaviour plans. The plans were based on *learning* the behaviours he needed to be a happier student and improve his learning: behaviours such as 'quiet voice', 'hands up without calling out', 'sitting on the mat', 'keeping hands and feet to yourself', 'facing the front', 'waiting your turn', etc. Unfortunately, he was still struggling with academic progress but his self-esteem was strengthening all the time. Fortunately, he had lots of extra support from a very talented teaching assistant who managed to relate really well to Troy and get alongside him.

Editor's note

In any school with students with challenging behaviours, teaching assistants play a *crucial* role. They often develop a close, positive, supportive and encouraging role as adult care-giver and mentor.

Their colleague support in developing individualised programmes is invaluable.

Setbacks

Everything continued to go well for a few months until about May. Suddenly, Troy reverted back to being the child he had been in September (term one in the UK). I found it hard to deal with that and felt that all the hard work we had put into Troy had been wasted. I had expected that it would take a good month at the beginning of the school year to teach Troy the expected patterns of behaviour, but after nine months of him being in the class with the routines and relationships firmly established, I was surprised and disappointed.

I discovered that his mother was pregnant again and Troy had not taken very well to the idea of having another younger sibling. This seemed to be challenging his place in the family and his feeling of being loved and valued. This all came out during a time when I was restraining him with another teacher present. He started shouting out at the top of his voice, 'My mum and dad have two brats already. Lisa [sister] is a brat and now they're having another brat like Lisa!' and so on for about ten minutes. It was helpful to know that it was a home influence rather than a school one that had really unsettled him as it helped explain his behaviour, but we couldn't excuse this behaviour; we had to work on a behaviour recovery plan yet again. The other major concern was that his self-esteem seemed to hit rock bottom again; he started to say he was 'no good at anything'.

We continued to tackle Troy's behaviour as we had always done with choices and consequences, and behaviour agreements to identify and practise helpful behaviours. The difference this time was that we chose to involve the other children more directly.

Involving the class group

I spoke to Troy privately about his behaviour and drew a picture of a ladder (on a postcard-sized card) which had a rung for each part of the day. If Troy behaved appropriately then he had a small 'reward' at the end of the session, or at the end of the morning or afternoon. The rewards were things like stickers, playing with a toy in the head teacher's room for two minutes, then five minutes (building up the time he was allowed throughout the day), trying on a soldier's jacket he had seen in the head teacher's room (a special treat!) and having a go on a special piece of equipment he had seen in the Hearing Impaired Unit. Each day, he had a new ladder with the rewards negotiated and written on at the start of each day. At the end of each day, if he had had a good day, he would get stickers ready for the rest of the class and would *give them out to the other children.*

I held a class meeting for the children to discuss Troy's concerns and this time Troy was there. He had agreed to let me talk to the whole class about his daily plans and wanted his classmates to be involved in helping him. I drew a mountain on a big piece of paper and talked (from experience) about how difficult it can be to climb up a mountain. I said that some people find it easy to climb up and want to run on ahead, and that some people find it difficult to get up and may need others to help them. Others find it so difficult that they just give up unless they have people encouraging them. As I was speaking, I drew figures on the mountain in different places. Some at the top, others struggling part way up with others helping them. I then spoke about how different people have different 'mountains' in their life. I said that for some of them their 'mountain' was reading, for others it was spelling and writing, for others it was maths, others found sports activities challenging, and for Troy, his 'mountain' was behaviour. I had discussed with Troy (prior to the classroom meeting) how we could talk about his behaviour with his classmates.

I shared Troy's plan with the children and showed them the ladder I had drawn. I asked them to think about ways in which they could help him climb his mountain. We talked about telling him when he was doing something that was good (helpful, thoughtful, kind, working on his classwork), 'ignoring' his inappropriate behaviour, reminding him of the rules and giving him two buddies to help him in the classroom and in the playground and several other ideas as well. I told the children that if they helped Troy, then at the end of each day they would receive stickers from him if he'd had a good day, or from someone else if he hadn't. We also planned a little visit to the nearby park, a celebration with drinks and biscuits, stickers from the head teacher and so on. I felt that it had to be worth their while to help him or they might not bother, or worse still, some students might copy his behaviour if they felt he had a better 'deal' than them with all the 'rewards' that he would be getting.

After this initial meeting, the children were really responsive and supportive. They helped Troy enormously, which in turn helped me too. Another idea that we came up with was to have a message board where we could write positive messages for Troy about the things he did. We drew a picture of him and at different times in the day children went there to write their personal message:

'Troy smiled at me.'
'Troy sat quietly at assembly.'
'Troy did a good picture.'
'Troy used the carpet rules.'

Troy took the message board home with him each time we did this. It became a favourite with the other children and on the days when I forgot to organise it, they got it ready themselves!

Two class buddies were chosen to help Troy. The two buddies were older children within the class. They were chosen by Troy from a list of suggestions that I gave him. They were very positive with him and thoughtfully firm. I gave them a piece of card with lots of squares on at playtimes so that they could draw smiley faces every time that Troy did something co-operative, positive, caring, thoughtful or kind. They felt that they had some control and responsible power in this situation, which helped them believe they could help Troy to change things for the better. Troy knew that he had to stay with them at playtime or he would lose his right to go outside.

Troy's self-esteem and behaviour improved enormously over the next few weeks until it was almost back to how he had been earlier in the year. It would be nice to think that the story has finished but I know that after six weeks of school holidays, he'll be coming back into my class with a different mix of children and he will need to re-establish himself in the classroom, what the expected behaviour is, how to belong to the group … and his mum will be having her baby this month too.

Now – though – we have our experience to give us confidence that the outcome is likely to be positive.

Colleague support

One of the key issues for me as a teacher has been to know that I have got the support and back-up of my colleagues. At times during Troy's story, probably all of our staff have had to deal with Troy in different situations, shared the load with me, brainstormed new ideas or supported the other children. It has been essential to know that Troy is dealt with consistently across the school by each person and for me to know that I was not alone in the situation.

Editor's postscript

This essay – again – demonstrates how much energy, effort, thought and goodwill teachers, and teaching assistants, give to children with social–emotional needs. Colleague support is essential to such enabling for the child. Our colleagues give us moral support in developing plans for these children. We also receive the essential assurance that we are (as much as it is possible) on the right track.

Educational psychologists, social workers and home–school liaison colleagues all give significant support to teachers but in the day-to-day, it is our teaching colleagues whose support is invaluable when seeking to manage children with challenging behaviours.

Debbie also engaged the positive support of the other children to support the child with socio-emotional needs and behaviour concerns. Children are often incredibly supportive and understanding and want to help classmates but need the sort of sensitive guidance Debbie and her colleagues were able to give.

Teachers often invite children with behaviour needs (at primary-age level) to work with 'behaviour-buddies' to help them and encourage them with their 'behaviour plans' (see also Rogers, 2003). This is a common – and very positive practice – in primary schools (and even – at times – at middle-school level).

Are there limits to what we can do?

Over the years, my colleagues and I have worked with some children (and their families) whose behaviours are so extreme, so protracted, so stressfully draining that we have had to recognise the hard reality that sometimes we cannot reach every child. Or put another way, we cannot reach every child *at this point in time, at this age, at this school* ...

Children with extreme patterns of behaviour (diagnosed or symptomatic) create significant stress for teachers and (other) students – this is natural. When such behaviours are ongoing (hour after hour, day after day, week after week, month after month); when the parental support is rarely given (or not given), or where parental trauma is ongoing and parents are unable to express the support needed for their child; where the child is unresponsive or resistant to the school-based support we offer and where such support is resisted well beyond bad-day syndrome; where we know we have exhausted strategies, 'plans', programmes and options – then we do need to consider an alternative placement for the child. This is never an easy choice for a school to make, but 'mainstream' schooling is not the best – or even the most workable – option for a very small percentage of children.

It is important that we do not easily blame ourselves – though most caring teachers feel some sense of guilt that they could not 'get through' to *this* child. Teachers can be very hard on themselves when they believe they are failing in their mission of supporting such children. It is important – crucial even – to remember that we 'get through' to, and make a significant difference to, most of the challenging children in our schools. There will always be a need – though – for specialist schools, pupil referral units, partial enrolment options, mixed schooling and adult-mentoring options (particularly in middle-school years and particularly with male students).

Colleagues need to support one another and assure one another that they have done their best; they 'hang in there' over countless hours, days, weeks, months ... They did so thoughtfully, with care, attention, and often incredible patience and good-will. They also do it at cost to their own health and well-being at times.

It is also important to remember the rights and welfare of other students affected by the persistent – at times, unremitting – aberrant, dysfunctional and even dangerous behaviours. School leadership must be supported in the difficult choices we need to make. Sometimes in saying 'we can no longer support you or your child with his continuing disruptive behaviour ...', Departments of Education (at local government level) need to support the rights and needs of local schools as well as the rights and needs of an individual student. This is never easy; due process that is realistic but practically supporting in its options *for the child* (and his parents) is crucial.

Good practice in this area begins with a due process that enables honesty and humanity coupled with practical options. It is crucial that schools are aware of what those processes (legal and practical) are and that they be supported (not blamed) on the rare occasions they need to use them.

Chapter 4

The Hard-to-Manage Class: When it is More than One or Two

Introduction

Bill Rogers

I came across the word *charivari* in an old *Punch* magazine (of the last century). I was intrigued by this word because it appeared on the front cover of the magazine unexplained. I looked it up in *The Oxford Shorter Dictionary*: 'a serenade of rough music made with kettles and pans or tea trays … used in France in derision of incongruous marriages, hence a babel of music …'. Apparently – in this unusual custom – a group of people disturbingly bang tea trays and kettles outside the home of those whom the mob believe have occasioned an 'incongruous marriage'(!)[1]

When reading the definition, my first thought turned to well-entrenched memories of 8D, 9C and 10E! Students noisily forming outside a classroom, pushing, shoving and 'testosteronically bonding' (the males play at pushing, shoving, 'strangling' and punching). When physically in the classroom, the noise level of the group rises (a minor Babel?); it then takes some time to settle 25 to 30 students prior to a hopeful teaching period. Then the calling out and the talking across the room – while the teacher is seeking to engage whole-class teaching time. Students who walk in late (and some 'grandstand' as they enter); students who 'wander'; noise levels during on-task learning time … 50 minutes, in a class period, can seem an awfully long time with such a class.

I have worked in many, many classes like this (mainly upper primary, middle-school level). I have worked with many colleagues in such classes as a teaching mentor – to rebuild a sense of personal goodwill that can easily be eroded when we have such a class on our timetable load! I can see why some teachers do not look forward to that class, that day ('do not look forward to' puts it mildly!).

---

1. I also came upon this word in a marvellous book, *Shakespeare's Language* (2000) by Frank Kermode. He suggests that a version of 'charivari' was displayed outside Brabantio's house, interrupting the wedding night of Othello and Desdemona in Shakespeare's play *Othello* (p. 167).

Rebuilding goodwill with such a class is not easy when repeated, widespread, distracting (and sometimes disruptive) behaviours seem habituated into the very social fabric of the class. Colleague support is crucial to assist colleagues (as early as possible) before negative *habituated* behaviours become the norm. Colleague support can enable that rebuilding of goodwill and a *sense of shared purpose with the class group* (Rogers, 2006a).

In the following essays, colleagues share how they gained a fresh perspective on the 'hard-class issue' and the approaches they found helpful within the context of colleague support. Chapter 5 takes these whole-class issues further when it addresses the issues of building co-operative classrooms.

The hard-to-manage class: reasons, options, support

Bill Rogers

Within any classroom group, up to 60 or 70 per cent of students are normally willing to co-operate with their teacher in building and sustaining a workable classroom community. In the establishment phase of term one of the school year, this 60 to 70 per cent will quickly habituate behaviour that is consistent with shared rights and responsibilities (Rogers, 2006a). This group of students will co-operate if the teacher is respectful, supportive and able to engage the class group with effective teaching and positive, respectful leadership. If, however, the goodwill of this group is diminished by teaching and management that lacks confidence, and a conscious and positive structure, it is much more difficult to manage that 30 per cent of attentional and challenging students present in the more challenging classes. If the teacher starts to lose the goodwill and co-operation of the 60 to 70 per cent, even some of those students will start to 'drift across' and collude with the attentionally challenging 30 per cent.

Those students who are emotionally and behaviourally disordered (1 to 5 per cent) are even more difficult to work with if the teacher has lost the goodwill of the majority.

Having worked with many classes at middle-school level (years 5–10), I've noticed that classes *may* become hard to manage for these typical reasons:

- Sometimes a *particular mix* of students that particular year (a skewed distribution) creates its own unique tensions as personalities vie for attention and power within the group. On some occasions it can help to reallocate students within the first two to four weeks if 'catalytic behaviours' do not change.
- Where a known 'harder' class has been given to a first-year teacher, this is unfair if there is no initial mentoring support. I find it professionally untenable

when a senior teacher replies with, 'Well, that happened to many of us in our first year so why not them?' A *known* hard class should be taken by the more experienced and competent teachers; or, at the very least, there should be a mentor working with any first-year teacher-colleague to assist the class teacher to engage the first few lessons (secondary) or first day (primary).

The research is clear: *how* the establishment phase with a class is addressed can significantly affect the general cohesion of the class in the weeks ahead (Rogers, 1998, 2006a). If a teacher has been given a known harder-to-manage class, then the establishment phase of their relationship with the class is likely to suffer. Particularly so if a challenging class group is given to a beginning teacher or a teacher with little experience of working with more challenging student behaviour.

■ The way the class is *characteristically treated* by their teacher significantly affects the co-operative goodwill of the students. If a teacher's leadership style is typically 'bossy', 'petty' (over-dwelling on minor issues) or evidencing a negative discipline style, it will have a significant effect on learning and behaviour. Mutual respect has to be *mutual*. And the respect of students is earned by teachers – through the kind of leadership and teaching we characteristically exercise. Conversely, a non-assertive teaching style will send mixed messages about a teacher's leadership of the group. There are teachers who ignore repeated calling out, butting in, 'grandstanding lateness', inappropriate language and banter or inappropriate noise levels. The ignoring of such behaviour – or the inconsistent management of such behaviours – may arise out of a misguided hopefulness that things will get better; they won't – not by themselves. Some teachers are anxious or 'fearful' that if they were to firmly confront such behaviours, the students would not actually take any notice anyway. This non-assertive pattern is quickly picked up by students as indicating that the teacher cannot manage the situation – or perhaps even that they 'don't care'.

■ Some students with 'attentional' or 'power-seeking' patterns of distracting and disruptive behaviour are not addressed early enough, and significantly enough, in the first few days and weeks of term one. Such students, particularly those with emotional behavioural disorder such as AD/HD, need *early* case supervision with a conscious focus on individual behaviour plans to teach them the essential behaviours for school life (Rogers, 2003, 2006a; see also Chapter 3 in this book).

■ The most common reason why classes become hard to manage is poor or inadequate establishment *as a class group* in the critical first meetings of week one. Students are psychologically and developmentally ready for their teachers to clarify the necessary rules and routines for learning, behaviour and the relative 'smooth-running' of a complex little community called 'our class' in those very first meetings (of term one).

I have worked with many teachers who have not established clear, workable, fair rules and routines on day one; have had inadequate seating plans ('Sit where you want, guys'); have not established, explained, taught and maintained positive learning and behaviour habits; have not explained, modelled and maintained appropriate noise volume levels; cues for entry to class and settling time; time-on-task behaviours, etc. Thoughtful establishment also means consistently and fairly following up inappropriate and wrong behaviour after class from the outset – *day one*. Consistent and early follow-up of inappropriate through to challenging behaviour is crucial in the establishment phase of the year. Such follow-up (one-to-one) – whether the 'after-class chat' or formal, due consequences – can be conducted respectfully – with fair certainty – to clarify the significance of behaviour ownership in the student (Rogers, 1998).

If teachers do not establish a class group with *conscious* planning, skill, positive leadership and management, some of the students within the 60 to 70 per cent of normally responsible and co-operative students may covertly – some overtly – collude with the more attentional and challenging students in distracting and off-task behaviours.

When a class has somewhat 'lost the plot'

When poor patterns of learning and behaviour are 'habituated' across a class group, it is essential that the class teacher work with supportive colleagues to re-habituate positive behaviours with the students. The earlier this is carried out in term one, the more effective the process and outcome will be.

If a teacher believes they are 'losing' their class, i.e. if a significant percentage of the class is *frequently*, *generally* and *durably* disruptive (more than bad-day syndrome), then a 'fresh start' approach is necessary – a re-establishment of the class group to re-engage their understanding, goodwill and co-operation.

Fresh start

A 'fresh start' process (Rogers, 2006a) will need to engage longer-term colleague support to produce a workable process and outcome: that re-engages the goodwill and shared rights and responsibilities of the teacher *and* the students.

A fresh start process will normally begin with a classroom meeting with the whole class, involving the regular class teacher and a supportive senior colleague (or at least a supportive colleague who has a good working relationship with the class) (see pp. 85, 86).

This classroom meeting allows an honest appraisal of how things are in the class *at present* in terms of behaviour and general learning. The teacher (with the support of a colleague) needs to utilise the classroom meeting forum as an opportunity for the class group and teacher to address the *current behaviour* (of a significant number of students in the class) as it affects learning and relationships. It is important that this meeting is not a lecture or some kind of hectoring verbal pay-back ('I'm sick and tired of this class …!'). Such tirades – obviously – only further alienate the *potential* (and residual) goodwill of the 60 to 70 per cent of students.

Three key questions my colleagues and I frequently ask of students in such meetings are:

- What's working well in our classroom at the moment? (and why?)
- What's not working well here at the moment? (and why?)
- What can/should we do to change things here? (so that we can get on with having a classroom where we can learn well without undue noise, calling out, time 'off-task' …).

These questions can be asked through a written proforma, or in an open-forum in a classroom meeting.

The basic rules for all classroom meetings need to be made clear at the outset:

- Focus on the question at issue and don't get side-tracked (see next rule).
- Use constructive responses (i.e. no put-downs of *any* class member, including the teacher!).
- Speak one at a time and within a reasonable time limit (to shared responses and length of meeting).
- Have a couple of students record the answers if conducting an open-forum classroom meeting. I have found it helpful to have one male/one female student recording the feedback (in print form) to leave the teacher free to conduct the meeting.

It can also help to break up the whole class into smaller sub-groups (the 2, 4, 6 method) and then use whole-class feedback for the whole-class meeting (see Rogers, 2006a). Students respond in pairs to the questions noted above (for ten minutes), then the pairs join to form a group of four (for a further ten minutes to share/add/refine) then finally, groups of six or thereabouts meet for a further ten minutes to fine-tune common responses. These responses are then shared with the whole class via a group mentor (or taken up by the teacher later and shared at a second meeting).

A second meeting will then be called to give feedback and responses to the questions raised at the first meeting. Normally, what happens here is that the teacher will list, on a few large posters (and a class hand-out):

- the *behaviours* that cause us *all* concern
- ways in which we can address and change those issues raised
- the *re-established* rules and routines to support these changes.

The routines often addressed include a change in seating arrangements (to enhance learning time); cues/routines for entry, settling and class learning time (particularly noise levels); cues/routines for engaging teacher assistance (these routines should never be assumed). The earlier in term one that this process of *re-establishment* occurs, the more effective will be the long-term outcome.

Some teachers publish the fresh-start outcome as a 'class-plan' (see Rogers, 2006a) and in some cases a copy of this is sent home to parents of this class (only after approval by the school principal/head teacher).

It can also help (with older students) to publish some positive class posters accentuating core rights and responsibilities, e.g. *We all have a right to learn. To learn well here we* ... [the poster then briefly lists the key positive learning rules/routines for this key right and responsibility, e.g. getting to class on time, having the necessary equipment, remembering the hands-up rule, (without calling out, or talking over others), using partner-voice during class work time]. *We all have a right to respect here in our class. We show respect when we* ... remember that we all share the same place, space and reason for being here. Respect is about treating others fairly, as we would want to be treated (no put-downs, cheap shots, no bullying of any kind is tolerated); respect is about helping others feel safe here; we use considered language and manners.

The published tone of such posters needs to be positive, constructive, clear and expectant – not simply a list of 'musts' and 'mustn'ts'.

It may be important, also, to encourage some teachers to re-appraise their behaviour leadership and discipline as they embark on any 'fresh start' process with a class group. Goodwill and respect (as noted earlier) is always a two-way street, with significant outcomes dependent on the quality of a teacher's leadership in behaviour management, and thoughtful and fair use of behaviour consequences (see Chapter 6). Most of all, the ongoing success of a fresh start is affected by the teacher's characteristic use of supportive encouragement and feedback to individual students and the class group.

While this process may – at first sight – seem labour intensive, it does give an appropriate and *guided* voice to re-engage shared understandings and responsibilities.

It is never too late to make a fresh start with a class group, providing we are willing to allow personal and professional appraisal, the opportunity for student input, discussion and invitation to co-operate and – most of all – colleague support.

My most challenging Year 8 class ever

Leanne Wright

In this case study, Leanne outlines her experiences with one of her most challenging classes. While they wore her down at times, with colleague support, some reflective planning, goodwill and energy, she saw a change in their behaviour and learning. Leanne shares the strategies that engaged a 'fresh start' with 8D.

I heard about 8D long before I 'picked them up' at the change of semester halfway through the year. Various staff members had thrown up their hands in horror after a lesson spent with them. And even though I must have taught a few hundred grade 8s in my 15 years of teaching, I have to say I wondered what had hit me. Every Wednesday afternoon, after 100 minutes with just them and me, I desperately wanted to resign!

In that class was Rebecca, a girl who had been living on the streets on and off in the last year or so and was only allowed to return home on the proviso that she attended school. There was Aaron (a student diagnosed with ADHD) who rarely took his medication at lunchtime and whose usual response to being 'told off ' was to fart; preferably as loud as possible. I'm sure his diet was designed to produce a smell that would attract lots of attention from his mates who enjoyed the opportunity to 'go bazza' (beserk).[2]

We had the elusive Sharon and Cindy who often had to be brought to class after being discovered in their usual wanderings in the corridor 'to find the social worker' or whatever. Angela's upper lip was permanently curled to one side in a sneer that can only be perfected by grade 8 girls. Her mate, Melissa, was nice but easily led. Throw in a handful of students with significant learning needs, some very silly boys, one bored intelligent one and a bright one who kept trying to be moved out of the class because he couldn't stand it, and we had quite an interesting 'cocktail'. I didn't mind the individuals but, boy, at times I hated that class.

Bringing pens and paper to write with was a big problem. I'd always solved that in the past by bringing spares but the other teachers warned me that they never got a thing back, so I named and numbered all my pens and rulers and had a 'library' system recording who everything went to each lesson. That at least worked. It was pointless trying to get them to give up their own time to solve the failure-to-bring-gear problem – they'd almost never turn up and they'd missed so many detentions it was impossible for senior staff to keep up with it all in supporting the staff, especially since they'd often just nick off or stay away from school.

Getting them to *use* the pens and paper was an even bigger challenge – except, of course, to write on each other or to 'fight' over. I reorganised my teaching and we did a lot of work on learning social skills in co-operative learning groups. This was somewhat chaotic at first because it was so different but ultimately I think it helped me to survive with that class. We changed activities about every 15 to 20 minutes from posters to quizzes to try to keep them interested. Unfortunately, it was difficult to get permission to take them on excursions because they were known for their shoplifting expertise and their ability to 'disappear'.

I even swallowed my pride and asked senior staff to 'track' them. I'd noticed

2. Interestingly, the genesis of the word 'berserk' is the title of famed Norse warriors who fought with unrestrained, frenzied, aggression! They wore 'bear-coated' apparel [bear-sark: Icelandic].

the shorter morning lesson was nowhere near as bad as the long afternoon one, so I asked the senior staff to organise a roster to allow someone to wander through my room a couple of times during the afternoon lesson. It was invaluable. Invariably, there was someone for them to 'chase up', or an issue to deal with while I was sorting out something else that was going on, and best of all I didn't feel isolated. It didn't always work perfectly though. Sometimes they'd forget and once I ended up with five colleagues in my room at once (they had all found something to deal with while they were there). I thought that was hilarious but I also thought it was wonderful that my colleagues made the effort – I felt very well supported. All the staff who taught them also had regular case meetings about them to share ideas that had worked for them and to work on common options.

I'd already done a lot of work on classroom rules which I'm sure the kids understood fairly well, even though it was more fun doing their own thing. I re-read a book called *You Know the Fair Rule* (Rogers, 1998). A colleague shared an approach with me that was very constructive in helping me to turn that class around. The idea behind it was based on a group incentive system. I went to a local hamburger restaurant and asked them if they would donate some free 'healthier' hamburgers to our common cause – they donated 35 hamburgers and a $5.00 prize. Then I explained to the kids that to be able to go for lunch with a hamburger – free – they had to earn points by supporting our class rules. The 'catch' was that they had to earn five points in each category of the rules:

- *Communication*, e.g. one person speaking at a time (during class discussions), quiet working voice during classwork time.
- *Learning*, e.g. coming prepared for work and letting others learn without disruption.
- *Safety*, e.g. not throwing things or hurting each other.
- Treating others with *respect* (e.g. no put downs).
- *Movement*, e.g. staying in seats unless it's necessary to move and then doing so in a *sensible* manner and for good reason. (*Fair Rule*, 1998, Chapter 7 pp. 248–58)

I put the headings on a sheet and ruled columns up for each lesson – for my purposes, it was actually easier to put in a cross if they broke a rule after being reminded, etc. I'd spend a few minutes at the end of the lesson filling in the information (using ticks and crosses for speed). I only gave them a vague idea of their progress at first in order to try to encourage them all. When they had a few ticks and it seemed more achievable, I'd tell them how many points (ticks) they had. I found it worked extremely well for the first two weeks but it was a bit too slow (maybe 25 points were too many) and they started to lose interest until I sped it up considerably.

Most of the class managed to get to the hamburger restaurant (although a couple were on suspension for something else – I gave them a couple of burger vouchers when they got back to my class). The ones who didn't make it stayed behind with the senior staff member in charge of my area. She was happy to see the progress made by the others. Meanwhile, I got to talk to the kids in a completely different setting – it was really helpful and I'm sure it affected my relationship with them from then on.

Three of the boys in my class got an A on a test I gave them – the first A they had *ever* had! It wasn't an easy test, although it was a topic they'd been fairly interested in (buying a car). They just about brought tears to my eyes – they were so thrilled. I also put a piece of work typed up on computer by each class member in a display folder and showed it to the principal. He came to tell me how wonderful it was one day (when I was away). When I returned, a few of them came barging excitedly into one of my other classes to tell me that the deputy principal had told them how impressed he was. I would never have believed that success could have actually meant anything to them.

I met up with quite a few of them again on a Year 11/12 orientation day – it was quite pleasing that they actually seemed to be happy to see me – it highlighted something for me that I've become really aware of over the last couple of years: that the relationship teachers develop with kids is *crucial* to being able to 'do anything' with them.

I'm not sure it was the actual strategy that I used with 8D that made the difference, but the fact that this approach made for a more positive atmosphere and better relationship building.

Another comment I'd like to make is that I'm amazed at how much learning it is possible to do in the area of behaviour management. I've been teaching for 16 years and am still putting new things into practice – I'm still reflecting on what it means to be a teacher.

I'll never forget that class and the rewards I gained from taking a few risks. I thought I might be seen as a hopeless teacher by asking for help, and chaos reigned at times as I experimented in order to get them to do something constructive. I'm really just glad that I survived at all!

P.S. I never could totally eliminate Aaron's farting.

Editor's postscript

Any time we use behaviour reinforcement strategies, we need to think carefully about why we are using *applied* reinforcers (ticks, crosses, stamps, stickers, charts, goals/targets, 'activities', even food!). Such an approach is *never an end in itself*; neither is it a disguised form of 'control'.

When used thoughtfully (as Leanne did), it enables the class to regain a sense of success and achievement. The reinforcers become a means to this end; they are never an end in themselves. As Leanne notes in her essay, it was the *relationship building* and *positive atmosphere* that made the difference. My colleagues and I also prefer to use the terms *encouragers* and *celebrations* rather than *rewards*. We are celebrating the group's/class's effort within our shared goals.

The 'class from hell'

Denise Frost

Denise writes about her experience with a class she initially described as 'the class from hell'. She was a new teacher to the school and several weeks into second term. It was a grade 3 class: 8- to 9-year-olds (7 girls and 14 boys). The class was causing a lot of concern for all the staff members. The expectation from the principal was to settle this very restless and challenging class – 'learning' was 'secondary'.

In this essay, Denise shares the frustration and stress that very challenging class behaviour can bring – even to experienced teacher leadership. With reflective colleague support and a dogged goodwill that re-engaged the children, Denise saw the class change for the better over time.

When I walked into the classroom, the children had taken an instruction from their previous teacher to 'sit anywhere'; a number of students had taken this instruction quite literally. Desk placement had no uniformity, with some desks even facing away from the blackboard to look out of windows or onto blank walls. The first day was discipline, discipline and more discipline. One maths sum (it seemed) and more discipline.

Beginnings

I began my first teaching day with, 'What sort of day do we want?', 'How can we achieve it?'

Very basic classroom rules were established, e.g. 'listen and eyes this way in instructional time', 'hands up', 'one person speaking at a time', 'stay in seats', etc.

Each day ended with, 'What kind of day did we have?', 'What went well?', 'What didn't?' Then 'the slate' was wiped. Each day began with a clean slate and a class meeting. 'What kind of day do you want today?', 'Who can make that happen? How?' Through these 'conferences', I was inviting the students to take some shared control with me of *our* class.

There were one or two ringleaders among several 'challenging' students. I roved the room with a notebook to record names of students I needed to follow up with and those who needed time-out (I did not rely on my memory alone).

I encountered many challenging behaviours, more than often all on one day:

calling out, roving students hassling other students, work refusal, breaking pencils and throwing books, sulking and swearing, up-turning desks, bullying and running away.

Strategies

Some of the strategies I used in my time with these students (from *You Know the Fair Rule*, Rogers, 1998) were:

- Daily meetings first up to begin the day positively, and also at the close of our day together to end positively.
- Remaining as 'calm' as possible (especially when replacing the decreasingly up-turned desks and broken pencils!)
- Planning for the daily disruptions – with clear routines and reminding of rules without arguing; like teaching to *focused* students by waiting for the majority to be attentive, acknowledging positive behaviours as much as possible (even hands up) and giving encouragement whenever possible (and the children loved stickers).
- Giving short-term learning goals (10 minutes initially then finally half an hour).
- Making contracts (behaviour contracts for 'ringleaders' and those with behaviour needs), giving clear directed choices ('we work now or make up time later') and having a supportive time-out plan (colleague support was fantastic here).

Editor's note

Having a *discipline plan* is as crucial as any lesson plan. We know that we will be facing some calling out; inattention; talking while the teacher is talking; students fiddling with objects *while* we are engaged in whole-class teaching time; students who wander in late; task avoidance; chair-leaning, etc. It is essential that we have *an awareness of what we will do and say* in such situations.

Obviously, we cannot plan for every contingency – we can, however, have a plan that will enable us to respond to distracting and disruptive behaviour in the *least intrusive way possible*. (This is discussed in some detail in Chapter 6.) Any such plan will need to recognise the *characteristic* features of our discipline language; how we restate rules; give *directed* choices; deal with students who want to prevaricate and argue; and how to utilise any time-out procedures calmly and with as much dignity as possible.

A discipline *plan* is not a formula (or panacea!) – it is a way of thinking about typical behaviour incidents and how we ought to respond in as positive, calm and clear a way as possible (bad day notwithstanding).

Such a 'plan' should also consider how we should follow up one-to-one with students to repair and rebuild. Repairing and rebuilding can be as basic as a brief – positive – after-class chat, or a more extended mediation session (say between

Continued

Continued
students in conflict). *Any* repairing and rebuilding should see the teacher:

- *briefly* 'tuning-in' to how the student might be feeling at that point (in their one-to-one talk about behaviour with their teacher). 'You're probably feeling concerned (or annoyed, or angry) that I've asked you to stay back for a talk about …'
- focusing briefly on the *behaviour issue* or *task* they have been kept back for. Avoid the reactive pay-back: 'You could be outside now, couldn't you?! But you're not, are you? You're in here now because you don't listen, do you!? …' and on and on it sometimes goes!
- giving the student a right-of-reply; at least a verbal right-of-reply. On some occasions, a written right-of-reply is helpful (see p. 116)
- referring the student back to the classroom behaviour agreement (the rights/rules/responsibilities). How did their behaviour affect others' safety, learning or fair treatment/respect?
- always finishing any one-to-one meeting as respectfully as possible and seeking to separate amicably (at least on our part as teachers). Avoid the temptation to restate it all(!) 'If you behave like that again, you won't just be speaking to me, or the principal, or your mother. I'll, I'll …!' (I'll what? Ring the Minister for Education?)

Outcomes

By the end of the year, thanks to colleague support over those challenging months, the class was starting to work well. Behaviour improved with an added bonus that learning had taken place – two sorts of learning:

- real learning (about what it means to get on with each other, as a class, *day after day*)
- the academic learning.

The *real* learning was the most gratifying. These students who had earlier displayed little self-control were now able to discern the impact of their actions on a class and to modify their responses to make a difference, a positive difference.

On the last day during our reflection time, one student responded for all when he said, 'We've come a long way, Miss. Remember the first day, we only got one sum done. Now look at what we get done in a day! It's great!'

The class agreed they liked it so much better this way and recognised that they, in their choice of behaviour responses, had made the difference.

Another colleague said of a similar class, 'Initially, I saw and felt that I'd arrived at "the class from hell" – in time, I found children …'

Classroom meetings to the rescue

Carmen Price

Many teachers have successfully used classroom meetings and friendship circles to support positive behaviour management. Carmen Price shares how she has utilised such approaches to enable conflict management, problem solving and repairing and rebuilding among students. In this primary classroom, Carmen was able to encourage the classroom – as a learning community – to reflect on, and take charge of, their behaviour.

The scene

It was the beginning of term 3 (often one of the hardest terms to get through) and a class of Year 4 students were becoming increasingly disruptive and challenging. This class was recognised throughout the school as one of the most difficult compositions of Year 4 students. They shared a demountable building with another group of Year 4 students who were also far from being 'angels'. The noise in the classroom often reached deafening limits as Jack complained about someone taking his pencil, Anne cried because she hadn't had a turn on the computer, Billy tapped his desk with his ruler just because he felt like it, and a low hum filtered through the air as children chatted and complained to their neighbours. Of course, there was also the fact that this class contained a large proportion of children with learning difficulties, most of them also displaying a variety of challenging behaviours and experiencing many social and emotional difficulties outside the school setting.

For the first semester, the children had very much been in the 'forming' and 'norming' stages of group development. Many new students had joined the class, some children had moved class and the children were getting acquainted with a new teacher. However, by the third term, the class was in full swing – 'storming' had begun and it seemed like they would never 'perform'. Needless to say, the teacher was at her wits end. She had struggled long and hard to understand the needs of each of these children and had suffered beyond the call of duty. Tried and trusted teaching and management techniques, individual interventions, provision of school support (learning support, teacher assistance time), even regular yoga classes and frequent holidays were not proving enough to get through this school year.

A closer look

At first glance, the situation seemed overwhelming. The givens were that the class composition could not be altered and that some circumstances beyond the school environment could not be controlled or modified (families will break down regardless of efforts made). However, at closer inspection, many positives and much potential existed. In the early stages, the teacher had worked hard to create clear expectations for the class. There was evidence that rights, rules and responsibilities for the classroom had been established. Reward and consequence systems were also in place; in fact, the teacher had gone to great lengths to use appealing and creative processes to motivate and regulate the students' behaviours. There were 'praise cheques', sticker books, bottle-top token economies, 'bank books' and positive points to recognise appropriate actions. More challenging behaviours were managed through 'steps' processes (e.g. Warning ⇨ Quiet Time ⇨ Time-Out ⇨ Office), the 'chill-out corner' and being on 'probation'. This class was filled with a wealth of behaviour management ideas, and yet there seemed to be a lack of co-operation and cohesiveness. The teacher was feeling utterly exhausted with trying to keep up with curriculum demands and the follow-through of the classroom behaviour management plan. Tension was mounting, and would grow worse by the end of the week, after lunch breaks, after specialist lessons (or any other change in the usual schedule) and when environmental conditions changed, e.g. it got hot, it rained, full moon(!), etc.

Help is at hand

All this did not go unnoticed and a more holistic approach prevailed. Strategies were implemented to control some of the environmental factors. For example, dividers were installed between the classes to cut down excess noise and some boundaries were more clearly established to cut down interference from incoming calls during teaching time. However, the provision and acceptance of colleague support was to make a real difference and generated different ways to view and handle this situation, and most importantly illustrated that *no one is alone in these situations*. I am sure we can appreciate what it is like to have a class just like this one or to have nightmares of such a class!

Together, the teacher and her support colleague began to gather information and collaborate. By putting the evidence together, it became apparent that the teacher was carrying much of the responsibility for the classroom functioning. While the behaviour management strategies were creative and abundant, there had been limited student involvement in these processes. With such a variety of strategies in place, it was also becoming difficult to implement and follow through with all of them effectively. Rights, rules and responsibilities once clearly displayed about the classroom had also slipped to the sideline as the class became more and more difficult to manage.

The students were also relying on the teacher to solve every little problem that was raised. Jeff would complain that Ben took his pencil, Ben would say that someone tripped him over, Kate would whinge that she couldn't work because the boy beside her was talking and Sally would continually ask what she should do when she was finished. Children would approach the teacher mid-sentence with seemingly minor problems without any attempt at finding their own solution. Even though the teacher tried using reminders and prompts to encourage the students to attempt to solve their own problems or follow class processes (e.g. 'What have you tried so far to work this out?', 'What is our rule in this classroom for asking questions?'), the frequency of these types of behaviours was so great that it was often easier to take on the responsibility of solving the student's problems (e.g. 'Give Jeff back his pencil, Ben!'). However, it was important to remember that every student in this classroom had some responsibility for its functioning. This was the aim – we sought to realise that aim by more directly involving the students as a class group.

The change process

It was decided to start with the least intrusive way to influence what was occurring in the classroom. The question was asked: what is the least we can do to make a difference with these kids? Many strategies and techniques had been tried, so what now? It was a process that came to the rescue. A process that could give some of the responsibilities of managing the classroom functioning to the students. A process that could help the children learn how to solve problems on their own, a technique promoting self-reflection and internal motivation. The decision was made to facilitate a class meeting and to use this process as a vehicle for change. While this was not a new phenomenon to this class, it was a different approach to the usual meetings where *the teacher addressed issues of concern with the class and explored the logical consequences.*

The teacher and the support colleague were to conduct the class meetings together. It was decided that the teacher would facilitate the meetings with her colleague beside her as 'a visitor' watching how the classroom worked to solve problems. This was to help to empower the teacher's role in the classroom. Furthermore, the teacher would be the one (together with the students) implementing the ideas generated from the class meetings and therefore should be the one to initiate and implement this change process.

The class meeting

The process for the class meetings was based on the ideas presented in the books *Cracking the Hard Class* (1997; 2nd edition 2006a) and *Behaviour Recovery* (1994; 2nd edition 2003) by Bill Rogers. A lot of energy was put into 'advertising' the first class meeting. Invitations were given to each student and flyers were sent home to explain the idea to parents. It was hoped that this would gain the students' interest and create the expectation that this was something new and different to the norm.

By the first class meeting, the children were eager and interested. The first meeting took place at the beginning of the week in the morning. This was aimed at establishing the idea of a 'fresh start' to the week (and to the year from the teacher's point of view!). Students were encouraged to sit in one large circle (away from their desks and the usual formality of the classroom), on the same level as the teacher. The class meeting was to be seen as a time for everyone to get together as a team. A time limit was set for the first meeting and a brief description was given on the purpose of class meetings. The teacher explained that it would be a time for group discussion on problems that were bothering the class. She explained that it would be a time for everyone to speak openly and to share their thoughts, opinions and ideas. The teacher then asked for students' thoughts on having frequent class meetings. The class agreed it would be a good idea. During this meeting, the class was on-task and focused.

The first meeting established some class meeting rules (with input from most students) and other processes for running the meetings. One thing that was decided upon was the use of a 'talking stick' in the meetings so that only one person would speak at a time (the person holding the stick). It was also decided that an 'issues board' would be used during the week to record any ideas for decision at the next meeting. The general framework for each meeting was based around the following questions:

- What is working well in this class (for you, for all of us) and why?
- What is not working so well and why?
- What can we do to improve things or make things better?

After each prompt, time was allowed to share observations and concerns, test out opinions, share ideas and look for solutions (evaluating the positives and negatives of each).

In the beginning, meetings were conducted twice a week as there were many issues that the class wanted to discuss. It also seemed important that the class received regular feedback on progress towards set goals. The teacher had the main role as facilitator during the meetings with the goal of modelling the process to the students. As time progressed, meetings became less frequent (once a week or upon request if an issue was raised) and teacher input became more subtle as students became familiar with the process and took on the key roles of facilitation. Students also progressed from addressing more problem-focused topics like classroom behaviour plans and peer conflicts in the classroom and playground, to more educational topics like wanting to learn social skills, conflict resolution skills and peer mediation skills.

These meetings became a regular feature of classroom life.

The outcome

The class meeting process demonstrated to the children that they were valued, involved and key participants in class life. It helped them to see that they and their concerns, ideas and opinions counted – they 'belonged' in the classroom. The meetings also led to a more peaceable classroom environment with simplified 'reward' and consequence systems and redefined rights, rules and responsibilities. It also became a forum for enlisting class support for understanding and working with more challenging students. Most importantly, the class meetings achieved outcomes that were agreed to by all the students and the teacher.

It would be nice to claim that this story ended happily ever after, yet in the real world we know that challenges are a natural part of our daily lives – life would be boring without them. Hence, the Year 4 class did struggle from time to time with issues they brought with them to school and still on the odd occasion approached the teacher for help with solving their problems. Yet this can be expected with students in this stage of development and in a society that relies a great deal on external approval and control. It is pleasing to say that by the end of term 4, the students were well and truly 'performing' as a team, were being more responsible for their own choices and actions, and were also achieving more curriculum outcomes through a more positive attitude toward the teacher *and* their learning.

The 'icing on the cake', so to speak, occurred at the 'parent day' – a day when the parents visited their children's classrooms to see some of the achievements of the year. On this day, the students got to facilitate their own class meeting in front of the parents to illustrate how their class 'worked things out'. The positive response from the parents was overwhelming, with many parents commenting that it would be wonderful if they could use such an idea at home (e.g. family meetings) to solve problems. This feedback was valued by both the teacher and students – it confirmed what they already knew about all they had accomplished as a team.

At first glance, some people would have given up on this Year 4 class; however, a caring and dedicated teacher, a team approach to intervention and a group of children willing to change moved this class towards positive outcomes. While it took hard work from everyone involved, the results and the learning experiences along the way made it all worthwhile.

Can you believe that it was hard to say goodbye to this group of children on the last day of school? What a journey it was!

A winner – in a hard class

Heather Fraser

Heather Fraser details the journey of her relationship with a 'class from hell' – in particular, a nine-year-old boy whose window-climbing exits and expletives and much more were a challenge. Meeting that challenge required some teacher soul-searching, time and patient goodwill.

Heather honestly shares the frustrations of what can often feel like a 'treadmill' when a small but significant number of students seem to hijack a class. Heather shares how 'focused time' and colleague support helped make a difference to these children.

Have you ever had the class from hell? You know the one. How could you forget? The one that is over-size in numbers, tending to be also over-size in big-headedness, the 'Let's stir things up and get lots of attention' (of the negative type).

How can you forget the body language of some of the children that says 'I am so cool in my latest gear', 'School sucks', 'I don't want to be here', 'I am doing you a favour when I actually do the set work expected from me' and 'It's fun to interact with me mates around the room', the latter being a euphemism for the friendly interaction of throwing comments and insults around the room. Then there is the sport of 'How many times can we interrupt the teacher when she is explaining things?' Not a scene conducive to other than survival teaching for a newcomer to a grade in term 4, regardless of her copious amounts of experience.

Now if you have all that in your memory, don't leave out the two students who stand out over and above the others – and, of the two, one not interested in any 'learning' at school, it seems, and the other, the ringleader, who sets his mate off, which in turn can set off the rest of the class!

It was this type of scenario I inherited in term 4 a few years ago. I took over this grade 4, enabling the class teacher to go on well-deserved long-service leave. I had not long returned from extended leave overseas. Bad news always travels quickly and I had certainly heard of this group. In particular, Johnny, nine years old, very unkempt in appearance, out of uniform most of the time, always grubby and his hands covered in leaking biro (which he also used to suck and chew.)

Johnny – a challenging student

Johnny was constantly in trouble. He spent most of his days in the principal's office or some other time-out venue. He would clear off home, some distance away from the school, if he could 'escape', which he tried on at least one occasion, cutting through the fly wire screen in the time-out room and attempting to scramble out of the window. On this occasion, only because there were staff covering every exit, he did not succeed but he did manage to call everyone within hearing distance names to make your ears curl!

Johnny was on the dreadful treadmill of 'anything that goes wrong is my fault'. His peers would easily and happily send blame in his direction and it so easily stuck! There was a high level of antagonism between him and most of his peers, both in class and in the playground. This boy's self-esteem and recognition was built on getting attention and always of the punitive kind. His body language strongly reflected a 'don't care' attitude. There was rarely any eye contact and he rarely spoke in other than short incomplete sentences, his head down.

Book work was almost non-existent. What he did produce was scrappy, illegible, incomplete, inaccurate, grubby and he often failed to start because he couldn't find his pencil. Not being able to locate a writing implement was a matter of course at the beginning of each session, not each day but every time he needed to do some application work. With this being the case, it was difficult to ascertain Johnny's academic ability. His quick-wittedness with 'smart alec' comments, his cunningness in covering himself concerning trouble and what he could actually do, as seen with the limited amount he did do under supervision, led me to believe that Johnny could learn, could be a competent learner, but his frequent pattern of task-avoidance was making this outcome seemingly unachievable.

At this point, I need to add that Johnny was very disorganised. His desk was a nightmare: papers everywhere, torn and screwed up and nothing in their folders; exercise books ripped; felt-tip pens loose and without lids causing more mess; bits of old lunch; hats (non-school hats) and old jumpers; other 'flotsam and jetsam' peculiar to nine-year-old boys and sometimes that elusive pen and pencil we couldn't find. It was little wonder it took so long for him to get started (see also p. 57).

My years of teaching experience and student management led me to believe this boy had backed himself into a big corner and was out of his depth on many fronts. It was not too difficult to work out that his frustrating behaviour was avoidance behaviour and the avoidance was a further cover for a number of obvious and not so obvious issues.

Starting to help Johnny change his focus – working together

It is always difficult to devote more time to someone in your class who already takes up huge amounts of your time, even if it is for purely discipline reasons. But the first step was to help with the seemingly absent organisation skills – that is, after I had positioned him in the class where he had no eye contact with certain other students and in the midst of students who had enough self-discipline so they wouldn't be too distracted by him.

So, to begin with, each morning recess, I stayed back with him for several minutes to help clean out his desk, sometimes finding the 'lost pencil' and getting the next books needed to the top of the pile. This was a consequence of his wasting time in the first session and, therefore, not being able to find anything. Over time, probably because of the daily desk clean out and finding things in his desk by himself, Johnny became more successful in his learning tasks and in his learning focus. My individual attention (seen as positive) and time was appreciated, although I only realised this when over the three-month period, he was slightly more relaxed with me and slightly more co-operative. Besides, this lad was missing out on some of his recess time; in itself a nuisance for him and me, but, in my case, in the long run, well worth it. Regarding the constant loss of his pencil, he had to hand it in to me before he went to play, lunch and home. The task for me was to remember to collect it because it was up to me to follow through to be effective.

The next bit of extra time from me (besides the necessary discipline) was to station myself near him or regularly move back to stand beside him and direct and encourage him to the next item. I would even get him started by doing the first item with him. I am afraid there probably is no other way, no short-cut or less teacher-intensive way – and I was fairly quickly rewarded in seeing a quantity and quality of work completed.

It must be noted that I was not setting unachievable goals like completing all the set work (or in the early period, even half of it!). We were coming from virtually no output to *some*. I would be grateful for any change, no matter how small at first – but in the longer term, aiming as high as I dared. I was encouraged and my delight must have shown, as Johnny began to respond. In the meantime, there were another 29 fourth-graders busily doing 'their thing'. Johnny wasn't the only distracting or disruptive student.

The days that Johnny didn't come to school – I must admit – were blissful. We were pretty much a normal energetic grade 4. However, there were very few of those days when Johnny was not there.

My principal was most supportive, encouraging me to send Johnny to him to give me some relief and restore some form of sanity to the classroom, but my pride and my self-esteem in terms of student management got the better of me most of the time. However, I did relent once or twice; after all, the students would benefit and so would I. I only had this class for the last term so I guess you could consider me 'fresh'. As I would not easily or quickly send him out, he realised this was where he was to be – in our class, not merely 'getting out of things'.

Johnny in Year 5 – making progress

When it came to student placement for Year 5, I was to have a Year 5 so I volunteered to have Johnny – yet again – and surprisingly no one objected! The fact was

I was seeing a glimmer of hopefulness that 'the worm had turned' but one term was not enough to consolidate the positive changes and for some reason I felt with another year change would be more enduring. To help even further, our principal decided to break the three groups of big classes of over 30 into four smaller groups. I had a tiny room and, now, only 23 students. This made an enormous difference. As well as smaller numbers for each class, the challenging students had more individual attention, and lost some of their 'punch'. That previous Year 4 level was heavy going. You seem to get that every now and again in a school's history. This demonstrated the importance of class size and student structure. It turned out that I didn't need to enforce the kind of focused and firm discipline needed the previous year in Year 4. The four new Year 5 teachers were extremely grateful for this rearrangement.

Teaching Year 5 was so much more positive for the reasons I have mentioned. The smaller class size and a dispersion of personalities also contributed positively to Johnny's behaviour. That was the year when, by accident (or fortunate opportunity), we saw another side to him. He was happier in the smaller class setting; he knew me as a helper (from last term) and the students who had reinforced his innappropriate behaviour were no longer in the same class. Also, with a smaller class and far more relaxed environment, we did more interactive and interesting things like formal debating (not the arguing with the teacher variety as in the past). It was here we saw another skill. This boy, who thrived on positive attention (like most of us), could get this undivided attention through debating, and his previously mentioned quick-wittedness became a positive attribute. I would often find him in a corner, by himself, reciting what he wanted to say before beginning a debating session.

He further came into his own when the class started practising for the annual school concert. It became a public way of showing all his peers and the whole school community a most talented side of a boy who in the past seemed to think the only way to get attention was the negative kind. At the dress rehearsal, some of the cast were absent, causing last minute panic. Without direction, Johnny – who had learnt all the roles – stepped into the various characters, saving the day!

I don't wish to suggest that this was 'magic'; there isn't any. It was about limit setting, defining the expectations (probably considered 'barriers' by the student), taking small achievable steps, *regularly encouraging the child* and in doing so allowing success – slowly turning the focus around. Once there is some positivity, and a feeling of success, there is a chance to find something the child is good at and help them to capitalise on this.

Family support is essential and early in Year 5, I did point out to his parents the wonderful changes we were noticing and sought their support. Daily reading and homework commitments were basically my theme with them and a noticeable change was seen outside the classroom. As my influence 'dimmed', there was continued improvement in Johnny's consistency and loyalty.

On the occasions when, as with most children, I had to bring back their attention, all I needed to do with Johnny now was to give a 'reminder look' (and not my 'fierce version' either). Gone were the days when disciplining him meant anger, denial and abuse. The nice thing was he would usually either give me a grin or say sorry and *get on with his work*.

This was wonderful for me as a teacher. As far I was concerned, all was normal. I should add that structured school work was usually completed without much of my intervention. Johnny still had some trouble using his initiative with tasks like projects by the end of Year 5. While he tended to stay at the job, planning was still his weakness unless a structure was agreed upon. I expected this would improve with a little maturity and when he moved into Year 6.

During his year in Year 5, Johnny's humour and quick-wittedness won him over with his class peers and he found new friends. Also, the fact that the students in our class saw that I had time for this lad, indicating he was not a 'lost cause', must have influenced them to develop a better attitude towards him. Johnny began to look people confidently in the face when talking to them. He was also more consistent with his school uniform – with a little help from a friend (the principal). He only had a few lapses.

Finally

To summarise, I guess when the need is great, we find that hidden reserve of patience and doggedness. Most essential, and I cannot emphasise this enough, *be prepared to put in the time for the student*: set realistic goals, be fair and consistent and follow up, follow up on everything – the good and the not so good. Once Johnny saw that I was out to help him and at the same time there were fair limitations for behaviour in our class and fair consequences, he learned to trust and change. (I knew I had really reached him when he felt comfortable enough to call me Mrs F.)

Johnny moved on to Year 6 (without my influence) to retain a reasonably calm demeanour, doing well throughout his Year 6 journey. Yes, he had the odd detention but took it without argument, faced his consequences and moved on. He stood there at the Year 6 graduation ceremony, receiving his certificate just like every other kid – happy, proud, special and in his case with an inkling of gratitude. He had made it – in more ways than one.

It is crucial not to underestimate the power of a teacher to influence their students!

Chapter 5

Working to Build a Co-operative Classroom Group: Classroom Meetings and Building Relationships

Introduction

Bill Rogers

Classroom meetings have been widely used in schools for many years. But a classroom meeting as discussed here is more than a normative classroom discussion, it is a structured format – a process – allowing students a *guided voice* on issues of common concern to them as individuals and as a group. Here is what one whole-class *classroom* behaviour agreement says about their meetings:

> In our class – Year 6 – we use classroom meetings for various purposes such as playing games, discussion activities, planning and as a way of discussing and solving problems.
>
> The classroom meeting is open to everyone in our class and everyone has the right to express their feelings or to remain silent. Sometimes we invite students from other classes into our classroom meetings.
>
> These meetings are positive and constructive, trying to help and support the individual whilst dealing effectively with the problem. We always try to make the person feel supported and understood at the end of a problem-solving discussion.
>
> Any consequences that are discussed by the students at these meetings must be real activities, related to the problem and respectful to everyone.

The following essays illustrate how teachers have used classroom meetings to help their students to:

- understand other students' feelings and concerns (perspective-taking)
- test out their individual views
- widen their own understanding of what others believe, and value, and are concerned about

- see where there is clear consensus on common concerns, feelings and needs
- develop communication skills and problem-solving skills. In each of the case examples shared by teachers, their aim is to *lead* the classroom group, not 'take it over'. It is important that the teacher sets fair rules and guides the agenda and then encourages and supports the students in *their thinking processes*. I have seen 'classroom meetings' fail because teachers use such meetings to only inform, 'tell' or merely seek to control student thinking.
- gain confidence in communicating their views and feelings to others
- meet basic needs such as belonging, fun and enjoyment.

In primary schools – notably – such a format is often part of the weekly process in the life of a class. One of the wider goals of such meetings is to build a mediation culture in schools; supporting students to problem-solve and mediate where possible. Such groups can enable teachers to hear their students' 'voice' in a focused way, to value that voice and guide and support that voice within shared rights and responsibilities. (See p. 86f)

Friendship problems: using a solving circle

Carmen Price

A group of five girls in Year 6 were referred by the classroom teacher for some difficulties maintaining effective friendships. The girls had received several detentions for 'fighting' (displaying verbal and physical aggression) with each other, and parents had started to express their concern regarding these girls playing together. Efforts were made by the teacher and parents to reason with the girls to 'stay away from each other' and 'choose other friends'. Consequences had also been put in place if the girls were seen together (e.g. playground passes, time in planning room). Yet, these strategies (based on external control) proved to have little impact. The move was made to look at other ways to improve the relationship between the girls rather than aiming to extinguish the friendship altogether.

Intervention process

With some background information on the girls and their issues, I began to plan the intervention process. While I would have to negotiate meeting times and the like with the group of girls, the school was prepared for me to work with the group for at least an hour each week over three or four consecutive weeks. Additional time was allocated for follow-up support with the teacher so that she could encourage the girls to practise any new skills in their natural environments.

The intervention process was based on the 'Choice Theory/Reality Therapy' approach (Glasser, 1992), utilising Glasser's concept of the 'solving circle' (SC) as the key intervention tool.

The 'solving circle' idea has been typically used as a marriage counselling technique; however, it can be adapted and applied with clients experiencing other forms of relationship challenges. The SC process asks five key questions:

1 Do you want to help your relationship?
2 Whose behaviour can you control?
3 What do you believe is wrong with the relationship now?
4 What do you believe is good about the relationship now?
5 Tell me one thing you could do that would make the relationship better.

It is based on the notion that the relationship is separate to any individual opinion or want in the group. Those involved in this process are prompted to physically step inside the SC if they want to work on improving the relationship (this may involve visualisation of a circle around them or moving into a designated area). Once inside the SC, the relationship can begin to be more reflectively understood and the process of rebuilding can be given potential.

Before meeting with the girls, I considered the visual tools I would use to introduce the idea of the SC. Since I knew the girls individually (from working within their classroom), I had already established some rapport and the foundations of a trusting relationship.

Session 1

The girls arrived as scheduled. I had arranged some seats in a circle and I encouraged the girls to take a seat. It was interesting to note the seating position each girl chose. The dynamics of the group were already becoming apparent. The perceived 'leader' of the group took a seat at one end of the circle (opposite me) and the remainder of the group seemed to split into two sections.

We went around the group and briefly introduced ourselves. I then asked the girls for the reason they thought they might have been approached to see me. The group looked towards the leader for a response. The response was simple: 'We keep fighting and our parents don't want us to be friends any more' and then, 'If T wouldn't keep annoying us we wouldn't fight so much'. The blame cycle had begun, just as I had suspected. I did not give this last comment any energy.

I continued by informing the girls that I knew everyone had been trying to keep the girls apart and that it hadn't really been very successful or helpful, so we were going to try something different. I was there for their 'friendship', not to take sides with anyone but to work for their 'friendship'. I wrote the word 'friendship' on the whiteboard as if it were a separate entity and pointed at this word every time it was mentioned. I then said to the girls that I needed to know a few things before we could go on with helping the 'friendship' and that we would spend the session finding out these things.

I emphasised the importance of the first question and then asked each girl: '**Do you want to help your friendship?**' The common response was, 'If she wants to help it' and 'only if everyone else does', so I restated my question again. 'This is just about what *you* want. Regardless of what the other girls say, do *you* want to help your friendship?' After some time to consider, the girls responded, 'yes'. I congratulated them for getting through the first difficult question, and stated that I, too, wanted to work on their friendship – we had a common goal. My aim was to put a lot of energy into setting this first question up and the idea of the 'friendship' being separate to any one of them and their personal needs.

I then continued on with the question: '**Whose behaviour can you control?**' To avoid the same people responding all the time, I directed this question to a different member in the group. All girls were able to reach the conclusion that they could only control their own behaviour. This may reflect learnings attained within the school setting, which has adopted a 'Choice Theory' approach (Glasser, 1986).

I then asked the third question: '**What do you believe is wrong with the friendship now?**' This prompted a whirlwind of blame (which I expected). I managed the exchange of this information with brief acknowledgments and redirection to the next person. Of course, there were a variety of reasons (e.g. 'She goes off and plays with other people', 'She bosses us around', 'They whisper about me', 'They leave me out of their games'). Yet these reasons were not what I wanted to focus on.

I was more interested in their response to the next question, and so I asked: '**What is good about your friendship now?**' The girls could each mention a few points (e.g. 'We look out for each other', 'We share with each other', 'We play fun games together', 'You always have someone to hang around'). This led on to brainstorming more general ideas (recorded on the whiteboard) about what makes a friendship good (i.e. friendly actions, words, etc.). I chose to extend this question a little further by asking: 'What do people *do* or *say* when they are being friendly?' I thought that this question might help the girls to consider what 'friendly behaviours' actually looked and sounded like.

This then lead on to the final question: '**Tell me one thing you could each do that you think may make your friendship better?**' I referred them to the ideas on the board to assist them in generating a goal. Each girl could come up with one thing with little effort. As they mentioned their idea, I got them to stand and step into the SC (which we called the 'Friendship Circle') that I had drawn on the floor with the word 'Friendship' written in the middle. Once we were all inside the circle, I explained the concept of the SC and explained that while they chose to be inside the circle, they were choosing to work on the friendship and what they themselves could do to improve it (as they can only control themselves). The girls liked this concept and asked if they could take the word 'friendship' away with them in case they needed to use 'the circle' during the week. The session finished with each group member having a 'friendly' behaviour to practise for the week and one more to think of and bring back to the next group meeting.

At the end of the session, I felt as though several goals had been achieved. The girls had gained more information on the concept of 'control' and whom this extends to (ourselves). They had a better idea of the SC, and they were working to improve the friendship rather than trying to change individual aspects of the group. Over the following week, I helped the girls to use the circle in the school setting and rehearsed this process with the teacher (who was helping the girls to apply the SC in the ordinary, day-to-day environment).

Session 2

The first session had focused on setting up the SC process and introducing the girls to the concepts behind this process. Over the next week, the girls had tried to apply the SC idea on their own and had experienced some difficulties in doing so. The classroom teacher had reported that the girls were approaching her with complaints that some girls would not step into the circle and were causing fights in the group. From this feedback, it became apparent that the girls were still stuck on the idea of external control (forcing others to get into the circle) and needed more practice with the ideas of 'Choice Theory' and the solving circle. The focus of session 2 was to review the week's progress and the goals they had set themselves, and to work with any challenges or positives experienced over the week.

The girls did not arrive at the session together (even though they were sent from the same class). Two girls arrived promptly and two others lingered behind. The group once again sat as though they were 'split' with a large space between the girls. Once seated, the girls launched into explanations of the week, which mostly contained blaming and complaints about other girls not stepping into the circle (e.g. 'We were having some trouble getting along and T wouldn't step into the circle to work it out. It was all her fault'). I worked to reframe their thinking by asking the girls, 'Who can you control?' Each girl responded 'Myself '. I followed this with a reflection like 'It sounds to me that some of you may have forgotten this, and were trying to control or get other people to step into the solving circle – maybe that was part of the problem you were having. Does that sound like what was happening?' Most girls nodded in agreement. With the process under way and the framework for thinking and behaving redefined, the session progressed more smoothly.

We reviewed the week by revisiting the goals set and used a 10-point scale to consider each girl's journey towards improving the friendship. The points on the scale reflected behaviours that we would see or hear if they were moving towards improving the friendship or, in contrast, moving away from the relationship. On occasions, I had to remind the girls that I was there for the friendship rather than any individual person. We practised using the SC and considered what we would do if people did not want to enter the SC. I highlighted to the girls that if they chose to stay outside the SC, they were still required to follow the school guidelines for getting on with others (in other words, being outside the SC did not give them the right to be unfriendly). There were rights, rules and responsibilities at school about how people should treat others, regardless of the closeness of their relationships. I also pointed out the natural consequence if the girls chose to act in unfriendly ways. My goal in presenting this information was to ensure that the girls were not using the SC as a means to justify their actions (e.g. 'I was not in the SC on the day I teased her'). They had to understand the rights, rules and responsibilities within the school setting too. The session ended with each girl choosing one way they could help the friendship over the next week.

Sessions 3 to 5

The next few sessions were of shorter duration. The girls started to arrive together (rather than split) which seemed to indicate that the relationship was improving. These sessions involved further practice using the solving circle, setting goals for change and probing deeper into areas of difficulty using 'Reality Therapy' techniques (e.g. 'What were you hoping would happen when you chose to say something nasty to T?', 'What did you do to get what you wanted?', 'Did that choice help the friendship or harm the friendship?'). We also regularly used the 10-point scale to review outcomes and the group's movements towards its goal to improve the friendship.

Further intervention involved practising the use of the SC in the girls' everyday environment and collaborative consultation with the classroom teacher.

Towards the end of the five sessions, the girls indicated that they had reached around a '7' on the 10-point scale. A score of '7' indicated the use of friendly behaviours like sharing, taking turns, speaking openly, and using respectful and friendly words and actions to one another. This score was a long way from the original response that showed behaviours like teasing, using put-downs, fighting and spreading rumours. The SC process seemed to have assisted the girls in changing their relationship with one another for the better. While outside assistance was still needed from time to time to help the girls to work on some of their relationship problems, the teacher, parents and administration were pleased with the progress of the relationship between the girls, and were happy for the relationship to continue.

In several 'booster sessions' that followed, the teacher and I assisted the girls in dealing with 'risk factors' that could influence or change the dynamics of their friendship. For example, if a new person were to join the group, they might need to use the SC to redefine each person's role in the friendship. Likewise, if someone chose to leave the group, the girls might also need the SC process and/or outside support.

Overall, Glasser's concept of the solving circle was a useful tool for facilitating relationship change. The SC prompted self-reflection and internal motivation to change within each girl and, in doing so, offered them an alternative method to solve their relationship difficulties beyond traditional external control techniques.

Relationships and conflict-solving (classroom and playground) with infants

Debbie Hoy and Ros Daniels

Debbie Hoy and Ros Daniels share how they help young children (infant age) rebuild relationships that are affected by friendship squabbles, exclusion tactics and 'bullying'.

Many of the fundamental skills of problem-solving can be introduced at infant level, given planning, structure, teaching (they are skills as well as attitudes) and school-wide support.

At the time of this case example, Debbie and Ros were senior early years teachers in a London school.

Issue 1 – friendship difficulties

Scenario

Molly and Kyrsten (ages six and seven) were having minor conflicts with each other in class and on the playground. A wider group of friends were also being drawn into the behaviour, which was causing some of them to be excluded from the group. It began with low frequency and low intensity behaviours and grew into high frequency and high intensity behaviours bordering on intimidation and bullying (including name-calling, using unkind speech and exclusion from games).

Both sets of parents were concerned about 'bullying' and about the effect that the situations were having on the children at home as well as at school; their academic work was suffering and they were unhappy. They each made appointments to talk about the situation and I reassured them that it would be fully investigated and that I would feed back to them.

School response

My investigation included:

- **Talking to the class teacher**

I spoke to the class teacher about the parental concerns and asked for some background information. She was already aware of the issues and agreed that I should get involved with investigating and supporting the children.

■ **Speaking to each of the two girls individually**

I went to the classroom and asked each child if they would be happy to have a chat with me. I talked to each of them individually and explained that I had spoken to their parents. I asked them to tell me what was making them feel unhappy in school and they each described incidents from their own perspective. I asked open questions as appropriate and reflected back some of what I had been told to gather a wider picture. I asked them if there was anything that could help to resolve the situation and gave them some suggestions (e.g. 'Would it help if we talked to Molly?'). We agreed that it would be helpful to set up a meeting where the two girls could talk together and I would act as facilitator.

■ **Meeting with the two girls together**

Both children were given the opportunity of telling the other how they felt about the conflict: 'Kyrsten, tell Molly how you felt when she left you out of the game'. They were then given the chance to respond. They both said sorry to each other, naming the behaviour that they were sorry for ('Sorry for not sharing our game with you') and I explained that sorry was a promise, which meant that they would try not do it again. We agreed that it would be helpful to meet with the other children and draw up some rules for the friendship group.

■ **Meeting with the group of five girls together**

The other three children joined us in the room and we met in a circle. I explained where we had got to so far in resolving the issues and that we wanted to draw up some rules or guidelines for the friendship.

■ **Agreeing on a list of 'friendship rules' and consequences**

We discussed what these might look like and I scribed for the group as they thought of the ideas. When they had been agreed, I wrote them out and we all signed the final copy. Each child was then given a photocopy to take away.

1 We will talk kindly to each other.
2 We will be gentle towards each other.
3 We will listen to each other.
4 We will share our games with each other.
5 We can play with other children if we want to.

We also agreed on a reporting strategy for the children if the problems continued. They were to report straight to the adult on supervision duty (in playground times) and also to report to me if there were any incidents. The consequence of breaking the friendship rules was that the child would lose the right to play with the group.

- **Feeding back to parents**
  Both sets of parents were informed of the actions and of the agreement that the children had made.
- **Monitoring**
  Over the next few days, the class teacher took responsibility for monitoring the behaviour in the classroom and asking the children how their playtimes had been for them. I also saw the children regularly during the first few days and no further issues arose. We continued to review this on a weekly basis.

Outcome

Although the process was time-consuming on the day, it was time well invested. The children were able to take responsibility in their relationships and had strategies for dealing with the difficulties. The alternative could have been constant interruptions after each playtime to sort out the difficulties they had been having. The parents said that the children had not had any further difficulties after the initial meetings.

Issue 2 – attitude problem

Scenario

Rupert (aged six) was a highly articulate, very able and self-assured child. He enjoyed school, and when motivated by the subject, was eager to learn new information. Rupert had made a positive start to the new school year and had responded well to the establishment of the shared class rules and responsibilities.

However, on occasions, he had an attitude that the learning in the classroom was 'beneath him'. At times like this, it was challenging to keep him on task and he could become verbally abusive towards adults and other children. After several incidents of exhibiting this behaviour and being sent out to the parallel class, it was agreed that we would work with him on changing his behaviour with a long-term plan. We set aside a day to achieve this.

School response

The process included:

- **Talking to the class teacher**
  I gathered a wider picture of when the incidents had happened and their frequency and intensity.
- **Withdrawing the child from the class**
  Having been given a choice with a consequence, Rupert was withdrawn from

the classroom with all of his school and personal belongings. Some of the time was used for him to catch up on his work, and the rest of the day was spent working on teaching corrective and supportive procedures.

■ **Working with Rupert individually**
Rupert and I talked through the behaviours that he had exhibited and he was very truthful about what he had done. He felt uncomfortable outside of his classroom and wanted to know what he had to do to get back into class. We had a thoughtful discussion about the definition of being sorry and what it looks like to be sorry. We built a mind map to show the negative behaviours and how to change them into positives. Rupert had to think very hard about how he was going to change the behaviours and with support he came up with realistic targets for change. Rupert was genuinely sorry and wrote letters to the people who had been affected by his behaviour (including his mother).

■ **Reintegrating him back into the class**
Towards the end of the afternoon, Rupert was ready to return to his own class. He took all his belongings and the 'sorry' letters. The children were in a circle when he returned and were very pleased to see him. After he had given out his sorry letters, Rupert received a card of friendship from the children. This was probably the most significant factor in the whole day, as he needed the reinforcement of being accepted by his peers.

■ **Monitoring**
The class teacher monitored his progress towards the behaviour targets and I also reinforced his progress throughout the day as he completed tasks.

■ **Feeding back to the parent**
Rupert's mother was fully involved with this process and is positively rewarding his school behaviours.

Outcome

Since that day, Rupert has continued to use his positive behaviour targets and is now – himself – supporting other children.

Telling the truth

We have found that children are more likely to tell the truth if we make it safe for them to do so. This involves the adult being calm, fair and consistent.

We usually give the child options, naming the incident, and telling them that if they do tell the truth, all we will say to them is, 'Thank you for telling the truth', and then ask them to put it right and help them to put it right.

Example of options given are:

■ Maybe you did *punch Tom in the stomach* and you did it on purpose and now

you feel sorry.
- Maybe you did *punch him* but you didn't mean to.
- Maybe you didn't *punch him* at all.

This usually results in the child taking the middle option and saying it was an accident. We thank them for being brave enough to tell the truth and talk about what they can do to put it right and resolve the situation.

A small minority will say, 'I don't know', and at that point it can help to ask them a question such as, 'If you thought you knew, what would it be?' If they still deny their involvement and you have evidence to the contrary, then allow them more thinking time. It is important to reassure the child that you are confident that they will be brave enough to be truthful and remind them that whatever they say, you will remain calm and fair and will be proud of them for being truthful, even if you don't like their behaviour.

Working with children using sharing in group meetings is time-consuming initially but always productive in its longer-term outcomes. Children begin to understand that they have a genuine voice and an opportunity to share their feelings and concerns. They can then work towards more constructive and co-operative solutions to their problems.

What may seem small or insignificant to a teacher can loom large in the minds of children. When teachers take time, and *make time*, to listen and to guide individuals and groups in both needs-sharing and solution-oriented thinking, the results are always more rewarding for all concerned.

Editor's note

I would like to strongly recommend a read-aloud picture storybook on bullying for infant and middle-school primary years called *No More Bullying* by Rosemary Stones (published by Dinosaur, HarperCollins imprint.) This book is a powerful awareness-raising option and starting point for any class or small group discussion. It clearly resonates with young children's experience of school and will assist both victim and bully, and raise awareness of the nature of bullying and how to address it within a school

---

Creating the peaceable school

Carmel Ryan

What is a peaceable school? What does it look, sound, feel like? Carmel Ryan (a deputy principal, primary) shares her thoughts. Her school has been consciously focused on developing a more 'peaceable' school through 'The Labrador Peaceable Schools Project' (Queensland, Australia).

Many people seem genuinely interested in the present state of play at our school. 'How far along the journey are you now? Have you noticed any appreciable differences since you developed a focus on a "peaceable" school?' Others simply remark, 'Oh, you're the experts!' (if only, I muse …) or 'Holy cow! I read your article on "peaceable schools". That seems like an awful lot of work to improve student behaviour. What about the rest of the job?' (Pay now or pay later, I think. There is a return on the investment but on the 'pay later' plan, interest accumulates. Personal choice.)

A snapshot of a peaceable school

And so I sit with pen poised trying to encapsulate briefly the spirit of a philosophy that is still evolving, still challenging, still frustrating but still exciting in its limitless potential.

Do I try to paint a picture of the peer support students, who, without external motivation (no stickers, no jelly babies, no play money) head up to the planning room during lunch hours 'just to help'?

Do I explain the 'planning room'? The place where students come in a climate of mutual respect to learn about the acceptance of responsibility for their behavioural choices, and where in an atmosphere of essential oils (smells nice), affirming posters, music – Bach (J.S.) – and bean bags, they are led through a thinking process which could be described as a 'cognitive State of Origin match' (Australian rugby). How do I describe the mediation I requested, having found myself spinning on my back wheels due to a communication problem between a Year 4 student and myself? At the mediation's conclusion, Sarah, a Year 7 student, asked, 'Do you think you two could ever be friends again?'

A success story

An extract from a student's journal:

> I have been fighting and pushing people around. I have been getting sent out of the classroom and parents have been complaining about me (to the police). Since I have been going into the planning room, I have learnt to co-operate around the playground and in the class. I am not going to blow it.
>
> (Year 8 student)

A challenge

Another student wrote:

> I am feeling happy because my problem has been solved by Mrs _____ and Mrs _____ and me, and we agreed to co-operate.
>
> (Year 10 student, suspended five days later)

In their own words

Student alternative plans are simple but powerful:

> I will only listen to those kids who tell me not to fight.
> I will no longer be a victim.

The starting point

A historical snapshot of student management at Labrador would show that the discipline was 'good'. Relationships were valued in the main, but, in the heat of myriads of daily bushfires, we sometimes would yield to the reactive model of stimulus–response.

On the door to my office are the words, 'If better is possible then good is not enough'. I began to realise that systems change when people experience personal change. As we engage in new dialogue about our shared perspective, we asked new questions:

- Is this going the way we want to go?
- If we keep going on this way, will it get better?
- Could things get worse?

Those questions finally drove us to look for new solutions: good becomes better, better becomes best. One can't change one's destination overnight, but one can change the direction. That direction for us was the exploration of William Glasser's 'Choice Theory/Reality Therapy'.

As we struggle to commit to a non-coercive environment where the concepts of non-violence, compassion, trust, respect and tolerance are the pervasive themes in the interaction of student–student, student–teacher, teacher–teacher and teacher–parent, we can focus on the real business of learning. I can hear the cry, 'But you don't understand. Our problems are different.' You're right. *Your* problems *are* different. To any school experiencing student management problems, I would say that what these examples will teach you is limited. It is necessary to know *why* a practice is successful. You cannot hope simply to duplicate a practice that may work in a particular setting. However, you can implement similar principles or guidelines and then it is a matter of trial and error – 'failing one's way' to success.

Would every member of the Labrador community agree that all attitudes, behaviours and activities have significantly improved enough to state that the journey is complete? I hope not! But it is undeniable that a metamorphosis is taking place – not rapid but sure; chaotic but organised; simple but complex; controlled but flexible; moving forward and getting stuck. New growth is always accompanied by pain. Six thousand years of recorded history reads: opportunity mixed with difficulty. Your journey (if you decide to accept it) will be no different.

If you are willing to accept that such behaviour management systems are more effective than exercising forceful authority over the learners, and are needed to deal with conflict in our schools, you will share similar changes in direction.

You will begin to move from external to internal control, from stimulus–response to behavioural choices, from positive reinforcement to self-evaluation, from coercive practice to collaboration. With so much more to relate, I will leave Haim Ginott (1971) to conclude:

> I've come to the frightening conclusion that I am the decisive element in the classroom. It's my personal approach that creates the climate. It's my daily mood that makes the weather. As a teacher, I possess tremendous power to make a child's life miserable or joyous. I can be a tool of torture or an instrument of inspiration. I can humiliate or humour, hurt or heal. In all situations, it is my response that decides whether a crisis will be escalated or de-escalated and a child humanised or dehumanised.

Good luck on *your* journey.

Quick scenario

An 11-year-old girl was sent to me because she was caught stealing pencils from a classmate's tidy tray. The teacher became frustrated because the child would not admit that she had stolen the pencils. After a lunch hour of discussion and tears and denial from the 'accused' (despite the accounts of at least three witnesses), I decided to continue the conversation in the privacy of my office. At the end of about 20 minutes, I sent the child back to the classroom.

The teacher rang through to thank me for finally getting the child to admit the theft. When I replied, 'But I didn't,' the teachers were perplexed. 'But everything is fine. The two students are happy. There are no tears. Life is back to normal in our classroom. What did you do?'

I related the conversation I had with the 'thief'. Forcing myself to take a completely different tack (I felt sure she was guilty as well), I asked Jane, 'What do you want?' She replied, 'I just want someone to believe me.'

'Okay, despite the mounting evidence, Jane, I believe you. But we still have a problem, don't we? What is it?'

'Well, Jackie doesn't have her pencils and the kids and teachers all hate me for all the fuss and my lying.'

'Okay, is there any way to make it right?'

'Well, I could give Jackie all the pencils I have in my bag and say I'm sorry for all the fuss.'

'Why don't you do that and come back and see me.'

About ten minutes later, both students returned smiling and happy. Jackie was more than happy with the pencils and the apology. Jane returned to the classroom and Jackie asked to see me privately. She said, 'I really still believe Jane took my pencils, but she is pretty poor and I think I know how she felt with everyone coming down on her. I think she's learnt a lot from this and she'll think twice before she does something like this again.'

We had a win-win situation. I could have been unyielding, humiliating Jane into admitting the theft. What would have been achieved? Some people who are into 'boss' management and punishment would call the outcome 'weak', with Jane getting away with it.

Weeks later, the students are still friends, the teacher reports no animosity, the 'thief' comes regularly to the planning room to help other students. We all know the truth, but the reality has more substance. The student still has her self-respect, relationships are being enhanced. Haven't we all made mistakes now and then?

People or events outside us never *merely* stimulate us to do anything. In this case, we all followed 'the rules of the game' to achieve the most meaningful outcome for us all – respect and value for the individual no matter what the choice.

A beautiful place: building a multicultural school

Larry Schwartz

In Noble Park Secondary College, children and teachers from around the world are building a harmonious, multicultural school that may be a pointer to Australia's future. Larry Schwartz reports. Peter D'Angelo shares how teachers can build confidence in their students and a positive sense of community – even in a busy classroom context.

Larry is a reporter with The Age *newspaper, Melbourne.*

Early afternoon in classroom B8. Tiny fish flit about a small aquarium. A blue-tongued lizard among lifeless specimens preserved in jars. 'You get a release?' asks the teacher. 'Of insulin,' says one of 17 students in this afternoon's Year 12 biology class. 'Diana, can you read that please?' says the teacher. 'Michael, have you done question three?' 'You all right, Scott?'

Nives takes notes diligently. Once she sat in a class in Trebinje, in her native Bosnia-Herzegovina. Then came a war.

'The bombing was probably the main thing,' she says. 'When you're seven years old, you don't expect that to happen in your own secure world.'

Nives' parents came from Dubrovnik, in Croatia. Among her closest friends, classmate Jenita is from Bosnia and Adriana is from Serbia.

'You don't look at the person for the background,' Nives says. 'You look at them as a person. We probably sometimes discuss the issues because being in a war is not exactly what everyone experiences or everyone would like to experience. (But) it's not a very big topic between us. We just talk about normal teenage things.'

Noble Park Secondary College is among Australia's most ethnically diverse schools. Almost half the 708 students were born overseas. Just three in 10 have an English-speaking background. At home, many will slip into one of more than 50 languages and dialects. They have come with their families from around the globe: Afghanistan, Croatia, East Timor, Cambodia, Thailand, Turkey, India, Chile, Ethiopia, Hong Kong, Western Samoa and more. Yet proudly displayed on a corridor wall is the Australian citizenship pledge.

Nives reads and write poetry – Keats' 'Ode to a Nightingale' is her favourite – but she hopes to study medicine or law.

Her family spent two years in a Danish town, Grena, before settling here in 1994. When Nives came here, she could speak several languages from the former Yugoslavia as well as Danish, Swedish and Norwegian. But she knew just one word in English.

'I think from cartoon the only word I knew was "dog",' says the 17-year-old, who learnt the language in a month of watching TV and reading newspapers. 'It's very weird.'

Created from the merger in 1994 of Noble Park Heights Secondary College and Noble Secondary College, the school is accessible through a side street, secluded from the hubbub of south-eastern suburbia by sporting fields and gums. Some of the factories that lured the rich mix of migrants have closed in recent years. Yet there is a buoyancy here, a sense that there are no limits in Australia.

'Really in this country you can do whatever you like,' says Jenita, 16, a Muslim born in Sarajevo whose family lived in Berlin for three years before coming here in 1995. 'No matter if you live in Noble Park or Toorak, you can do it. That's the kind of society it is.'

A classmate, Francesca, 17, was four when her family arrived here from turmoil in Romania. 'Whatever was back in our countries was back in our countries,' says Francesca, who joined the Army Reserve last year. 'We're in Australia now. We're friends. We don't look for where we come from.'

A visitor may wonder at this harmony in diversity, but it seems natural to Richard, 18, of Anglo-Australian descent, who stacks shelves at a supermarket before school, sells second-hand mobile phones afterwards, has his own band and plans to be a sound technician.

'Being Australian,' he says, 'I've always felt safe here and when other people come I feel no resentment. I welcome them because it's … giving Australia more diversity.'

You wonder, too, about the changing nature of Australia's identity. 'The rate of change is still too fast to freeze in an identity,' says Bill, 17, who isn't sure when his British forebears came to Australia. 'The rate of change has to slow down to get a real identity.'

The friendship between Nives, Jenita and Adriana has impressed their English teacher, Peter D'Angelo (see Chapter 1, p. 15). To him, the bond epitomises how national tensions can be transcended.

'You'd think there'd be racism but there isn't,' he says of the school. D'Angelo taught some of the students here when they were newly arrived refugees, at nearby Noble Park English Language School, one of four Melbourne schools for migrants and refugees. He is now integration co-ordinator and one of nine teachers of English as a second language at Noble Park Secondary. He is also a poet and author who has written extensively on the migrant experience.

Now 47, he was four-and-a-half when his family migrated from Italy's Abruzzi region. His maternal grandfather had a gift for him as he prepared to embark on a converted cargo vessel, the *Oceania*, with his mother and two sisters for a 31-day trip to a faraway land where he would meet his father, who had gone on ahead before he was born. 'My grandfather gave me a pair of sunglasses – and I know this sounds corny but it did happen – and he said: "Put these on when you reach Australia and you'll see a beautiful place".'

His grandfather had told him, too, to use the sunglasses to look out for dolphins. Once he did. But the glasses were broken by a boy on board. There was a borrowed grey car to collect them from Station Pier. The house his father had set out to build was not complete. The family slept on a concrete floor.

In the title poem of his collection *Folk Songs*, he writes of migrants hurried down gangways to shouts of 'bloody refos!', hard times on production lines, and domestic discord with a widening gap between generations.

We sent our children to school but they came home with more than English; strange tongues crept into kitchens, began questioning customs, then dividing our lives ...

It's an experience familiar to Yoko, 17. 'I think there is a gap because my parents are from Japan and they still have that Japanese culture,' she says. 'They don't get as much exposed to Australia as I do because I go to school. I meet all these people and they're from different cultures. I think everyone gets more exposed to Australia than their parents do.'

D'Angelo has watched some students progress from their first months in Australia. Lino, 18, was 12 when he arrived from East Timor. D'Angelo says Lino has grown in confidence but the bright smile was there from the start. Lino plans to learn carpentry before returning to Dili to help rebuild his country.

'I would rather go back,' he says. 'I've got more relatives there. When I go back I can find a job easier because the war isn't happening.'

Nives has already been back to her birthplace. 'At the beginning I didn't feel like going much,' she says. 'I wanted to see my family and all but I didn't think I wanted to go back to that place because obviously the memories were a bit mixed. So I was overwhelmed when I went over there. I absolutely loved it.'

'But even though it was a great experience, it was very hard for me. I think I still call Australia home, as clichéd as that sounds. I was happy to come back here.'

We meet again in a conference room. Of four students attending a Student Representative Council meeting, one was born in Australia. The others came from Romania, Afghanistan and New Zealand.

'I knew how to spell my name, that's all,' says quietly spoken Farooq, 14, recalling when his family fled Kabul four years ago. 'We just wanted to stay there but we couldn't because there was killing and everything. We had to leave our house behind us ... We just wanted peace.'

His mother worries that her three sons might marry outside the Muslim faith. 'Most parents want their kids to be in their religion,' he says, 'and they want them to be strict. But they just can't because they drift away with others at school and everything.'

Farooq has a passion for Australian Rules football. Last year he won a best and fairest vote in the Dandenong district league. His family lived in Sydney before coming to Melbourne, so he barracks for the *Swans* (a famous Australian football team). He first played in the under-11s for a local club and still cringes at an early mistake.

'I remember I handballed through the goals. I thought there was going to be a goal. I remember that. I grabbed the ball and the goals were in front of me. I thought "easy goal", I just handballed it through. It was quite embarrassing ...'

Demons skipper David Neitz, *Kangaroo* Glenn Archer and *Collingwood's* late Darren Millane came from the same club.[1]

Farooq dreams of one day playing for the *Swans*. 'My mum wants me to quit. She goes, "You're going to hurt yourself." I have to go in my bedroom and watch telly when the footy is on. The whole family just hates it totally. Probably one day I'll hopefully get into the AFL (Australian Football League) and my mum can see me on the telly or something. Then she'll realise that I did it.'

Peter D'Angelo knows the trauma some have endured. 'Any sudden noises from a car exhaust, they'd flinch,' he says.

D'Angelo was inexperienced and the language school poorly equipped when he faced the disconcerting silence of Vietnamese and Cambodian children in the early 1980s. It took a while before he heard stories of rape by Thai pirates and other horrors. A Cambodian wrote a poem that perplexed him. She explained that it described how her father's face had been hacked away to reveal the white skull beneath.

The Romanians came with their stories of brutalities. Latin Americans too. 'The talk of what happened in El Salvador is also frightening,' he says. The Afghanis, fleeing Soviet invasion. Bosnians in the early 1990s. Again and again he told himself, 'It just can't get any worse than this.' *Teaching was so much more than a job.*

---

1. The Demons, Kangaroos and Collingwood are also Australian Rules Football clubs (a bit like Arsenal and Chelsea in the UK!).

'I realised that I had to give them the best I could because it wasn't a job anymore. It was a … true vocation.'

But his approach demanded so much that he came to withdraw and, for a while, tried not to give so much of himself. A 16-year-old Bosnian girl he taught had a spirited good nature and ready smile despite kidney and liver disease, loss of sight in one eye and post-trauma epileptic fits. Her father had been beaten and taken away. She and her mother were raped by soldiers. One day, she showed him some lines she had written:

> I am the essence of my people
> And the spirit of my past,
> In this new land
> I will take as always
> The good and the bad …

Her example inspired him. 'I was teaching kids to write poetry in a very detached way,' he says. 'It clicked that I was doing it without the real feeling there. I think she clicked too. She wrote a poem and thanked me for teaching her English so she could write about her feelings.'

'Here I was, doing it by rote. I was cheating my students. I was becoming like a zombie. She made me come back. That's when I decided to extend it. I wanted to see these kids in another context, which was this school here.'

D'Angelo initiated our visit to the school and organised a discussion between more than 20 students. Such was the diversity, it seemed this might be emblematic of a future Australia. He believes Australia is more confident and tolerant than when he came here as a child. 'I feel it's at a stage where it needs to take a final step and we can be anything we want to be. I think these kids have got it in their power to do that.'

A human story

Unsourced

A colleague of mine found this on the Internet (unsourced). I do not doubt its veracity – or its universal message.

A few years ago at the Special Olympics held in Seattle in the United States, nine contestants, all physically or mentally disabled, assembled at the starting line for the 100-yard dash. At the sound of the gun, they all started out, not exactly in a dash, but with a relish to run the race to the finish and win. All, that is, except for one boy who stumbled on the asphalt, tumbled over a couple of times, and began to cry. The other eight heard the boy cry. They slowed down and paused. Then they all turned around and went back. Every one of them. One girl with Down's syndrome bent down and kissed him and said, 'This will make it better.' Then all nine linked arms and walked together to the finishing line. Everyone in the stadium stood and the cheering went on for ten minutes. People who were there are still telling the story. Why? ... Because deep down we know this one thing: what matters in life is more than winning for yourself. What truly matters in this life is helping others win, even if it means slowing yourself down and changing your course.

Chapter 6

Principles and Practices that Enable Us to Make a Difference with Individual Children and Classroom Groups

Bill Rogers

> *We learn from each other as teachers. We teach each other; by default or design.*
>
> *Entering into a colleague's classroom – even in print – can provide a shared collegial awareness of our common task, our common struggle. It can also remind us how we find the energy, goodwill and support to build the kind of relationships that effect the sorts of changes these accounts detail.*
>
> *These are children and young people whose thinking, attitude, self-esteem and learning have been directly affected by the colleagues we read about here. There are common themes, understandings, skills and teacher behaviours that clearly brought about those 'differences' in affect and behaviour.*

While there is obvious variance among schools in terms of school populations, local areas, teaching styles, leadership styles, policies, the physical resources in a school and the quality of its colleague culture (in terms of support and teamwork), common understandings, principles and practices clearly emerge across all these teachers.

Colleague support

In each account in this book, teachers note the crucial nature of colleague support.

Moral support

This is the collegial attitude that shares the 'common lot'; that *colleague watchfulness* where we consciously look out for one another, particularly in times of crisis (as when a student's behaviour is – effectively – 'holding a class to ransom'). Teachers are not criticised or blamed when asking for help – colleague support is offered early, before things get too out of hand.

In some schools, there is that tension between a teacher needing and wanting support (sometimes desperately) and the anxiety that if they do ask, they will be perceived as inadequate, ineffective, or – worse – incompetent. The issue of a teacher's competency is, of course, a significant factor that sometimes needs to be painfully addressed. However, a school should distinguish between long-term professional 'performance' concerns and the need to offer *early* and *strategic colleague support* to a colleague who is clearly struggling with a challenging child or class.

No teacher should have to suffer in a kind of degrading 'survivalism' because of the anxiety that they will be signalling that they are a teacher who 'cannot cope', is 'not up to the task' or who is incompetent.

There is wide research that demonstrates a significant correlation between teacher stress, coping, welfare and teacher effectiveness on the one hand and the quality and extent of ongoing colleague support offered in a given school (Rogers, 2002a). In the schools we read about here, colleague support is offered early, without censure or implied 'blame' and clearly with a sense of shared struggle.

Structural support

Structural support describes those expressions, or 'forms', of colleague support that a school 'factors in' to its daily organisation and culture. It is colleague support that is consciously developed around colleagues' espoused needs. The research indicates that colleagues value a collegial interdependency based in supportive plans, programmes and structures *as well as moral support.*

In each of the accounts noted in this text, any meaningful change in student behaviour begins to develop when some structure or plan changed the focus of teacher and students' attention from the natural stress of whatever is occurring, to the possibilities of seeing things, and doing things, differently. Each teacher finds some 'plan', 'key' or 'process' within which to support an individual or class group. This always arises out of a genuine desire to 'connect' and engage with the student and then to support the student to gain awareness of their behaviour and effect change. Any such plan has its relative success because that plan is a whole-school response.

The common forms of 'structural' support noted by colleagues are:

■ A behaviour, welfare and discipline policy with a clear focus on positive discipline practices (rather than reactive, ad hoc practice) – any policy has to be built on a whole-school needs analysis and will address common aims, shared discipline practice and common discipline planning in areas such as: the way we address and manage behaviour in the classroom; all duty-of-care contexts where we need to manage and enable safe environments (playground, wet-day supervision, meals supervision, bus duty ...); and supporting students with special needs and students at risk.

Such a policy also develops and applies due behaviour consequences based on the principle of 'negotiated' options (including mediation, restitution and, even, classroom meetings) as well as non-negotiable consequences for serious behaviours such as violence, bullying, drugs and weapons.

■ Seeking to keep the focus of any behaviour consequences on the *fair certainty* of due process rather than 'severity' – teachers do not use a behaviour consequence (such as follow-up beyond the classroom, detention or withdrawal of privileges) as an opportunity to berate the student or engage in some kind of 'emotional pay-back' (tempting as that might be). Further, they always emphasise the need to repair and rebuild with the child and to help the child repair and rebuild with their peers. While this is a labour-intensive aspect of our teacher leadership, it goes a long way to achieving a more positive and peaceable school.

■ Adequate, and school-wide, time-out options for repeatedly distracting and disruptive students – such time-out planning needs to have its least-to-most-intrusive stages such as: class time-out options; colleague-assisted time-out options (including directing a student to a colleague's classroom nearby); senior teacher assisted time-out options and what to do in a crisis management situation. Staff need to carefully consider how they communicate with students when they are angry or hostile or aggressive. Our ability to communicate calmly, clearly and be supported with *immediate colleague back-up is essential in a crisis*. How the teacher manages behaviour at the point of crisis – in that emotional moment – is also crucial. Staff need to discuss and plan for such situations with very challenging children. Any use of time-out practice must be developed from a shared professional understanding of *why we need (on occasion) to utilise time-out practice*.

Key policy questions will address:

■ what we *say* and *do* when we direct a student to time-out
■ what the options are regarding *where* we direct a child to calm down/think about their behaviour away from their class peers
■ what ought to happen for/with the student *during a time-out episode* (particularly how we enable the student to calm, settle, refocus). The role of the supervising adult, here, should be thoughtfully discussed. Time-out is not – primarily – a counselling session, though we should encourage the child to respond to some key focus questions *when and if he is calm enough*: What happened ... ? What rule/what right was affected ... ? What's your side of the story ... ? What can you do to fix things up? ... make things better? How can I help? Younger children can draw a few pictures around these focus questions.
■ on what basis the child goes back to his host class *after* designated time-out?

■ the crucial importance of the initiating teacher (the class teacher) following up with the student later that day. Repairing and rebuilding is a crucial feature of support and understanding by the teacher – later – when the child has well and truly calmed down.

Chapter 3 outlines a common 'structure' or form of support: that of colleagues developing individual behaviour management plans with children with repeatedly attentional, distracting, disruptive or emotionally disordered behaviours. The concept of *individual behaviour management plans* is widely and commonly used in supportive schools. While their main emphasis is to give the child behaviour and learning skills, they also give individual teachers a *structure* within which to reflect and modify their teaching focus and support for the child.

Professional support

Each teacher (in this book) values the insight, problem-sharing, analysis and shared action planning offered by their colleagues. Sometimes this involves team meetings and the ongoing reassurance that we're 'on the right track'; at other times, it involves mentoring with a colleague in the classroom to work with an individual child, or to help conduct a classroom meeting or to help a colleague develop a 'fresh start' process with a challenging classroom group (see Chapters 4 and 5).

One colleague writes about how colleague support helped rebuild her confidence in the utility and benefits of classroom meetings.

> When I conducted my first classroom meeting with a composite grade 5/6 they were a very difficult class and I was hoping to use the meeting format to readdress where we were going as a class – to move towards a 'fresh start'.
>
> The meeting was loud – raucous in fact. Frequent calling out and students saying things like 'Shut up!! I'm talking ...' There were put-downs ('Stupid', 'Won't work!') when solutions were proposed. I stopped the meeting after 20 minutes! I changed the activity to the class now writing an evaluation of their behaviour at the meeting. It helped regain some sanity.
>
> I shared what I'd gone through with colleagues and got immediate support. A colleague and I discussed what had happened and they came into class with me to help me conduct the next classroom meeting; we had a separate place for the classroom meeting (not the classroom); used name cards (to be turned over when anyone in the group wished to speak or contribute); had a set routine for listing, discussing and offering solutions to problems, choosing workable solutions and having a time limit for the classroom meeting. (Rogers, 1992: 54)

Anne notes that it was the reassurance and confidence garnered from discussing and planning the meeting before they went into the classroom that made the difference. *Having a colleague in the classroom with her* – as a supportive mentor – gave the insight, modelling and emotional support that informed, challenged and strengthened her professional practice.

Whole-school emphasis

In many of the schools, the individual teacher's struggle with a challenging student or class is an issue addressed on a whole-school basis. Teachers are not left in moral, 'structural' or professional isolation. As one teacher said to me recently, 'In our school a, "problem-child" is not just *your* problem, it is *our* problem ... If an incident has occurred with a grade teacher's child on playground duty, nobody goes up to that teacher and says, "Do you know what *your* Johnny or Tracey did in the playground?". When a child's behaviour is an issue in the playground, that child is everyone's child not just 'the grade teacher's child.'

Whenever a child's behaviour is *frequent* (in its disruptive expression), *general* (across several teachers/classes) and *durable* (more than bad-day syndrome), then the individual teacher is enabled, with colleague support, to develop an individual behaviour management plan with the child. Such plans (see Chapter 3) often give the student the structure they need within which to learn and supportively develop new skills for behaviour and formal learning.

The whole-school emphasis also includes well-developed time-out options (noted earlier pp. 116–17) and mediation and restitutional opportunities.

In colleague support, *form follows function*; the *function* of colleague support is to meet teachers' needs (their espoused, not *assumed*, need). In consciously supportive cultures, senior staff engage that process of espoused needs analysis on a regular basis and work with staff to provide dependable *forms* of colleague support (structures, plans, policies, professional teaming options – formal and informal). When teachers believe their needs are being heard, engaged with and realistically addressed, they feel better and take on their professional role with more confidence and goodwill (Rogers, 2002a).

An ongoing willingness to persist, coupled with a commitment to respect for the child

Children who frequently display attentional and challenging behaviours in classrooms and playgrounds are not always easy to 'like'. Liking a student is not something we can easily 'manufacture' – dependent as it is on mood, circumstance, weather, available time ... Respecting the essential person is no mean feat when they are driving you 'round the twist' or 'up the wall'. One of the metaphors my colleagues and I have often used is a drawing of a large square on a piece of paper (see over page); at the centre of the white square is a dark dot. As a metaphor, it highlights how easy it is to only see, and focus on, the dark dot in the centre of the white square; it is *as if* it is the only thing we 'see'. It is *as if* the dark dot draws one's attention to it and we do not 'see' the larger – much larger – white space.

When dealing hourly, daily, with student behaviour that creates stress (for teacher and students alike), it is so easy to only see the worst in the student (or the class) and miss those times when the student (and class) do behave thoughtfully, considerately and more co-operatively. In a harder-than-average class, it is easy to over-focus on the four or five 'catalytic' students rather than the 70 per cent of students who behave co-operatively *most of the time*. So too when developing a whole-school policy on behaviour management, it is important to make it *for all*, not merely the 10 per cent of challenging students. It is about focus *and* perspective.

These teachers have managed to gain a perspective – within their stressful circumstances – so that they have learned to see the 'white square' as much bigger than the 'darkish dot' in its centre. It is easy, so easy, to *just* focus on the dot at the expense of the space in the rest of the square.

I've also used this metaphor with students. Initially, all they can see is the dot when asked, 'What can you see here?' When asked different questions, they eventually see that almost all of the square is the 'space'. The metaphor is developed conceptually as the space representing what is better, more helpful, positive, less stressful, more realistically possible, in contrast to the 'dark dot' – the stressful or difficult aspect of life at the moment. When using this visual metaphor with colleagues, some have said, 'The dark dot is too big!' Our collegial response is, 'How can we make the white space bigger?' The 'white space' is the colleague support offered in good faith, giving whatever we can to manage the 'dark dot', as it were.

These teachers *persist* with the child, with the class. That persistence is based in a communicated respect for the individual coupled with a belief that things *can be different*.

This persistence and belief is given psychological and relational 'flesh' through structures and programmes, but in the end, it is the teacher's belief in the child, and the group, that comes through to make the difference.

When children's behaviour is rude (and crude), lazy, arrogant, selfish and insensitive, hostile and aggressive, it is not easy to keep the relational focus on the fundamental person. It is always a challenge to ask how we can discipline *and support*, with some dignity. These children chip away at our natural and professional goodwill. If we choose to work with challenging children, it is, naturally, stressful and there is a frustrating 'normality' about this stressful reality. That stress is better managed, and our coping resources are far more effectively engaged, when we have ongoing colleague support. It helps when we know that we're all 'in the same boat' – a little leaky at times, perhaps a bit rusty, but assured the boat is still viable, and working, the rudder and compass are OK ... and we're 'getting around those icebergs' (as one colleague deftly put it) so we're *still* stressed but not *as* stressed, *as* often, *as* long ... (Rogers, 2002b).

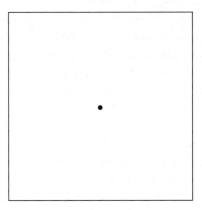

The 'bad-day syndrome': accepting fallibility in ourselves and in others

These teachers also acknowledge that within their naturally stressful role, they do have bad days when they 'snap' at students, say the 'wrong thing' (to a student or class) or forget to encourage (when it would have really helped ...). Teachers can be incredibly hard on themselves, not least when they start comparing themselves to teachers they believe (or perceive) are more successful with challenging students (or groups).

All humans are fallible; this is our axiomatic humanity! We recognise that we fail (we are not *failures*); we forget; we make stupid mistakes and, of course, we get tired and fed-up – and why wouldn't we? Mentally kicking oneself ('I *should have* done this ... or that ... I *never* get it right ...', 'I'll *never* get through to that kid ... that class') is understandable, but detrimental to our professional responsibility, our professional esteem and may negatively affect any workable options. In his book *Learned Optimism*, Martin Seligman (1991) speaks about 'characteristic explanatory styles' that people utilise for stressful and bad events (p. 8f, this volume). These assumptive beliefs significantly influence not just a teacher's behaviour and response (when under stress), they also affect a teacher's emotional well-being and coping. If I *characteristically* say things like, 'It's *all* the student's fault ...' 'I'll *never* be able to manage that class ...'; 'They *shouldn't* answer back ...'; (they do – sometimes) ... 'Students *should* do as they are told ...' (some do not) such explanations are *themselves* stressful and unlikely to be supported by social reality!

A cognitive demand ('they *must* ...'; 'they *should* ...') is different from a realistic preference and expectation: 'I don't particularly like swearing; how can I better address this issue with the student/s?' is a more realistic way of addressing reality than the 'explanatory style' that says, 'Children *mustn't* swear ...' If our characteristic explanatory style for stressful events is to 'globalise' – 'all', 'never', 'no one', e.g. 'All the kids in my class are animals!', not only will that add to our stress, it will significantly affect our coping ability and our ability to focus on, and orient, any helpful or meaningful change (Rogers, 1996, 2006b).

There is a big difference, however, between accepting fallibility and unwillingness to address what we know is repeatedly, and *characteristically*, working against our shared aims and shared practices as a collegial team. There are times we need to confront our behaviour when it is self-defeating and overly negative. We do this best in a climate of positive and supportive collegiality. When we accept our fallibility, we accept our humanity – without excusing our responsibility to work for improvement and change where it is needed.

Separating the behaviour from the person

This is a message as old as the Human Family. Whenever an adult is in a role of leadership with others, they have to learn to see the person beyond the inappropriate, the thoughtless or the wrong behaviour, while at the same time not excusing the inappropriate or wrong behaviour.

This asks a lot of us as teachers – yet the teachers writing here respond to that call. They see the 'white space' as well as the 'dot', while not allowing the dot to constantly take 'centre stage'. (pp. 119–20)

They also do not 're-victimise' the child because of his family background or where he comes from. They recognise that while we clearly cannot control the many factors outside of the school setting affecting a child's attitude and behaviour, they can help the child to believe in themselves and bring about positive change in behaviour and learning *while at school*.

Focusing on the child's effort towards change

Merely telling the child they should (or should not) behave in 'this' or 'that' way will rarely bring about necessary change. Worse, simply telling them louder, or longer, will often reinforce avoidance, attentional or power-seeking patterns of behaviour. Unless a child sees a need to change, has a reason for change, and is given motivation, ongoing support, hope and, often, a 'plan' for change, they may resist what we believe are our good motives in any discipline we apply, or any support we offer.

Of course, children need discipline but discipline is never an end in itself; it is always a means to an end.

Children need, and want, to 'belong'. It is a primary social need (Adler, 1957; Coopersmith, 1967; Dreikurs et al., 1982; Erickson, 1970; Glasser, 1986;

Maslow, 1970). *Some* children feel and believe (with relative degrees of consciousness) that they can only really belong when they are drawing significant attention to themselves, or engaging their teachers in power struggles. Teachers variously describe these children as significantly attention-seeking or power-seeking. Their behaviour is – in effect – their goal; seeking to *belong* to their social group/s at school. The behaviour they exercise within that 'goal', while appearing disruptive and negative to many teachers, does self-confirm in many children in that they often achieve the 'goal' they seek: the attention or power within their peer group/s, or from their teacher. The 'private logic' of the child confirms the belief of 'significance' and 'belonging' gained through disruptive behaviour and negative behaviour (Dreikurs et al., 1982).

When we *overly* attend, nag, engage or threaten students who repeatedly call out, clown around, answer back or challenge, we re-confirm in these children their goals of attention or power. And it is so easy to get overly drawn into a child's attentional and challenging behaviours, to get caught up in pointless arguing, 'scoring' and – even – threatening behaviours. At the point this happens – of course – we are not thinking that our behaviour (as the teacher) is reconfirming the student's 'goal' (of seeking to 'belong' through negative attentional and power-seeking behaviours).

It is not easy to *consciously* step back and ask ourselves (in the less stressful moment): how can I re-engage this child so I can give them the beneficial help they need? How can I reframe – positively – the student's sense of personal power in a way that will strengthen their self-concept? These teachers have managed to do that – to balance appropriate discipline without overly reinforcing the child's mistaken goals.

Supportive interventions in schools help children in their need to belong, giving them hope in the purpose and direction of behaviour change. When children (indeed adults) feel, believe and behave as if they have meaningful control over their lives, they feel, and do, better; they relate to others in more positive and co-operative ways.

When we need to discipline our students, we can do so in ways that keep the fundamental dignity of the child intact while still addressing the inappropriate, disruptive or even dysfunctional behaviour. It can help to consciously plan for this challenging feature of our leadership so that our *language of discipline* is not merely left to the vagaries of mood or chance. The way we intervene in situations where behaviour is disruptive, challenging, needs as assiduous a level of planning as anything we do as teachers.

Focusing on the 'primary' behaviour or issue

When children 'sneer', 'pout', 'sulk', 'sigh', 'raise their eyes to the ceiling' and display other such irritating non-verbal behaviours, these teachers consciously seek to keep the focus of their discipline engagement on the primary issue or behaviour, rather than focusing on 'secondary' behaviours such as the pout, the 'tut-tutting', the overly drawn sigh! This is a daily (hourly) challenge for teachers in those 'emotional moments' when a child responds to a teacher's reminder, direction or question in a 'sulky', 'pouty', 'sighing' manner. When the student looks like you've asked them to fly to the moon because you've asked them to 'put up your hand', 'wait your turn', 'go back to your seat', 'carry on with your work', 'remember our rule for …', it is not easy to keep the focus of your discipline on the *main* or *primary issue* in the student's behaviour at that moment when emotions are naturally raised.

I was working with a challenging class in Western Sydney a few years back. As soon as the noisy, restless students came into the classroom (including a couple of lads 'testosteronically bonding' – 'We're just mucking around!'), three girls raced to the back of the room and began to loudly rearrange the last row of tables and chairs moving them to the far back, right corner of the classroom (I suspected to create a small 'bloc').

Instead of formally beginning the lesson (from the front of the classroom), I walked over to the girls (the rest of the class sensing, watching …). The girls were sitting in their chairs but had pushed their tables right away from all the others to the far back corner of the room. It was my first meeting with this class so I asked them for their names. 'What's your name, please?' I believe I was pleasant as I made eye contact with the first student. She leaned back in her chair, raised her eyes, sighed and said, 'What do you want to know my name for?!' I sensed a barely controlled insolence as she accented the pronoun; her tone, her manner needed to be addressed without getting into unnecessary confrontation. I also wanted to keep the focus of my communication on the main or 'primary issue' of the students having moved the furniture – now added to by the tone and manner of her response. I also wanted to do this as quickly as possible, realising the potential audience-seeking capacity of this student.

'I'm not speaking rudely to you, I don't expect you to speak rudely to me.' I kept eye contact, but also looked at the other girls (might they collude with her?). The Year 8 student leaned back: 'Rude?! What's rude!?'

I added, 'I'm not speaking rudely or defensively to you, I don't expect you to speak that way to me.' In this very brief exchange (it nearly always seems longer in the immediate, emotional moment), I was conscious of speaking calmly but with relaxed assertion (open body language and not conveying a threat). I'm facing a 14-year-old girl. She's not my enemy, she's a student.

I repeated the first question: 'What's your name, please? I'm one of the new teachers here.'

'Talia.' It came out as a sigh, with raised eyes, folded arms: these are 'secondary behaviours'. We can learn to *tactically ignore some aspects of the student's behaviour (the rolling of eyes, the frown, the sibilant sigh …)* in the emotional moment and keep the focus on the main or 'primary' issue. 'Talia,

Sophie and Hailey' (the other two girls were co-operative in response, in manner), 'you've rearranged the furniture – it belongs back there.' I pointed back behind me.

In this exchange, I was also aware that the whole class was watching this interaction, making their 'judgements' – why wouldn't they? I was also aware that the young girl's behaviour (the attentionally challenging behaviour) was, no doubt, seeking peer audience. I was conscious of seeking to lead this situation so that the wider audience (of peers) would more likely accept the necessary teacher leadership, thus minimising the student's attentional goal. This, of course, is never easy in the emotional moment.

In response to the incidental direction to put the chairs back to the 'normal place', Talia leaned back with a feigned 'hurt' scowl: 'But we're only sitting here 'cos we're friends!'

A bit of *partial agreement*, however, goes a long way. 'I have no problems with you sitting together as friends (the partial agreement). However, the furniture belongs back there. That's where I expect it to go. Thank you.' At that point, it helps to non-verbally give the student/s 'take-up time' by 'disengaging' and physically moving away – while conveying expectation of co-operation, commonsense or (at least) compliance (Rogers, 1998). All this happened reasonably quickly (it often seems longer).

As I turned and moved away from the back of the room, I could 'see' them move the furniture back. Talia was muttering and sighing, 'Gees, new teacher, new teacher … na, na, na …' (at just above sotto voce). Again, it is this sort of 'secondary behaviour' we tactically ignore, keeping the focus on the main ('primary') issue at that point: the furniture going back (and having addressed the initial rudeness). Aspects of 'secondary behaviour' such as attitude expressed in sighs, raised eyes, muttered whingeing (unless overtly rude or unsafe) can often be addressed later – away from the audience – by follow-up with the student in a calmer moment. Sometimes this follow-up may need to be a brief five-minute chat after class (if time), or an informal behaviour interview at lunchtime (see p.83).

At that point, I went back to the front of the class and formally started yet another lesson (albeit with a new and challenging class).

NB: If Talia and her classmates had refused to move (as I requested), I would have given a deferred consequence. 'Talia, Sophie and Hayley – if you choose not to move the furniture back now, I'll have to follow this up at recess.' At that point, it is helpful to – again – give the student take-up time. If the student mutters, 'Don't care,' a brief 'I do' (and take-up time) is enough. It will be essential, though, to follow up later with fair certainty. What is important, in such cases, is to put the responsibility back on to the student (particularly at adolescent level) and avoid getting into a verbal stand-off.

It sounds as if this approach is time-consuming. It is actually less time-consuming, both in the immediate emotional moment and in the necessary follow-up with the student (one-to-one) later, away from their peer audience.

Editor's note

It is important to avoid using interrogatives in such discipline situations (above), e.g. *'Why* did you move the furniture?' or 'You shouldn't have moved it, *should you?'* or the really unhelpful interrogative *'Have you* moved the furniture?' It is enough to describe the 'obvious reality'. 'You've moved … they belong there …' (This acts as an 'incidental direction'.)

Where we do use questions, in discipline contexts, a quiet 'What …?', 'Where …?' or 'How …?' enables the student to focus on what (or where …) they need to be doing. Teachers will often use the 'what' question in reference to a rule/procedure: 'what's our rule for mobile phones?' (this to a student texting, surreptitiously, in classwork time …). A *direct* question enables a student (at least) to be behaviourally aware. If he does not know the answer (rare!), we can redirect; if he argues the point – again – we can redirect the student to the expected behaviour (or the fair rule), or clarify the deferred (or immediate) consequence.

Discipline

My colleagues and I have learned that when we need to discipline our students, we seek to follow these guidelines:

- **Avoid *unnecessary* confrontation** (most of the time) – when we do have to use assertive direction (or command), we do so with *firm* calmness and *clear* direction or command.
- Keep the **intervention as least *intrusive*** as possible, or if we need to become *more intrusive,* make sure that does not equate to becoming more hostile or verbally aggressive – it will mean becoming more assertive. Assertion is a skill, it can be learned. For example, rather than phrase questions as 'don'ts …' we seek (wherever possible) to phrase them as 'do's'. For example, 'Don't call out' becomes 'Hands up, thanks.' or 'Hands up without calling out.' 'Don't talk when I'm teaching' becomes 'Looking this way and listening, thanks.' We may need to add the qualifier '… without talking.' 'Don't fiddle with the window blinds' becomes 'Jason … Dean … leave the window blinds, thanks and face this way.' Of course, with any discipline language, our positive and expectant *tone and manner* are as crucial as the positive language.
- Keep the **corrective language positive** (where possible) – note this typical example of settling a class at the beginning of a lesson: the students are rest-

less, several are chatting to each other, a few are calling out, several students are loudly fiddling with pencil cases/water bottles ... Teacher A is pacing up and down at the front of the classroom and says (in a rather loud voice), 'Will you please be quiet ...?!', 'Can you stop talking and listen *now*?!' He addresses two boys fiddling with the window blinds, 'You two, yes, *you two*; can you stop doing that *and listen*?' His pacing (to and fro) is itself telegraphing a corresponding restlessness (and unhelpful energy) to the more restless boys. His loud voice is also kinaesthetically unsettling (rather than helping the class to settle ...). His directions to the class to settle are actually questions: 'Will you ...?', 'Can you ...?'. Teacher A is not a 'bad teacher' – but may be unaware that his behaviour, too, is part of the dynamic mix in the class that will help or hinder a sense of calmness and focus.

Teacher B seeks to keep her classroom management – and discipline – least intrusive wherever possible. As the class comes into the classroom restless, chatting, with a bit of pushing and shoving, she has a brief, quiet word to students as they file in. Several students are chatting, 'fiddling', etc. She waits for the residual noise to settle ... Scanning the room, she makes brief, transitional eye contact; she lifts the voice a little ... 'Settling down everyone,' (she pauses briefly and repeats the group direction ...) 'Eyes and ears this way.' (She pauses again to allow some take-up). She feels – and sees – the group settle. Several students are chatting, and she does not ask them why they are chatting: 'Rebecca, Chantelle, Suzanne, why are you talking?', nor does she use a negative direction, 'Don't talk when I'm teaching.' She *briefly describes* what she sees: 'Rebecca ... Chantelle ... Suzanne, you're talking. Looking this way and listening. Thanks.' Sometimes the *descriptive* aspect of the direction is enough, e.g.: 'Michael, you're cracking the water bottle – it's really distracting' (her voice is calm; her tone and manner expectant). It has been a few minutes now since the class have come in. The teacher has had to quietly, briefly direct several students in the class settling phase (as did Teacher A) but she has kept such interventions consciously least intrusive.

■ Keep the corrective discipline **focused on the 'primary' issue or behaviour** and avoid getting caught up in 'secondary' issues or behaviours such as those noted earlier (p. 122f). How many times have we heard students say: 'But other teachers let us sit where we want'; 'listen to our iPods'; 'chew gum'; 'wear hats in class'; 'dance on the tables in an east wind ...'. The answer here is, 'I don't know what other teachers do, in our class we ...' or ' ... our school rule is ...'. It is important not to get into arguments about which teachers let students sit where they want, etc. It is important to refocus the student's responsibility through a question or rule reminder, back to the fair school rule.

■ Keep the fundamental **respect** for the student – as a person – intact. *Always* easier said than done.

■ **Follow up** all repeatedly distracting or disruptive behaviour on a one-to-one basis after class, or some time later that day. This says, 'I care', 'It's important', 'We need to think about behaviour now and for the next time we're together in class ...'. It also demonstrates the **fair certainty of appropriate consequences**. It is also important to use such time to **repair and rebuild**. Even a few, brief, positive words and 'separating amicably' can enhance repairing and rebuilding (see p. 83).

Where distracting and disruptive behaviours are ongoing, it is crucial to seek colleague support and pursue individual behaviour management plans (Behaviour Recovery – see Chapter 3).

■ **Distinguish between 'negotiable' and 'non-negotiable' consequences** – non-negotiable consequences are those we apply for any *repeatedly* disturbing or unsafe behaviour, or for any aggressive, hostile or bullying behaviour, or for use of violence, intimidation, drugs or weapons. 'Negotiable consequences' are those we *work through with the student*, using focus questions (see below) – and referring to our fundamental rights and responsibilities. We work with the student (at a calmer moment) to enable some restitutional outcome.

■ When applying behaviour consequences, **emphasise the certainty** of the behaviour consequences rather than the severity of the consequences. In other words, we let the consequence do the work of teaching accountability and responsibility. The 'certainty principle' – when applied with respect and dignity – is a more powerful and effective tool than an attitude that uses consequences merely as a punitive tool to make the child feel worse. It is fundamental to keep the respect of the student intact when *applying* the consequences.

■ *'Negotiable' consequences* – when establishing behaviour consequences, seek to **establish a relationship between the disruptive behaviour and the outcome**; where appropriate, ask the student what they think they should do to address the behaviour in question. Key questions that can be asked (or responded to in a written response sheet) are:
What happened – i.e. your behaviour? (to cause you to be in 'detention time');
What rule (older children: *What right/rule*) *was broken?*
What's your side of it all? (right of reply)
What can you do to fix things up, make things better?
How can I help? (the initiating teacher asks this question)

■ Degrees of seriousness regarding consequences – at the school-wide level, establish **degrees of seriousness** with respect to behaviour consequences (especially detention practices). Some teachers will use inappropriate detentions (even formal detentions) for behaviours that are more effectively addressed by a personal one-to-one talk with the student. It is always worth a school reviewing its detention policy to address what behaviours lead to formal detention and internal or external temporary exclusion from classes.

■ **Establish year level and school-wide processes for exit, time-out and follow-up** of any students whose disruptive behaviour has necessitated 'exit' from the classroom (safety concerns; *persistent* refusal to work within the fair rules and within reasonable teacher direction; verbal abuse).

■ **Remember the importance of re-establishing working relationships and reconciliation** between teacher and student(s). We avoid holding (nursing) grudges. We deal honestly and as fairly as possible with the challenging student (or parent!). Where the relational issues between teacher/students are serious, it will be important to employ supporting mediation (from colleagues) for problem-solving and resolution.

The power of leadership – using our power for, and with, our children

When we are engaged in the disciplining aspect of our role as teachers, it is easy to fall into the assumption that we can actually control others, that we can make others do what we want. Power and authority in our leadership means more than 'controlling power' – our ability to 'control' others. When working with very challenging children, the exercise of power – as 'control', and any use of assertive force – without responsive moral authority leads only to reactive confrontation and relational resentment. Moral authority always superintends 'role' authority. The power associated with one's role authority (as teacher) needs to be understood as more than power *over* others – it is more to be considered as the power we use (as adults) *for* and *with* our students. Our aim – within such *relational power* – is to use our 'power' to motivate, engage, assist, teach and encourage our students to control their own behaviour. Even in situations where we have to physically restrain a child who is a significant danger to himself or others, we consciously seek to use our power to enable the student to 'calm' himself, regain self-control and work to repair and rebuild (O'Brien, 1998; Rogers, 2003; Rogers and McPherson, 2008). In each of the accounts in this book, teachers share how they began to understand and use this *kind* of power for the benefit and welfare of their students.

To use a deceptively basic example here: I've worked with some teachers who will snatch a toy, comic, iPod or mobile phone off a student's desk. It is annoying when students 'secrete' such items on their desk (particularly during whole-class teaching time). Some teachers will seek to control the event, *and the student's behaviour*, by simply taking the object. In 'challenging schools', taking, or forcing a student to hand over, an iPod or mobile phone is a recipe for conflict. I've seen students quickly directed to leave the classroom over such pointless power exchanges.

A student is listening to his iPod during on-task learning time. His teacher notices this and 'marches' over ...

(Teacher) 'Right, Troy – give that to me.'
(Student) 'I can work with it on. I'm not hassling anyone!'
(Teacher) 'I don't care if you can work with it on. You know you're not supposed to bring those into class. Now give it to me.'
(Student) 'No way – I'll put it away if it's such a big deal!'
(Teacher) 'No you won't – you'll give it to me now! I said, give it to me!'
(Student) 'No – no way – it's my iPod ...'
(Teacher) 'Right – if you don't hand it over, you can get out of my class now.'

The student gets up, banging his chair, adding (as he storms off), 'It's a sh-t class anyway ...!' and (of course) drawing attentional significance in front of his classmates (at least in his 'private logic'). He bangs the class door as he leaves ... Who won? Why was it *defined* as a conflict; as something that has to be 'won'? Does the issue have to be defined in this way – *contestably*?

Other teachers will use their 'power' to control *the situation* rather than the student, using their 'power' to work with the student.

A teacher notices an iPod on the student's table and comes across to the student. She does not immediately comment on it. She asks how the student is going. He mutters, 'OK.' She has a brief chat about the classwork he is doing and then ...

(Teacher) 'Travis, you've got your iPod here.' (Brief 'description of reality'.)
(Student) Student frowns, 'Yeah,' adding, 'other teachers don't say anything, as long as we get our work done.'
(Teacher) 'Maybe they don't' (brief , and quiet, partial agreement). 'What's the school rule about iPods in class, Travis?'
(Student) 'I told you Miss – other teachers let us.'
(Teacher) 'You did' (brief partial agreement). 'You know the school rule ...' (reminder). 'I want you to put the iPod in your bag or on my table, ta' (a directed choice).

At this point, the teacher walks away, giving 'the control' back to the student, giving the student some 'take-up time' and disengaging any potential power struggle. She realises, of course, she cannot simply make him hand over the object, or put it away. However, by giving a directed 'choice' (within the fair, known rules), she has put the responsibility back where it belongs – with the student. If he refuses ('chooses') not to put it away (he'll hardly put it on the teacher's desk), the teacher will go back – a little later – and give the student a deferred consequence: 'If you choose not to put the iPod away, I'll have to follow this up with you after class' (i.e. following up later, after class or at break – away from 'the audience of peers').

Most students do put their 'trinkets' away, with muttered sighs and whinges (which we'll *tactically ignore*). It will then be important to briefly acknowledge this and *resume task focus* a little later in that phase of the lesson by coming back to the student and quietly affirming: 'How's your work going? Glad to see the iPod is away for now (wink) – let's have a look at your maths, Travis ...'

When the student puts an object away, they are – in effect – (at that point) granting the teacher the authority that the teacher exercises *at that point*. The teacher's tone, manner, respect, confidence and emotional intelligence all play their part – naturally. This is the creative tension of teacher authority: that our *relational* power is seen in the reciprocity of characteristic student responses. As such, our power to lead comes not merely from assumptive role power ('I am a teacher, therefore students *should* do what I say') but from *earning* such authority by the nature of our leadership; how we *characteristically* communicate the shared rights, responsibilities and rules that assist the relatively smooth running of a busy classroom. We also earn our *relational* leadership authority by the quality, and effort, of our teaching. How we seek to cater for abilities and understanding of our students; how we seek to find connective teaching points; how we seek to cater for the mix of learning styles; how we seek to encourage *all* of our students will go a long way to building the trust of our students and their willingness to co-operate with us as teacher leader.

Is such a leadership style more than personality? Is the ability to relate well to young people something one just *has* or can it be learned? One of the terms used for the social, relational dexterity and intuitiveness that characterises such relational leadership is 'emotional intelligence', the other is 'social intelligence'. In our daily practice, these kinds of terms (emotional/social intelligence) describe our expression of humanity, goodwill, empathetic awareness, care, encouragement and – yes – necessary discipline. While some teachers do seem to have an innate sense of how to tune in, look for and sense others' needs and feelings and respond with some 'connective awareness', it is my view that we can learn to develop the sorts of attributions, understandings and skills that these teachers clearly exhibit. *The ability to teach and lead effectively* (with all the expected bad days and fallibility) *is about wanting and learning to be an effective teacher.*

Descriptive feedback to encourage students

We all know that people respond to encouragement. We know that children need (and want) encouragement and supportive feedback in their learning, and in their behaviour. However, when we give overly 'global' and ebullient praise to students (especially those who have struggled with learning and teachers' authority at school), they may well not believe it. Praise such as, 'That's fantastic/great/marvellous/wonderful/brilliant!', because a student has done a few sentences or remembered to *sit* on the mat (without rolling, pushing or touching) may see them reject such praise and become even more attentional in their behaviour. With some students – however – they may only make an effort if we keep telling them they are 'wonderful', 'great', 'brilliant', and keep giving them rewards to prove it(!) There is a place for using behaviour enhancement and encouragers (rather than rewards as something *earned*). Overall, though, it is important to develop an encouraging/feedback style of teaching that looks out for and affirms – and builds on – a child's effort.

When giving encouragement and feedback, it is important to have a modicum of *joie de vivre* while at the same time keeping the emphasis on *descriptive feedback*. We do this by affirming what the student has *done* (in effort, attitude or behaviour). The focus then is on affirming the student's effort (or at least the direction of their effort!).

'You remembered to start straight away, Craig. You've already answered those first two questions. How do you think you'll go on those decimal fractions in questions 4 and 5? Remember the rule about the decimal point and multiplying by 10. I'll come back and see how you're doing later.'

For example, if a student has remembered to use his 'inside voice' (in classwork time), his teacher will *quietly* affirm, acknowledge and describe: 'You remembered to use your inside voice, Sean. It makes it so much easier for everyone to work when we use our inside voices.' (This to a grade 3 student on a behaviour plan emphasising a quieter 'working voice' or 'partner-voice' in classwork time.) The teacher will then re-engage the student within his task focus: 'How's your writing going?'

It is also important not to devalue descriptive affirmation by qualifying it: '*Why* can't you do that all the time?', '*If* you only put your hand up like that all the time, we would have a much happier class, wouldn't we?', '*But* you could have done much better *if only* you had ...' Such qualifying is demotivating and may well see the student not acknowledge the preceding encouragement.

Conveying empathy

All the students in these studies responded to their teachers' empathy – not feeling sorry for the child but being aware of, and responding to, the child's perspective; giving them a voice (even a basic 'right of reply' in a detention!) and valuing their voice. Empathy is what a child sees in us, hears in us and senses in us *over time*. It is always more than words. It is about our characteristic manner and tone as we relate to them, not what we say as a result of 'the bad day syndrome'. Children are almost always forgiving of our bad days.

Branwhite (1988) notes that it is a teacher's empathy that is the most valued teacher quality cited by pupils (in Kyriacou, 1991). I suspect it is also one of the most valued qualities in human relationships generally.

Keeping a sense of humour

In every study I've read on what students like and positively respond to in their teachers, 'a sense of humour' is always in the top five.[1] This does not mean telling jokes *as such*; it is the ability to see the lighter side of life. We are, after all, stuck in that small classroom space, hour after hour, day after day. We know that laughter can help lift the spirit, defuse and reframe tension, even assist stress and coping in positive ways:[2] repartee, *bon mots*, dry wit, irony, farce (plenty of that in schools) and even satire can all have a place in the classroom.

In the one-to-one modelling we often engage in with children with EBD, the teacher's 'acting out' of the student's disruptive behaviour often occasions laughter and such laughter is healthy (p. 47). Effective teachers, while clearly jaded at times from working with overly challenging students, do not resort to labelling, sarcasm, put-downs, cheap shots or point scoring. When teachers use sarcasm, they are seeking to 'score' off a child's behaviour, temperament or personality. We do not use humour to intentionally hurt, whatever the temptation. Humour is all about defusing tension, or at least reframing the tension so we're less stressed (that obviously includes the students!).

Victor Frankyl, the eminent Viennese psychiatrist – who was interned in the concentration camps of Dachau and Auschwitz – said, 'One could even find a sense of humour there as well; of course, only the faint trace of one, and then only for a few seconds or minutes. Humour was one of the soul's weapons in the fight for self-preservation. It is well known that humour, more than anything else in the human make-up, can provide an aloofness and an ability to rise above any situation, even if only for a few seconds or minutes ...' (in *Man's Search for Meaning*, 1985: 63. Frankyl first published this after the Second World War in 1946.)

Giving students a voice through classroom meetings

This is a recurrent practice used by teachers throughout this book. They believe that the forum and process of classroom meetings gives a 'voice' to students as individuals and as members of a *classroom group*. Such meetings need to have structure and fair rules to enable that 'voice' to be heard and engaged (see Chapter 5).

These meetings can also assist a class group to understand, even empathise, with a classmate who presents with challenging behaviour and emotional behaviour disorders. They do not often use the 'labels' we use; they see 'Troy', 'Jason', 'Dean' or

---

1. See McInerney and McInerney (1998); Rogers (2002b).
2. Rogers (2002a: 114–15) suggests that humour can help a person 'to some extent deal with his repressed emotions'. This is of the group as well as the individual (ibid: 117). Malcolm Muggeridge reminds us that 'We can bear to be human because, as humans, we can laugh' (in Nicholas Bentley's *How Can You Bear to be Human?*, 1957: 10). Frank Muir has noted that 'essentially laughter is a kindly human characteristic' (in his preface to *The Oxford Book of Humorous Prose*). Sir Peter Ustinov notes that 'it is humour that distinguishes us from the other animals' (in *Ustinov at Eighty* CD).

'Michelle' (or) … who needs understanding and support. I am frequently encouraged at the nature, and degree, of support students will give troublesome and challenging students *if* the teacher is able to lead and guide, and manage the classroom context with care and consistency. I have seen this countless times myself when conducting classroom meetings to address the behaviour of an individual (or several students) in the context of the group (see also Rogers, 2003).

Such meetings need skilled leadership if they are to work towards the aims envisaged. One of the common uses of classroom meetings is the 'fresh start process' for a hard-to-manage class group. The classroom meeting format often gives the class that has drifted into poor (often unreflective) patterns of behaviour its guided voice as a means to a 'fresh start' (see p. 86f). In such cases, however, it is normally advisable that the class or subject teacher conduct the meeting(s) with a supportive colleague (who also knows, and has the respect of, the class).

Balancing the short term with longer-term aims

As noted earlier, there are many factors we cannot control in the lives of our children (p. 27f). Even while they are with us at school, we cannot simply 'control' the behaviour of these children for good; we can lead, guide, expect, even confront (where necessary), but we cannot simply 'make' them behave well or learn well.

In the immediate short term – in the many emotional moments in a busy lesson – we will need to both encourage and correct our students. It is in the longer term, however, that teachers normally build up any lasting success regarding behaviour changes.

From the after-class chats (week one), to *supportive* use of time-out, we convey that:

> While we will not – cannot – allow you to hold the learning and safety of other students to ransom, we will always (beyond time-out, detention and other consequences) support you to make better choices about your behaviour while you are with us here.

The teachers writing here made a difference because they gave that extra time to the student *beyond* the classroom context. This is noted over and over again by these teachers. In the classroom context, children seek to 'belong' – and most do so in co-operative, considerate ways. But the children noted in this book often seek inappropriate, highly attentional or challenging ways to meet the need to belong to their social grouping (in a school context).

These teachers made time (away from the peer audience) to help the child understand their behaviour and come to terms with this need to belong. They helped these students to believe that this fundamental need could be met in positive ways. This is where the individual plans (noted in Chapter 3) are often a much more effective *longer-term* support for the children than short-term discipline and consequences alone. What the children themselves note most strongly, however, is the fact that their teacher cares enough to spend this time, this attention, this care and this support – one-to-one with them.

Whenever we spend such time on any supportive strategy, we need to distinguish it from 'consequential' time (e.g. time-out, detentions, withdrawal of privileges). Due consequences are essential in a school behaviour policy but they always need to be balanced by longer-term *support*.

Caveat

All long-term support is costly; it is labour intensive. Many teachers (at primary level) spend a lot of non-contact time supporting children with behaviour and learning. They spend a lot of time contacting – and discussing with – support agencies and other professionals. They spend a lot of time working with parents and caregivers. Beyond any natural whingeing, these teachers always say it was worth it.

Key principles and practices
- Appreciating, embracing and enabling the critical nature of *consistent colleague support*.
- Establishing *whole-school approaches*, providing 'structures' within collegial relationships.
- Being willing to persist, coupled with holding a respect for the child's humanity.
- Accepting fallibility in ourselves and others; acknowledging 'bad day syndrome'.
- Separating the behaviour from the person.
- Focusing on the child's efforts towards change.
- Keeping the focus on the 'primary' behaviour or issue in discipline contexts.
- Developing key discipline skills; using our leadership power *for* and *with* our children.
- Using descriptive feedback to encourage.
- Conveying empathy to our students.
- Maintaining a sense of humour.
- Giving students a voice through classroom meetings.
- Balancing the short term with longer-term aims.

We become more effective as teachers through personal and collegial reflection. Such reflection needs to occur within the values, expectations, behaviours, principles, goals and skills we hold relative to concepts like 'effective' or 'good'. In this sense, it is not mere utility that drives us; we are purpose-driven as well as needs-driven. Based on the fundamental values of mutual respect, mutual regard and the dignity of the individual, we seek to be 'a good teacher' – we reflect (from time to time) on what such 'effectiveness' and 'goodness' might mean for us. The teachers writing here have reminded us about what good (and fallible and tired) teachers are like, and why.

> Aristotle (in his Nichomachean Ethics) makes the point that 'of every art' we become 'good or bad as a result of building well …' and '… this makes it our duty to see that our activities have the right character, since the differences of quality in them are repeated in the dispositions that follow in their train. So it is a matter of real importance whether our early education confirms us in one set of habits or another. It would be nearer to the truth to say that it makes a very great difference indeed, in fact all the difference in the world.[3]

---

3. See Aristotle's *Nichomachean Ethics* Book Two, Chapter One, in J.A.K. Thompson's translation (Penguin Classics, 1969: 56).

Chapter 7

Supporting Parents of Children with Challenging Behaviours

Communicating with parents who challenge ...

Bill Rogers

Many years ago, I was sitting in a principal's office with an angry mother and her seven-year-old child (whose behaviour – at school – had 'created' a very large file). The principal had asked me to sit in on the 'interview', as I had been working in 'Jackson's classroom' as a teacher–mentor. I had worked with Jackson's teacher to enable a behaviour plan to help Jackson with his low frustration tolerance and attentional behaviours. My colleague and I had seen some hopeful, early, changes in his behaviour.

The principal also wanted some moral support at this meeting with Jackson's mother – it can be taxing when a mother storms in with obviously hostile body language. Before we had finished a 'welcome' and a careful focus of, 'We wanted to talk with you about Jackson ...' she started a tirade of, 'Ever since he's come to this sh_t school you've had it in for him ... He was alright at the last fifteen schools ...!' The tirade continued ... with f___ing, and sh_tting about the 'bastard teachers in this school ...'. We let her run with 'this' for a few minutes.

I directed Jackson to sit outside the office and gave him a box of toys to play with. It took us another five minutes or more to calmly find a 'break into, and through', the 'psychological traffic' of her 'spleen-venting' (as it were!) and reassure her that this meeting had been called so that we could share Jackson's 'success' with his behaviour plan (Chapter 3).

- We assured her that we knew she cared for Jackson (as did we).
- We focused on the link between his behaviour 'plan' and how it would encourage and support his learning at school.

■ *We invited her understanding and support. We asked if she had any questions ...*

It took time and patience (in that meeting) to gain a sense of connectedness with Jackson's mother. I also experienced – yet again – the principal's good-will, grace and patience with this mother.

In the following essays, my colleagues recount a number of situations where they have sought to defuse tension – with stressed, anxious, demanding, challenging and angry parents – while at the same time seeking to be professional and supportive. No mean feat! Increasingly, it seems, we have to deal with very frustrated, angry and even abusive parents.

An article in the Sunday Express *(14 September 2008) suggested that as verbal abuse and physical intimidation from parents who fail to see that their children had behaved badly increases, teachers are more likely to let bad behaviour pass rather than risk parents' anger. Not only do teachers fear the reactions of such parents but there is widespread concern that these parents are not taking responsibility for their children nor are they playing their part in the bargain in making teachers authority figures. This feeling of being undermined isn't helped by the fact that in the 2007–08 academic year, more than 70,000 pupils who assaulted teachers were let back into school.*

Editor's note

A provocative headline in an Australian newspaper, 'Workplace is a war zone' (*The Age*), notes that research from the Australian Institute of Criminology, conducted among police, doctors, nurses, taxi drivers and teachers, indicates that these professions face the greatest risk of verbal attacks and, even, assaults, injury through employer negligence, physical and verbal abuse, racial abuse, bullying, sexual harassment and (even) malicious gossip (*The Age* newspaper, Santina Perore, 22 February 2000).

In each of these professions – of course – those members of the public are vulnerable, often feeling anxious, confused, in pain (psychological or physical or both); in our case as teachers, this is mostly parents or close relations of the student/s in question.

Wherever a sensitive – and disturbing – issue like this is raised in the press, it can seem as if we are overwhelmed by difficult parents; we are not. Most parents (thankfully) are co-operative and supportive, even when their son or daughter is presenting with behaviour and learning concerns. However, there is a small but significant group of parents who can create significant stress for their own children and teachers. It is for this reason that my colleagues and I have sought to address this issue severally to enable a practical, yet supportive, response when supporting parents. Although these colleagues work at primary- and secondary-age levels in 'regular' schools, pupil-referral visits and schools for students with emotional and behaviour disorders, there are common shared practices that enable supportive and positive relationships with parents and children.

Dealing with – and supporting – difficult parents

Gail Doney

We know that the greatest influence in any child's life is their parents. Yet as schools and teachers, we often seem to concentrate on trying to provide for the academic, social and emotional needs of our students within the boundaries of the school, believing that we can have little or no influence on the parental influence of a child's life. In this essay Gail seeks to share how she communicates with the more challenging parents to enhance parental support.

Connecting with the parent

As a classroom teacher – some years ago now – I always made the relationships with my students' parents a priority and especially targeted the extremely quiet parent, the over-anxious parent and, most importantly, the parent of students who had obvious behaviour or social problems. I would always welcome the parent warmly, often approaching them in the morning and after school to have a personal chat, sometimes sharing my personal experiences and family with them, and most importantly ringing them now and again to tell them how proud or pleased I was with their child. I would make a point to congratulate them as a parent saying such things as: 'You have done a wonderful job to produce such ... a lovely child; a confident child; or a child with an enormous exuberance for life.'

Taking the time and effort to remember a parent's name *seems basic* but it is imperative. Children tell us one of the most important things a teacher can do is call them by name – it develops and contributes hugely to a sense of connectedness and belonging. It is the same for parents. School can be just as terrifying for some parents – new people, not quite knowing the expectations or how things work and being anxious about fitting in and finding a sense of value and worth. Enabling a positive connectedness with the parents of my students in this area as a classroom teacher was a crucial aspect of my teaching but now, as an Assistant Principal, how was I going to transfer this practice to a whole-school level? That was my challenge!

> **Editor's note**
> Parents also come to a school with their own memories of schooling (good, bad or in between). Some parents have had a negative, failing, even punitive experience of schooling; this will quite likely colour how they feel as they make any visit to school. Obviously, those first visits are crucial in engaging some sense of connection and acceptance. *Our* perspective-taking is always *helpful*: how do we feel as a new parent in a new school (see also p. 152).

How much of this can we plan for?

Strategic planning to develop parent relationships on a whole-school basis is critical to achieve success when dealing with difficult parents. The more 'deposits' you have in the *'positive* relationship bank', the more easily the more negative situations can be resolved.

Training teachers and even giving them time to role-play, practise and consolidate their skills in developing relationships with parents is the first step. Practise 'making conversation' and discuss behaviours that enhance parent connectedness. Many teachers are nervous enough about their grade, much less in taking the time to worry about how they will connect with and relate to parents. In particular, young teachers are often more 'frightened' of the parents than anyone.

The transition phase from pre-school and kindergarten to 'big school' is probably the only time that schools will get 100 per cent of all parents together at one time – listening attentively and (mostly) with great eagerness and expectation – a bit like classrooms on the first day. How we run that first session and the rest of the programme is crucial to our success. It will be important to have activities that promote positive relationships between parents, educating parents on the rules and programmes at the school and the reasons and purpose for them, giving parenting tips and articulating repeatedly how and why we should always work together. *The children are the first priority for all of us.*

All these factors are important but we do not live in a fairytale world. Since becoming Assistant Principal, there have been a number of occasions on which I have had to deal with angry parents. One important thing I have learnt over my many years in education is to try to understand the values and behaviours of parents sometimes described as 'living in generational poverty'. This attempt at understanding has been fundamental to any success we have had as a community of teachers in gaining parental trust and enlisting their understanding and support.

The immediate emotional moment

When a very angry parent presents at the school, they may well be extremely agitated, psychologically and physically. They may well have a mindset intent on 'getting their way', insisting the school do … (this or that) 'now!' They may even want revenge for what they perceive as an injustice to their child or to themselves.

At this point, the parent may be verbally hostile, or provocative, using swearing or even threatening language. The swearing may not be directly 'attacking' but rather an expression of their anger (and difficulty in relative self-control). We too may have experienced these feelings *and* behaviour ourselves!

We avoid getting drawn into the secondary stage of an angry or aggressive situation: swearing and rude behaviour to some extent can be tactically ignored, depending on the time and place. Listening to what is being said – giving the parent an opportunity to vent, and to feel that their concerns have been given acknowledgment – is essential to discovering the core reason for the anxiety and coming to a satisfactory solution for all concerned. Never become defensive. We can, of course, be assertive as it is imperative to adhere to our duty of care for students and other community members. Above all, though, stay calm! At times this can be a difficult mental state to control (see p. 163f).

The following two examples illustrate how we might seek to deal with extremely difficult parents in a way that is likely to engage a workable – even a positive – outcome.

Ann

Although skinny, frail and poorly dressed, Ann looked excited with anticipation during her first visit to our school. She wanted the very best school for her child and decided that this was where he had to be. She talked nervously about anything and everything on the school tour. I made particular care to refer to her by name and help her feel at ease; I instinctively felt that our 'journey' with Ann would not be an easy one for all of us. Before her child started school, I had ten requests from parents for their children *not* to be in her child's grade. Ann had been described to me as rude, loud and aggressive. Her son Bobby was boisterous and often antagonistic but it was actually the mother the other parents did not want to be near.

It did not take long for Ann to make her mark. The first incidents included swearing and name-calling at other parents in the schoolyard, abusing and cursing parents in the school car park and even chasing our School Council President through the streets in a road rage incident. On each of these occasions, I would escort her quietly into my office and talk to her about what was acceptable at school and what was not. She would change from an aggressive, out-of-control person to an insecure 'little girl' who cried uncontrollably – the sign of a person under enormous stress! I would always ask her what was going on in her life and she would tell me. We would discuss strategies and then seek to put them in place; she freely admitted that she had an anger-management problem. It is very important when working with someone like Ann that we always show empathy and understanding, no matter how irrational some of the things they say. Just listen, and always bring the conversation back to *their children*. We would say such things as, 'You have to understand, Ann, that if someone was speaking and acting like that in front of your children, you would not be happy. We teach the children to use their manners and be respectful and I know that's what you want for your children; look at the wonderful job you've done with Bobby.' I also spoke to her about the repercussions of her behaviour on her son. We talked about how she was perceived by other parents when she was behaving in this manner (regardless of how unfairly she felt she had been treated) and that the result of this would be that parents would tell their children not to play with Bobby. Did she want that?

I discussed with her the value of anger-management skills and encouraged Ann to attend an anger-management course. We also organised regular sessions with the school psychologist. I made a point of seeking her out, a few times a week – in the mornings and afternoons – when she was picking Bobby up, to ask how she was and comment positively on Bobby's behaviour and learning. I asked her to help me with the sorting and packing of chocolates for the school chocolate drive – a situation where she would have a chance to meet and talk with the other parents. I worked alongside her all morning, encouraging conversations with the other mothers that would give all of them a chance to get to know Ann. She had a very enjoyable time and for some time after seemed happy, relaxed and feeling better about herself.

Yet, still we had another incident. Her close friend (and she didn't have many) told her she was no longer welcome in her home as she and her husband did not like the way she swore in front of their children. Of course, this made her very angry and increased her feelings of rejection and insecurity. The end result of this was that, a week later, she walked across the school hall, screaming and cursing and hit the friend's husband over the head with a book in front of a school assembly of 600 children and their parents. She was assertively escorted out of the hall, and as the situation was very volatile; she was asked to go home immediately. I spoke to the other family involved and they admitted having made gestures across the hall that were intended to antagonise her. Both families were informed that this behaviour was unacceptable and would not be tolerated at our school. I spoke to Ann at length, but made it very clear that if there was one more incident, she left me no choice but to ban her from the schoolyard. I also requested that she come to the office whenever she came to the school and I would escort her to and from the classroom to protect her and others. She did not like this at all and complained bitterly, even contacting the Department of Education, but not liking or wanting the alternative, Ann did adhere to our conditions. We stood firm on our decisions despite a number of tantrums.

The school still continued to focus explicitly on maintaining and building a positive relationship with Ann. The office staff, class teacher and teacher aides *were always very friendly and welcoming.* Things went along nicely for quite some time. However, only a month later, as a result of a private family dispute, Ann verbally attacked her Year 4 niece, before school, in the schoolyard. The child was hysterical for an hour afterwards. Mothers came running from everywhere calling for me to do something quickly! The duty of care for my community, students and parents had to be my immediate priority. I walked up to Ann and said, 'Ann, your behaviour is totally unacceptable. Please leave the schoolyard now and when you have settled down, I want to see you in my office before 3.30 p.m. today.' She started to yell about what her brother had done and I put my hand up, repeated my first statement and then said, 'If someone had spoken to Bobby like that, you would have been furious. Please leave. I will talk to you when you are calm.' Much to my relief, she did.

I had my conversation carefully planned for when she came to my office later that day. I would have to ban her from the school. At midday, she rang me to say she would not be coming to my office as she had decided she no longer would come into the school as she didn't need to put herself under the stress of having to deal with *those* people! Such a relief! I thanked her for making a decision that was probably the best option at this time and I promised to keep in touch with her. I made a concerted effort to periodically ring Ann and see how things were going. She has gradually been allowed into the school over the past two years. She had one small incident at the transition meeting for her second child where she had an altercation with another mother and I am pleased to say she very quickly pulled herself together, apologised and the two of them actually sat down and had coffee together. I whispered in her ear how impressed I was with her and since then she has clearly made a positive effort. I am 'keeping my fingers crossed'.

Relationships are important. Yes, she was difficult but there were many things contributing to her anxiety. My core responsibility – however – is the children at our school. The happier the parent, the happier the child and, I am pleased to say, Bobby is thriving academically and socially.

Faye

Addison had attended the local kindergarten. On one of my visits, Helen the teacher and Sue the assistant, informed me of how much trouble and stress his mother, Faye, had caused – she had taken up a petition saying the children where all being abused at the kindergarten which was a total fabrication. Prior to the new school year, many parents came quietly to me requesting that their children be placed in a different grade to Addison, Faye's son, as they wanted nothing to do with his mother. Warning bells of potential trouble rang in my head!

Faye was a huge attention seeker. She was pleasant enough but very much 'in your face', wanting recognition and acknowledgment. She thoroughly enjoyed the five two-hour weekly transition sessions and laughed and talked with other parents. She was obviously excited about her child beginning the journey into his school life. I made a point of talking to Faye and discovering that she was a single parent; Addison's father was not involved in the children's lives in any way. She had no job, preferring to live on benefits so she could be at home with her two children. We both talked about our families and quickly built quite a positive relationship. The next year, school started well and I frequently stopped to talk to Faye in the playground or corridor. She seemed happy.

One month into the school year, a very distressed graduate teacher came to me saying Faye had come into her room aggressively and in front of the children, called out to her across the room, 'YOU ARE A LIAR! Yesterday, you promised my son a sticker and he didn't get it!' In actual fact, we had sent this young teacher home at lunchtime as she was extremely ill and she did not have the opportunity to fulfil her promises to any of her students that day.

The next day, I quietly walked up to her just as she had delivered her son to the classroom and asked her if I could speak to her. I started the conversation by saying I had heard from the teacher that she had been very upset the day before. I let her unload her grievances about the sticker and listened respectfully. I then explained the situation to her – the teacher having to go home – and empathised that I was sorry Addison was disappointed. However, there was a protocol at the school, and what she had done was not acceptable, *especially in front of the class*. I then stated that she appeared to be very stressed and asked if everything was all right. The tears flowed steadily for the next half hour as she told me all her woes. Faye was a very lonely person with low self-esteem, who was struggling to do her very best for her two children whom she loved very much. We talked about what she should do if she was ever worried about anything and I suggested that she train as a reading tutor as a stepping stone to developing skills and qualifications that may help her gain employment when her youngest started school.

Faye was one of the most committed and enthusiastic workers for our school and we were most thankful for her wonderful contribution. We did not have an entirely seamless transition, as she was innately a gossip and something of a 'busy body' and had to be spoken to a few times about confidentiality and appropriate professional behaviours in our school. We survived these situations due to a long-standing positive relationship. Eventually, she completed an integration aide course and provided casual relief for staff absences. We helped her find employment at another local school as a teacher aide. She is currently a kindergarten assistant and has one more year before she graduates with a Bachelor of Education. *I am so proud of her.*

Understanding each case on its merits with empathy, encouragement and openness creates far more positive outcomes for the parent, child and the school.

> ## Supporting the parents of children with challenging behaviour
>
> ### Cathy Whalen
>
> *Dealing with parents who are upset, confused even angry, is 'par for the course' in most schools. Cathy is a head teacher in an early years school and shares how she seeks to work with her colleagues to establish supportive communication and practical support for parents with challenging children. It is not only some children who have special needs – some parents, too, have special needs. Balancing dignity, respect and practical support in dealing with parents is addressed in this essay with experience, empathetic skill and a sense of realistic possibility.*

A little about our school and nursery

As a head teacher of a nursery and infant school, with children from 3+ and 7+ years old, I am in a very privileged position, as I meet parents and carers when their children are still young and the vast majority feel positive and optimistic about their children, school and the future. Parents want the best for their children and want to know what they can do to work in partnership with the school for the benefit of their child.

Each day, parents and carers are welcomed into the school and nursery to bring and collect their children, and over the course of time, I see bumps become babies, toddlers and finally new admissions to our nursery and school. I try to be around and available at the beginning and end of session times, to meet and talk with parents informally. Some people would not contemplate coming to see me in my office, but will catch me when I am wandering in the classroom or on the playground. This creates opportunities to watch the interaction between parents and their children, to see how they relate to each other and their friends, and to build positive and trusting relationships with them. This can prove invaluable if and when life or behaviour goes a little 'pear-shaped', as it does for so many of us at some time or another.

If and when difficult situations do arise, parents hopefully feel they know me quite well and are able to approach me confidently, knowing I am ready to listen and support if I can, or put them in touch with someone else if they need specialist guidance.

At our school and nursery, the behaviour policy is deeply embedded in daily practice. It applies to everyone involved in the school: children, staff governors, parents, carers and visitors, and is based on respect, and on those essential rights and responsibilities – the right to feel safe; the right to dignified, fair and respectful treatment and the right to learn without undue or unfair distractions or disruptions. It has created a calm, safe, purposeful ethos in which enjoyable learning and teaching takes place and where people are trusted. Many of our children come from homes where there are a range of difficulties and challenges, and life can be very hard:

- Some of the children and their parents have special needs.
- For some, the environment and behaviour of adults and children at home is challenging, erratic, sometimes frightening and abusive.

By trying to support the needs of the individual children and their parents and carers at our nursery and school, we are creating a safe haven for them, a place where they can talk confidently and hopefully move forwards and face life and events more positively.

So what do we do when a child's challenging behaviour is proving to be beyond the level a class teacher can manage, or beyond what parents can manage at home?

Sometimes, a child's behaviour at school is 'manageable', but at home they are out of control and the parents feel desperate. If you cannot manage your child's behaviour at the age of five, how will you manage when they are 15? Most parents under these circumstances want help and guidance. They want to be in control. Some are frightened of their children and give in easily to their demands for constant attention, refusal to go to bed, eat their food or get up and come to school.

Encounters with parents of children with challenging behaviour can come in a variety of forms and for a variety of reasons. It is worth remembering that sometimes they are flooded with a range of strong emotions triggered by nothing to do with school. It is essential not to take their comments personally. They may be angry and demanding of your attention and time now, like their children, or they may be embarrassed by their children's behaviour and defensive. Sometimes they are in denial that the behaviour is unacceptable and feel the school's expectations are unreasonable.

Other parents may be perfectly happy with their child's behaviour at home and surprised and shocked that the child is behaving in unacceptable ways at school. Personal circumstances also impact on people's responses and needs. They may be depressed, sleep-deprived, mentally or physically ill, or even bereaved and grieving. Some single parents are coping alone with a range of challenging circumstances at home with no family or friends to call upon and they arrive weeping, feeling helpless and hopeless about their situation, desperate for guidance and support to know what to do.

Being aware of the above helps me to deal with what it feels like to be faced with an angry or distressed parent, but even after all these years, it can still feel like a personal attack, threatening or frightening, disturbing and distressing – and I can feel the adrenaline coursing through my body, making my heat race and my mouth go dry.

Under these circumstances, as with managing children's challenging behaviour, it is crucial to stay outwardly calm, allow some 'cool-off time' if possible, be a supportive listener and take the time needed to resolve the situation. If a parent is angry and behaving or talking abusively, either on the phone or within the school situation, it is important to remind them calmly but clearly that they are breaching the school's expectations for behaviour, and to arrange a time to meet later in the day. This gives time for emotions to subside and time to think, plan and investigate a situation further.

Amber

Lunchtime play is just over and the children are returning to their classes. A flushed member of the support staff comes to find me. Seven-year-old Amber has scratched another child on the face as she was hanging her coat up, and is now in an extremely disturbed state in the toilets, refusing to come back to her classroom. Would I please come and help. This is a familiar scenario with Amber at the moment – a child who frequently engages in unprovoked attacks on other children from mild pushing, to kicking, biting, punching and scratching others, for no apparent reason. She also defaces their work, calls out during whole-class teaching times, crawls under furniture and invades others' space – anything to get attention. The class teacher is highly skilled in the management of children's challenging behaviour, including Amber's, but there are times when the next step of the whole-school's behaviour policy needs to come into action. Having her in the classroom is like sitting on a time bomb. The children and teacher visibly relax when she is removed. They need recovery time too.

I find Amber lying on the floor, screaming and out of control in the cloakroom area, with a learning support assistant watching her to check she is not going to run off, hurt herself or injure someone else. The sound of her distress can be heard throughout this part of the school as the classroom areas have no doors. Her wailing is distressing for other children and staff. I approach her calmly, talk quietly to her. I tell her she needs to come to my room and that she can either walk there by herself or we will need to help her. She knows what is going to happen, but is so out of control of her emotions that she does not seem to hear me. She is reluctant to come but I insist, and carefully the support assistant and I help her down to my room where she crawls under the furniture, ending up lying under my desk, still screaming. With the door closed, we can watch and wait until her anger and frustration subside. She knows she is safe here, that we are here to help her. It takes some 20 minutes before she finally falls asleep under the desk. She has totally exhausted herself.

As head teacher, I have a responsibility to contact the parents of the injured child as well as Amber's parent. I need to see the injured child, talk with Amber about what has happened and meet with her parent, and to reassure the class teacher, support staff and her peers that all is okay. This takes the remainder of the afternoon and goes well beyond the end of the school day and takes up time later in the week, as we put into place the following plan of action.

- When Amber has calmed down in my room sufficiently to be left under the watchful eye of her classroom assistant, I return to Amber's class to talk with the injured child, check that she is okay and listen to her account of what happened.
- I reassure the class teacher and Amber's classmates that she is safe and has calmed down.
- I phone the parent of the injured child to explain what has happened, that their child is okay and to explain what we are doing to follow things up. I do not tell this parent the name of the child involved, but invite her to see me at the end of the day with her child.
- I phone Amber's mother and ask her to come to the school as soon as possible, as Amber is still asleep under my desk. She is distressed but not surprised to hear there has been another incident.
- When she arrives, it is close to the end of the school day and Amber is beginning to stir. Mum greets her lovingly; there is no reprimand, she only appears concerned about her own child, not the one who has been injured.
- Amber is calmer now, but still in a dazed and weepy state, just wanting her mother to take her home.
- I talk with Amber about what she has done and how she has behaved. She knows she has broken our safety rule and agrees that her behaviour was unacceptable. I explain that she will be spending her break times tomorrow working with someone on her action plan. When asked what she might do to make amends, she suggests writing a letter of apology to the injured child and one to the teacher and class, as well as behaving appropriately in school the following day and keeping the school rules. (She knows the school rules and behaviour policy well, but has huge difficulty keeping to them when she is flooded with emotion.)
- Mum and I confirm the date of our next meeting with the Educational Psychologist and myself at school. This is one of a series we have arranged to support Mum managing Amber's behaviour at home.

Meetings with parents and carers

When I do meet with a parent or carer, I always thank them for coming and try to put them at ease by offering a drink (usually a hot one) and a quiet, undisturbed place where they can talk in confidence. It must be a bit scary if you have been asked to come and meet with the head teacher, especially if your experience of school as a child was not positive. Confidentiality is essential, as is empathy, understanding and respect.

Working in collaboration with other professionals

Throughout the years, I have learned a great deal from others, particularly professionals such as educational psychologists, speech therapists, bereavement therapists and health visitors. They see children and their parents in different settings – sometimes at home – and can bring insight, expertise and a new dimension to our understanding of how we can best meet individual needs.

Over recent years, I have worked in close partnership with the Educational Psychologist assigned to our school, focusing our time on parents and carers with children showing the most challenging behaviour either at home or at school, children who are at risk of being excluded if their behaviour does not improve. The approach is preventative not reactive, offering help and guidance before things have reached crisis point. She has expertise and training that I lack, but I know the children and parents well, so together we are well placed to work in tandem to support parents and indirectly their children.

Sometimes, a child's behaviour can be challenging because we do not have the full picture of what life is like for them (see Amber's story above.) Our Educational Psychologist has shown me an approach that has worked successfully with many children and their parents. Sometimes, a child's teacher or one-to-one support worker will also be present, or will have written an account to share. With complex needs, we work together, but now I frequently use the approach myself and find it provides a clear and helpful framework to move a situation forward positively.

The basic collaborative framework for the meeting with parents is as follows:

- *Welcome and thank* the parent/s for coming to the meeting.
- *Emphasise confidentiality.* Explain that everything shared is totally confidential, unless there are child protection issues involved.
- *Ask parents if they mind if notes are taken* of the meeting as a report will be written and sent to the parents and school after the meeting.
- *Briefly explain the outline structure of the meeting*:
  - time limit – one hour

- share strengths
- share concerns
- share early background (going back to before the child was born, pregnancy, baby's early months and childhood). *Please note – I do not ever do this if I feel it is beyond my role and expertise as a head teacher*
- agree on an action plan for home and school
- put another date in the diary for everyone – about two to three months in the future.

Jason

Jason is a very able boy of six, physically large for his age. He lives with and is cared for by his father, who is separated from his mother, although she still sees him with his father regularly. Dad works full time and Jason spends his time before and after school with a childminder. Academically, Jason is making good progress, but his behaviour at school has been giving cause for concern since he was in reception, aged four. His face seldom shows emotion and he frequently hurts other children, usually by pushing them over, hitting or kicking them. He can tell you how he should be behaving and knows the school's behaviour policy and procedures extremely well. He can tell you the inevitable consequences of breaking our rules and yet he regularly continues to do so.

In his first year at school, his teacher spent most Fridays after school talking with his father, giving feedback about Jason's week, the positive and the negative, listening to the father's reactions and offering support and guidance. The father is a shy, quiet man who is always defensive of his son's behaviour and quick to blame other children for 'provoking' Jason. He says he never has any problems with Jason's behaviour at home. As head teacher, I have often joined the teacher at these Friday meetings, trying to understand why we seem to move forwards with improved behaviour for a few weeks and then slip back again.

Dad has agreed to meet with me and our Educational Psychologist to see if we can improve things, as he now generally agrees that Jason's behaviour can be dangerous and unacceptable. Recently, Jason was responsible for a nasty injury to another child when he pushed him into a metal fence.

We follow the format described above and then:

- Start by asking the parent to describe the child's strengths. Parents of children with challenging behaviour frequently find this hard, and slip into negative descriptions at such times. It is necessary to immediately redirect them to describing positive traits, interests and abilities. Parents' outward appearance often changes at this point and they start to smile and relax as they share good experiences and memories. In Jason's case, this is different. The father is pleased with the progress Jason is making with reading and writing and feels there have been fewer incidents of him hurting others. He says he plays independently at home and is very imaginative. He is keen to write and draw. He says he plays well with the younger children at the childminder's.

■ Next, the school or teacher shares the child's strengths. These often coincide with those of the parents and give the meeting an upbeat feel. The teacher is similarly pleased with Jason's work progress and says his behaviour in class has improved.

■ We share concerns from the father and school. The father is concerned that he does not play with children of his own age out of school. Jason and his dad spend a great deal of one-to-one time playing together, with Jason leading the direction of the play. He feels Jason is not being stretched at school. The teacher feels that he isn't fulfilling his potential, as he is frequently interfering with and distracting others at work times. He makes negative comments about peers' work and will take ages completing a written task. He is regularly involved in incidents at playtimes where his 'friends' get hurt or upset.

■ We share Jason's early background (going right back to before the child was born, pregnancy, baby's early months and childhood. I have omitted this for reasons of confidentiality). *Please note again – I don't ever do this if I feel it is beyond my role and expertise as a head teacher.*

■ We agree an action plan for home and school. Dad will try to enrol Jason in some clubs outside school where he can mix with children of his own age. Jason will miss a couple of days' outside playtimes, spending time with his class teacher or another skilled adult talking about how he can play well with others. At school, we will assign one of our playtime learning support assistants to engage Jason in productive play with other children. (We have many resources available at playtimes, including bikes and scooters, large climbing equipment, board games, construction toys and small world play resources.)

■ We arrange another date to meet in two months' time, with Jason's mother present too.

In the interim period, we monitor Jason's behaviour at school, and continue with our daily/weekly, teacher/father meetings, as and when necessary. We always try to focus on the positive and improvements, whilst never losing sight of the day-to-day expectations of behaviour from across the school, and that what we expect and will accept from Jason is no different from our expectations of anyone else within our school and nursery.

At subsequent meetings, we learn that:

■ Jason's mother and father have very different views on what is acceptable behaviour at home.

■ Both parents dote on Jason, and he has lots of one-to-one adult attention from both of them.

- Dad seldom makes demands of Jason, tending to follow his lead, allowing him to dictate much of what will happen at home. Dad thinks it is okay for Jason to throw a ball repeatedly at his dad's face.
- At school and home, Jason does not appear to show or feel remorse when he has hurt someone, and will justify his behaviour by saying someone provoked him.
- Jason is very competitive when playing board or computer games with his parents and has to win. If not, he gets very angry and will have a tantrum, although this doesn't last for more than about five minutes. He hates losing under any circumstances. Many of the computer games are violent and involve fighting and killing. Both parents say they are highly competitive too.

Action plans include:

- The parents will encourage Jason to play more independently of them at home, and will ask themselves how much Jason is controlling their lives.
- They will consider inviting Jason's peers from class home to play.
- The class teacher will set up a 'circle of friends' with Jason and children in the class. With the guidance of the teacher, between them, they will set some targets for Jason to improve his behaviour at school, and the circle of friends will help him to achieve these.
- The head teacher/teacher undertakes some observations of Jason at playtimes from within the school, so that Jason is unaware he is being observed. (This reveals fascinating evidence of Jason dominating and controlling play with his peers on the playground. When Jason resorts to violence, it is usually because his friends have changed the rules of a game in some way, so that Jason is no longer dictating the roles and direction of play.)
- The class teacher will establish a chart to record Jason's good playtime behaviour, i.e. when he does not hurt another child. This will be shared daily with the father, and some kind of agreed reward given if Jason achieves six out of ten good play times, initially, building up the frequency of good play times over time. (This proves to be highly motivating for Jason and his behaviour improves.)

As a result of the work with the parents and children in the case studies described above, the behaviour of both children improved considerably. There were still occasions on which their behaviour deteriorated but the frequency decreased. Without this work, there is a strong possibility that they could have been excluded from school. Amber's relationship with her mother improved dramatically, with the mother taking more responsibility and control of the situation at home. All parents worked in partnership with the school and said they found the meetings valuable.

Children are more likely to learn and thrive when they feel secure, safe and cared for and that applies to their parents too. Sometimes we succeed with both parents and children, sometimes we enable the children to find ways of coping, and occasionally we fail, but whatever the outcome, we know we have tried to make a positive difference, and hopefully the parents and children know that too.

Working with difficult parents

Maureen Smyth

How can we realistically enable and support parents of very challenging children in a way that meets their needs for unconditional positive regard? Maureen raises a fundamental human question that is always held in some tension with our need to protect the safety and welfare of all of our students. As head of a school for emotionally and behaviourally-disordered students Maureen seeks to share how she, with her colleagues, seeks to face this daily reality.

It is difficult to be a parent and to an extent all parents are difficult. When my first baby would not sleep, I (eventually) went along for advice and support to a sleep clinic organised by the local child and family consultation service. How hard was that, to specialise in managing difficult behaviour and find myself less than perfect, with a child who would not play by the rules? What were these 'rules'? How come I did not have a copy? 'Parents like you are the worst' said the community psychiatric nurse reassuringly. My first-born never did sleep much, was strong-willed and challenging. 'Who does he take after?' mused the nurse, thus teaching me a valuable lesson. While I admire my son's spirit and would never squash it, his non-conformist ways down the years have ensured that throughout my professional life I dare not become complacent or judgemental. The challenge is, do not judge, do not patronise and try to walk in the other's shoes.

To work with difficult parents, we first need to check out their value system and our own. Most parents want to do the best by their children, even if their way of doing it is not to our liking. School evokes strong feelings for most adults, especially those who were not successful there; so turning in to the school gates, they can meet with feelings and thoughts long suppressed. Being called to account for the difficult behaviour of their children, some parents feel as if they are back in their own schooldays, summoned before the head teacher to account for some childish misdemeanour. 'Difficult' parents are often those in denial of any problems or those who feel responsible, guilty or humiliated that their child's behaviour has come to this.

The extent to which the parents negotiate the first meeting is largely dependent on the experience they bring with them and the reception they receive. Very few people want their child to attend a special school for children with behavioural, emotional and/or social difficulties and it can be a tough job to encourage parents to see the value of such a school for their child. Some protest that the problem lies with the school, any school, not their child. This could be true, but is less likely to be so if the child has attended or been excluded from several schools.

Parents are susceptible to strong feelings of guilt, humiliation and shame and these are easily identified with, or projected on to the school. Acknowledging that your child's behaviour is a problem can mean that you may have to acknowledge your part in creating or maintaining the problem. It is much easier to blame the school or *that* teacher than to take on board your part in it. It is important for schools not to be blaming either. Some children are hard to bring up.

One way to obviate the blame and guilt is to look at the challenging behaviour as causing a problem rather than being the problem itself. When I ask parents and children if they have lost friends because of the child's behaviour, the answer is often yes. Eventually, people stop inviting troublesome children to play, and parents are marginalised at the school gates. A new school with new support systems for children and parents is often a new opportunity to get life back on track, to understand behaviour and the feelings behind it, to take responsibility and to change.

It is a hard lesson for parents to learn that children do not arrive exactly the way we expect them. They come as themselves, with their own personality and idiosyncrasies. As one parent said to me recently, 'I am so quiet and reserved. Where did this angry, feisty child come from?'

As I write, the headline reports in the British press are about the tragic and cruel death of baby P, aged 17 months, at the hands of his mother, her partner and/or lodger. While the leading stories vilify the social workers and system which did not protect this child, there is little comment on the parent and adults who tortured and killed their child, or an examination of what their experiences of childhood were.

Parents who hurt their children or do not seem to like them are, in my experience, the most difficult to deal with. They operate on a continuum of abuse from ridicule and put-downs to physical harm and murder. I remember teaching a Spanish lesson many years ago to a class of 13-year-olds who were learning numbers and the names of family members. Suddenly, one boy rose up from his seat and hurled the table across the classroom. It transpired that as a small boy, he had witnessed his father put his baby sister in a cardboard box and kick it around the room. The girl later died. How, then, to answer the seemingly innocent question, 'How many brothers and sisters do you have?' The less innocent speculation is, will he go on to become a parent who abuses his child and about whom we will read in our newspapers in the future? Sadly, this is possible.

Sometimes the best we can do is to support children in spite of their parents. I sometimes wonder if our task with older children is to teach them to 'withstand' their parents. We have recently readmitted a girl in her last year of schooling who is on the point of permanent exclusion from the mainstream school to which she transferred from us four years ago. Her mother has never forgiven her for being referred to a special school, as if her challenging behaviour was all her doing and nothing to do with her. In the intervening period, she had made her daughter's life so intolerable that she has left home and is living with ageing grandparents some distance away. The mother has since thrown out her daughter's bed, given away her things and given away her room. Mum is vociferous and self-righteous in her anger. The girl just wants her mum to say sorry for the hurtful things she has said to her, for the blame she has heaped on her, for not loving her enough or caring for her at all.

In these circumstances, 'unconditional, positive regard' is the biggest test of all.

Editor's note

Maureen highlights several valuable reminders about working with difficult parents:

- Consider the term *unconditional positive regard* – developed by Carl Rogers in the late 1950s. Rogers believed that human beings have a basic and innate need to be accepted and valued; they have a fundamental need for positive regard from others, most essentially – and obviously – from their parents. One's very life concept is linked to others' regard. *Unconditional positive regard* (in this sense) means our acceptance of the child regardless of their behaviour (but not, of course, merely ignoring or excusing their behaviour). For us – as teachers – this means we address our discipline to the behaviour while accepting the child and not rejecting them. He contrasts this with conditional positive regard where praise, acceptance, love are conditional on the individual's conforming to parental or social standards (Halonen and Santrock, 1996).
- Remember that, as parents ourselves, we, too, have struggled and questioned and doubted: why are our children so different? Am I too hard a parent? Too lax? Could I have done better?
- Ask why does my child/my son/my daughter, behave this way? Is it my fault? *Our own perspective-taking* (as a parent) is helpful when we face a parent who is struggling with doubts, anxieties, fears and anger.
- Avoid the temptation to patronise; yet – notwithstanding – we sometimes need to confront parents whose behaviour is causing disturbing and dysfunctional relationships for their own children or other members of the school community (p. 25).
- Recognise that the behaviour of a child is not only problematic *in itself*; it is part of a wider frame of relationships. This is probably our biggest concern, and challenge. We cannot ignore the challenging behaviour nor can we excuse it, but we can *try to understand and support the child* within the range of his behaviour.

As Maureen notes, this is the 'biggest test of all'.

Working with parents/carers of children with challenging behaviours (primary)

Alyson Dermody Palmer

Building trust and common understandings are crucial to working with parents and children, particularly children with behaviour-disorders. Children in pupil-referral settings often have a jaded and troubled history in mainstream schooling. Alyson shares how she, and her team, seek to re-build trust, and positive – workable – relationships with the educational community for parent(s) and children alike.

'That's the first time anyone has ever said anything nice about my child.'

I was really shocked when a parent from the unit said that to me after I told her what a lovely boy her son was and that he had had a good day at school.

Building relationships and trust, and common understandings

A large proportion of my role is working directly with parents of children in the Pupil Referral Unit. When children with challenging behaviour are in mainstream schools, a lot of the contact between the parents and the school is negative. Parents say that towards the end of their child's time at their previous school they are often receiving daily phone calls to go and pick up their child and take them home early as the child's behaviour is too challenging for them to be at school. When I first meet parents/carers, I make a point of saying, 'Please answer the phone if we ring you because we try hard to phone with good news rather than bad.' When children first start at the unit, both the child and their parent/carer can be disillusioned with the education system and wary and unwilling to engage with staff. They often mistrust school staff and when a child has been excluded from school, relationships between home and school are at the best fragile and at the worst completely broken down.

A lot of parents I work with feel isolated and often have no one to talk to. They feel people do not understand their situation and what it is like having a child with very challenging behaviour. The vast majority of our parents/carers are lone parents and an increasing number are grandparents. I have been told many stories about when their child was in their last mainstream school and other parents in the school would not talk to them in the playground and would tell their children to move away and not play with the child with challenging behaviour. Over two years later this is still a very poignant memory for one grandparent I work with. Another parent told me the day after her son had been permanently excluded from school, she still had to take his older sister to the same school. As she walked through the school gates, the other parents moved back, whispering and sniggering as she had to make her way across the playground. The mum told me how upsetting this was and how dreadful she felt to be such a public figure of speculation and gossip as she took her daughter to school.

Effective working with parents is extremely time-consuming. Our unit obviously has a lot less children than a mainstream school so it is easier for us to get to know parents well. Regular contact both by phone and in person is essential to sustain a good relationship. I have weekly/bi-weekly meetings with some parents because they need that high level of support. A lot of time is spent listening, sometimes being shouted at, not necessarily because they are cross with me directly but because I happen to be there. We explore problems together and we come up with solutions and ways forward.

In the past year, our Family Support Worker and I have introduced weekly parents' coffee mornings in the unit. We are developing these informal sessions where we chat about whatever parents want to. Other sessions are more focused and we have covered topics such as sleep issues, internet safety, healthy eating and rewards and sanctions. This term, an ex-parent, Pauline, has joined our coffee mornings. Her son has a wide range of special education needs including Asperger's Syndrome and ADHD and he left the unit over two years ago. Whilst Pauline's son attended our unit, we developed an excellent relationship and stayed in regular contact with her and her family after he had moved to his new specialist placement. Pauline spoke to me at the beginning of this term and said she would really like to do some voluntary work with parents who were in a similar situation to her when her son was permanently excluded from his mainstream school. This was too good an opportunity to be missed. Parents respect Pauline's views and listen to her advice because they know that she understands exactly where they are coming from and all the different emotions that go with having a child with challenging behaviours. Hopefully, Pauline's role will continue and develop over time. We try to maintain contact with families of children who have left the unit. We often get ex-pupils and their families coming back to visit which is wonderful.

Home visits

Home visits can sometimes be a vital part of my work with parents. It is not appropriate to make home visits to all parents but for some it is the right thing to do. Last year, one of the parents at the unit had a serious illness which meant that when she was not having treatment, she was often very weak and walking was difficult so I regularly made home visits to help support her. She always thanked me for going and I never felt like I was intruding. We built up a strong relationship and although we often had to discuss very difficult issues, we were able to maintain this relationship. Thankfully, the parent's health improved and sometimes she was able to meet me at school which her son loved. She even managed to cook lunch with him at school for everyone else!

Inviting parents to 'the visit'

We also encourage parents to spend time in the classroom. We model behaviour strategies and quite often it is good for a parent to have time with their child away from the rest of the family or with some external support. Sometimes, they are reluctant to actually be in a lesson with their child but feel more comfortable cooking a favourite dish with their child in our kitchen. This is really successful – we have had some delicious food and the parents/carers and child are very proud of each other and what they have produced.

We invite parents to our Christmas play which in a Pupil Referral Unit is always an interesting event – you never really know what might happen next! It is often the first time that the children have been allowed in such a play and that alone is an enormous thrill for everyone. After the performance, the parents say how proud they are of the children and how well they have done, which sadly is not something they are used to saying.

All the children in our unit regularly go on school trips, either topic-related trips, e.g. to the Science Museum, or trips they have 'earned' by regularly meeting the targets in their Behaviour Support Plan. Occasionally, we invite parents/carers on these trips, particularly if a child's behaviour is very difficult to manage out of school. These trips are generally very successful and parents always enjoy them. We also have the usual newsletter, reports, parents/carers evenings to communicate with parents and a parents/carers questionnaire about their views on the unit and their child's progress at school.

'Rewards' and behaviour consequences

Supporting parents with rewards and sanctions (behaviour consequences) is also a large part of my work with them. I devise and make sticker charts for parents to use at home with their child. The focus is on one specific behaviour that the parents want to change at a time. We provide stickers and ongoing support to maintain the charts. Children at the unit are used to these types of charts at school. Therefore, they understand how they work and they feel secure with them. It enables a visible and tangible framework for parent and child. I spend a lot of time discussing rewards and sanctions with parents. I try to encourage them to give children rewards which are more to do with special time with each other than material goods (see also p. 130f). Discussing sanctions (behaviour consequences) can be a much trickier thing to do. I always advise parents to make the sanction something that the child will mind, and not like losing, but also not so difficult for the parent that it makes their life even more difficult than it already is! I also advise them not to make hasty decisions when they are angry but to try and make a calmer more measured decision later on – a strategy I try to use with my own children! For example, do not ban the computer for six months – it is too difficult for everyone involved.

Parents of children with challenging behaviour have lots of different professionals with whom they need to keep in contact. I communicate with outside agencies on parents' behalf including Social Care and Safeguarding, Health Services and Play Services. Often an introduction, a letter or making an appointment, is enough to start the ball rolling. Sometimes, more is needed and I attend appointments with parents at a variety of meetings to support them and sometimes to make sure they attend! I help parents to complete application forms for a variety of things, most commonly the Disability Living Allowance (on which I have become something of an expert!). Receiving extra financial support can often make a huge difference to the lives of the families we work with.

Beyond our support

When we are thinking of a child's next placement after leaving the unit, we have a lot of discussion with parents/carers about possible schools. I accompany them on visits to those schools and talk through any concerns, worries etc. with them. When any child changes school, it is often a difficult and stressful time for families. When children with challenging behaviour are changing schools, the process is even more difficult and stressful. Parents and their children worry about being excluded again and the placement breaking down. Concerns about whether they have made the right decision are even more prevalent for these families.

Parental perspectives

Above all, at our unit, we value the parents' perspective and knowledge of their child. They live with their child and often have to manage their child's very challenging behaviour, alone and in difficult circumstances. At school, we have the luxury of excellent support from our staff team and a 'soft room', which is a safe place for the children to calm and settle, and focus. We also say goodbye to the children at the end of the day and do not have to manage their behaviour 24 hours a day, seven days a week.

The better the relationship staff at the unit have with the parents of the children we work with, the more progress the children make with both their learning and managing their behaviour. It is crucial for parents to support and back up the work we are doing at school, and it is just as important that we support and back up what parents are doing at home. We must remember how isolated, desperate and lonely some parents/carers of children with challenging behaviour can feel, and one of the most important things those of us who work with them can do is listen – this listening enables our understanding and invites their trust.

Working with children with challenging behaviour is a great but demanding job. Living with them, well that is a different matter!

An extended note on anger (primarily from Aristotle)

Bill Rogers

Can you remember the last time you got really angry; what it felt like; what you did when you were angry? Imagine how difficult it can be for children when they get angry.

In reflecting – yet again – our dealing with frustration, and anger, in others (and in ourselves) I have re-visited the writings of Aristotle. There are many understandings, and principles, about managing anger that immediately touch the reality of this most powerful, and often troubling, human emotion. Aristotle enables us to find the difficult 'middle way' between the disturbing extremes of behaviour that anger can generate.

I have also tried to summarise the key ideas, principles and practices from all the essays in Chapter 7 in the light of reflection on the philosophy of Aristotle in the Nichomachean Ethics.

Aristotle (in the *Nichomachean Ethics*, 1969) notes that, ' …we must not forget that it is human to be painfully affected by anger and to find revenge sweet' (Book Three: p. 100). He is not saying we *should* find revenge sweet – but many will take recourse in forms of revenge and 'justify it' because of their anger. In Book Seven (Chapter 6), he further notes that 'anger and bad temper are common human frailties' – it is hard to bring reason to bear upon those things, circumstances and people that occasion our anger, hard but not impossible.

He says (in Book Four) that our 'anger may be produced by a variety of causes, but, however that may be, it is the person[1] who is angry on the right occasions and with the right people and at the right moment and for the right length of time who wins our commendation' (p. 128). He contrasts those who are overly (and overtly) tame when there is a good (just) reason to express appropriate anger with those who are choleric. In fact, he says – in such cases – that not to speak with 'proper spirit' when one has 'due right' to be angry 'looks like insensibility' (ibid.: 128).

Then there are those who 'lose their tempers easily, quickly and completely' (the

---

1. I have taken the liberty of substituting *person* for *man*. When Aristotle uses *man* in the generic sense, he does so as standing for humanity in general.

choleric) and 'who refuse to make a quarrel up unless they are allowed to inflict some vengeance or some punishment ...' (op. cit. 128). I have worked with some teachers (and parents) who believe that it is not enough to exact an appropriate behaviour consequence for a child who has been overly disruptive or who has cheated, lied, stolen or bullied, but that we must also vilify them and make them feel really bad *as well*. This – of course – is the constant tension between justice and punishment, and between guilt, revenge, reconciliation and restitution.

For Aristotle, the general principles of 'anger management' (he does not use that term) can be drawn from the *Nichomachean Ethics* as 'those we are to lay hold upon (in) the middle state ...' (Book Four: 129). Finding a 'middle way' between losing our temper easily, quickly and intemperately, and conversely 'holding our anger in' for fear we might ill-manage our emotions is no mean feat. Such skills can be learned.

Because the emotive states of high frustration and anger are impulsive and sometimes even irrational, it is difficult for reason to be exercised *at the point of high emotion*. As noted later, when we are dealing with others who are impulsive or angry, it is *our own calmness* that can enable the *degree* of impulsivity in the other start to defuse (p. 163). So too when we – ourselves – are angry (hopefully on issues that matter), when we communicate *our anger*, then *our calmness* enables some clarity in that immediate emotional moment.

Of course, a *sustained* expression of anger to another is normally self-defeating. A clear, assertive expression of what we are angry about can be effective if we allow some cool-off time at the point of significant frustration; reason can *then* 'play' a restorative role. At its most expressive, this is sometimes called (as it is by Aristotle) 'righteous anger' (Book Seven, Chapter 6: 208). And in Book Three, Chapter 1, he notes, 'There are some things at which we *ought* to feel anger ...' (Aristotle's emphasis). 'Righteous' anger was expressed by Jesus on several occasions and directed against pompous, lying, cheating, hypocritical leaders (certain priests, politicians) in high places.

Aristotle says (what psychologists would later say) we should never deny our anger simply because 'feeling angry (or frightened) is something we can't help' (Book Two, Chapter 5: 63). It is the *feeling* we cannot help when it arises in us; what we do *when* that feeling arises is something we can learn to do something about. In this sense, general 'anger management' is possible. As Aristotle goes on to note:

> We are not spoken of as 'good' or 'bad' in respect of our feelings but of our virtues and vices. Neither are we praised or blamed for the way we feel. A person is not praised for being frightened or angry, nor is he blamed for just being angry; it is being angry in a particular way. (ibid.: 63).

This is a crucial principle and a very helpful teaching point: while we cannot immediately control our feelings (our feelings – *as such* – cannot tell us what to do), we can learn to control what we do when we have those feelings. There is, says Aristotle, the 'element of the will' in what we do *when* we feel angry. This, though, is affected by our 'general disposition' and is also open to learning. We can learn to express and communicate those issues and concerns about which we are frustrated or angry, in a better way. This is what Aristotle meant by 'getting angry in the right way'; there are better, more effective ways to communicate our anger. Aristotle dares to say what the post-modernist often would not say – there are 'right ways' (just ways) to express and communicate our anger. (p. 160f)

To summarise some understandings about anger and how we address it, and express it (from the *Ethics*):

■ Feelings – mostly – just *come* … What we do *when* they come is a different matter.
■ We cannot directly, and immediately, control how we feel (in the immediacy of the moment).
■ We should not blame ourselves (or others) *because* they are angry. After all, it is our emotions that make us uniquely human.
■ There are many issues that contribute to our anger.
■ We do not always have control over the issues that contribute to, or affect, our anger.
■ There are issues, concerns, that we *should* get angry about. Some issues clearly merit *just* anger.
■ It is pointless trying to 'reason' with someone who is irrationally angry: 'The person who is passion's slave will not listen to or understand the logic of anyone who tries to dissuade [them] from going on as [they] are doing. When a [person] is in that state, what chance have you of changing [their] mind by argumentation?' (Book Ten, Chapter 9: 311). In a sense, it is very difficult to even *think* when we are angry. We need cooling-off time!
■ There is a significant difference between the emotion of anger (that which we cannot immediately control) and what we can do *when* we recognise, and feel, angry. That is, we can learn to *manage* our feelings of anger *when* we feel them *and acknowledge them*. We also cannot directly control another's anger; we can contribute to *their calming* and, then, occasion the possibility of working on the issues that sparked their anger. That management (even when we need to be assertive) can be more effective for the expression of anger in the emotional moment, when we consciously legitimise our need to express (not sublimate) our anger. Whether we do it immediately or after cool-off time and reflection may depend on the context, situation and people involved.
■ When we communicate our anger, we do so on issues that matter. In this sense, we would not say to a student, 'I am angry that you haven't done your homework.' 'I'm angry that you call out a lot in class.' These behaviours/issues, while contributing to our frustration, do not merit *anger*. More appropriately, our emotional language (in degree) would see us saying, 'I'm *concerned* you haven't done your homework – how can I help?' 'I'm *annoyed* when you call out a lot in

class because the other students – your classmates – don't get a fair go. Let's work on a plan …' (this conversation would obviously occur one-to-one).

As a parent, we would not *reasonably* say, 'I'm angry because you haven't put the lid back on the peanut butter and the kitchen bench is *still* messy!! What's wrong with you; you're just like your bloody father!!!' We are annoyed by the mess – yes – and our children need to hear that (plus the reminder to clear up *their* mess). Annoyance, and 'cheesed-offness', though, are different in *degree* from anger.

The issues, circumstances and behaviours that *merit* anger need some moral weight, some effect of injustice, rather than equating *anger* (a 'big league' emotion) with being annoyed, fed-up, irritated or frustrated. In this sense, as teachers, we are careful not to easily debase the word anger, so that it can carry moral/justice weighting. Getting angry on issues that matter is part of our learning and part of our moral perspective on life. How we *communicate* the *degrees* of frustration through to significant anger is something that can be learned. This conception about 'moral weight' regarding anger is important to our professionalism as teachers.

■ This gives us hope that the *habits of anger* (in ourselves as well as those we teach) can be modified. Behaviour is not universally, immutably fixed. If that were true, we could help no one. Developing more positive 'habits' of anger management is possible – thankfully. Aristotle quotes Evenus: 'Habit, my friend, is practice long pursued that at last becomes the [person] themselves' (Book Seven, Chapter 10).

The articles in the newspapers I noted earlier sound dramatic (p. 137) – and they are. It is important to note, however, that it is mostly only a small percentage of parents who get so angry they become temporarily irrational and hostile. Many of us have had an angry parent storm into our office (or even a classroom) demanding – with a raised voice – why we have been *so* unfair to their child. Sometimes, the parent is so angry they will be swearing and even threatening. 'What kind of f___ing school is this!? What'd you suspend my Craig for!!? What did he do?! What about the other little sh_ts …?!!' Upset? Yes, sometimes a parent will present with irrational anger. Yet even that anger is motivated (one hopes) by care for their child and not merely a poor sense of justice. As Aristotle notes, it takes some *conscious will* to address another's anger (as well as our own).

Habits of anger

In each of these essays, my colleagues note key understandings that enable more positive 'habits of anger':

- The first person to calm in such a situation is ourselves. We cannot actually 'calm' someone else (adult or child); it is hard enough to consciously cue ourselves to be calmer when we are really frustrated or angry!

  As the adult self, we cue our calmness to enable theirs.

- It can help – initially – to let the other person 'run out of psychological steam' (as it were). It will be important, though, not to look at your watch – frowning – as the angry parent remonstrates(!).

- We take a deep, cognitive breath as it were, and communicate (non-verbally) that we are not a threat to them, that we are ready to listen. It is important not to *immediately* react to the other's hostility.

- When we cue our calmness, the parent will – often – regain some self-control, enough for us to ask them to take a seat ... Having run somewhat 'out of immediate steam' – and seated – it is less likely they will feel so psychologically angry.

- If you sense any significant threat, or *any* danger, immediately call for a colleague. It is crucial that class teachers call for senior teacher support *immediately* if a parent storms into a classroom and demands an *immediate* audience, or verbally abuses or threatens a class teacher.

- Once the parent is 'calm enough', it will be important to *tune in to how they are probably feeling at that point.* We avoid saying, 'I know how you feel.' (We do not know how they feel.) We can say something like: 'I can see you're really upset about Craig being temporarily suspended from school, Mrs Whinger ...' If the parent butts in ('... too f___ing right!!') and wants to begin another tirade, it will help to wait for the next 'break in the psychological traffic'. We can then repeat, 'Mrs Whinger ... I can see you're upset and angry ... please take a seat.'

- Reassure the parent that we know they care. This is important; we know (ourselves) that this is what would drive us as a parent in any similar situation. 'Mrs Whinger, I know you care about Craig. So do we ... You wouldn't be here if you didn't care ...' This may well be the 'door' that opens to a more positive communication.

- If the parent has directly sworn at us, or used threatening swearing about us, or other staff, it will be important to *briefly* make the point: 'Mrs Whinger, I'm not swearing at you, I don't expect (or 'want' or 'like it when ...') you swear at me. As I said, I know you care about ... We're here to try to help and support ... We can do this without swearing and accusing.' If we say nothing about their swearing (or hostile language), it in effect excuses, or discounts, their behaviour. We acknowledge their anger, we do not – however – have to accept, or merely 'tolerate' their swearing. On these occasions, I believe we need to be quietly, *briefly* and calmly assertive and move on.

- Focus – then – on the issue of concern. Keep the focus on the issue; avoid getting overly involved in 'what happened at the other 15 schools(!)', or 'what happened with the other teacher last year(!)', or ....

- Yes, we have to listen to a parent's concern (however skewed, confused, misinformed, or – even – frivolous) yet it is important to address the issue within the school's policy (relative to the issue). While it is always important that a parent knows that they will be heard and that they will always have an appropriate right-of-reply, we do not need to *defend* the school's behaviour policy, or defend what we believe about aggression, bullying, or racism or … We keep the focus on the central, core rights and responsibilities relative to the issue at hand.

- Get the facts about the issue or concern (or have them ready at hand wherever possible). It can help to have it in writing from (we hope) reliable records. This will aid clarity and focus.

- We should seek to be honest as well as caring; not hiding the unpleasant details but not attacking the character of their child (or the parent!) tempting as that might be on occasion!). We work towards a solution that will address the issue *in light of the student and the parents, and the school's rights and responsibilities.*

- It may sound obvious, but it is important to avoid taking a querulous or argumentative *stance* (even if we think we are right on 'all this …'). It is still tempting though!

- When we invite early support to parents, it can often minimise (or eliminate) messy and often inaccurate disclosures in the public domain (local gossip, the press, the media).

- There are (again rare) occasions when a parent will *continue* to vent, vilify, accuse or threaten despite our calmness and our cueing of care and concern. On these occasions, it is wise to direct the parent to leave, calmly, clearly, firmly, assertively. Some parents, when they arrive on school property, may be affected by alcohol or drugs and unable to effectively control thought or speech. Some are so driven by an insistent passion for misguided justice that they will refuse to see anything beyond their emotive state. Some parents are simply bullies. Either way, it is pointless trying to reason with them – at least for now.

  It is pointless trying to engage a parent when they continue to stand and threaten. Hold up a 'blocking hand': '… Mrs Whinger, I want you to leave now. NOW. I'm not prepared to continue with this while you're swearing at me and threatening me.' If you can also get in the words, '… When you've calmed down ring and make a time to talk …' – do so. If not, show them the door.

  If they refuse to leave (it sometimes happens!), walk out yourself; they will most likely follow (by now a colleague will have appeared to give support). As they leave, they may well still be chanting their mantra, 'You bunch of gutless bastards; I'm taking Justin out of this shit, f___ing school!! I'm going to tell the Department about you, you f___ing a___hole …!!'

- If any teacher has been on the receiving end of a disturbing – or dysfunctional – parent tirade, it will always help to debrief with colleagues before leaving school that day. Many schools (these days) have internal policy guidelines on managing parental concerns, complaints and crises. Such policies will normally reflect the sorts of approaches my colleagues and I have raised here in this chapter.

Caveat

There are occasions when a parent's behaviour is so bizarre, so threatening or potentially dangerous that we will need to contact the police. Schools – normally – have good relationships with their local community policing team. No teacher should have to be the victim of continual threats, haranguing or harassment. Even on these (thankfully rare) occasions, we would normally contact the parents – later – and invite them to another meeting. The messy business of restraining orders on some parents (regarding visiting a school) are also (thankfully) rare. Our overriding concern on these occasions is the safety and welfare of our students and our colleagues.

> ### Editor's note
> None of this is easy to describe – in print. When we talk about the natural tension between *our* calmness and our assertion when addressing angry parents, it is not easy to describe it without sounding tendentious, patronising or pompous. Yet it is this – precisely – we do not want to communicate. It is one thing to say 'we need to be calm in such situations …' – we do; it is communicating our calmness in such a way that is likely to *enable the other* (child or adult) to cue potential calmness in themselves. Perspective-taking (how would we want to be 'treated'?) is at the heart of how we behave towards others.

Chapter 8

Narratives: How Teachers' Stories Connect Us, Support Us, Encourage Us and Enable Us as Teachers

Sharn Donnison

> *Sharn Donnison has written a thought-provoking essay on narratives in the teaching profession: their place, their purpose, their effect. Sharn's essay encourages us to consider the place of reflection inherent in our narrative journey. Such reflection within – and from the narrative – enables us to gain meaning from what happens to us as we interact with, and teach, our children. Such stories further enable our professional encouragement and growth.*

Stories

Stories have surrounded us from our earliest years. They have formed the warp and woof of the fabric of our lives. As children, we sat in silent rapture as we were transported to another time and place by the stories of our culture and cultures less familiar. For some, it was Sunday School stories of floods, famines and a baby born in a manger. For others, it was stories of conquerors and heroes, goblins and ghouls. These stories enriched our imaginations and added to the storehouse of our knowledge. Now, as adults, the narratives of movies, television shows, books and magazines, advertisements, photos and news reports become our daily reality. We have formed the stories that we have told, and those stories have formed us. They have become us and we have become them. Like the Borg in the television story, *Star Trek*, we are 'assimilated'.

The purpose of this essay is to provide a framework by which to understand and reflect on the stories in this book. I draw particularly upon the work of Stephen Preskill (1998) who has identified five narrative types. Bruner (1996) maintains that there is one prime rule for all narratives. He suggests that there should be a reason for it that distinguishes it from silence. Preskill's narrative types provide five reasons as to why the silence is broken by teachers' stories. The following reflects on some of the stories in this book in terms of Preskill's five narrative types. I also draw upon the stories that surround us in our world to explain and exemplify these narrative types.

Narratives as representations of reality

Jerome Bruner (1996) acknowledges the link between ourselves and our stories. He suggests that narratives are representations of reality. They are not merely fabricated stories meant to amuse or entertain, but are encapsulated fragments of what people find real and meaningful in their worlds. It is, as Bartlett explains, People are still longing for a story because they are still longing for meaning (in Wall, 2000). In this sense, narratives are active and not just passive retellings of events gone by. They are a way of making meaning out of the experiences of everyday life, of visualising the world, organising the past and explaining the present. They help one identify, create and justify one's place in the world.

As the embodiment of beliefs, values, fears, hopes and dreams, narratives become precious and meaningful. They are one's private experiences of the world. When narrating these stories, that private world becomes a public utterance (Cohen and Shires, 1988). In sharing their stories, the teachers in this book not only mediate their private experiences to make them publicly known, but also proffer themselves. As such, their stories are precious. They are gifts offered in trust. In each of these teachers' narratives, they paint a picture of who they are, what they deem important and how they relate to the world. In Langellier's words, 'in a most profound way, our stories tell us who we are and who we can – or cannot – be, at both surface and deep level meaning' (1989: 267).

Narratives as representations of culture

As well as being a vehicle for the presentation of self, each story expresses an element of the teaching culture. They are, as Bruner (1996) declares, signposts to what is culturally relevant. They provide a window through which one can glimpse the teacher's world and contribute to an understanding of what it takes to be a good teacher. Preskill (1998) acknowledges this. He offers that teachers narratives are guides to the challenges, adversities and wonders of educating children and that each narrative offers a vicarious experience of life in the classroom:

> The protagonists in these narratives grapple with all of the difficulties that make teaching in contemporary schools so daunting, but their stories highlight the imagination and commitment of teachers who see possibility in the most trying of circumstances. They reaffirm the role that teachers can play in humanising and democratising students and in unleashing their ability to make a difference in the world. (1998: 344)

While teachers' narratives are of general public interest, practising and pre-service teachers especially respond to narratives of the classroom. This is particularly true of pre-service teachers who thirst for 'real' classroom stories. These stories encourage and fuel their sense of purpose and provide them with an experience of the classroom, however vicarious. For the veteran teacher, these stories are vehicles through which they can interconnect and reflect on their own practice.

Types of narrative

Preskill's five narrative types are essentially the identification of five different 'plots'. A plot is the result of action taken in regard to events. Actions have reasons and what people (in this sense) do does not happen merely by chance. Beliefs, thoughts, values, desires and theories motivate their actions. A narrative combines motivated action in response to an event to form a 'plot'. Preskill's work on teachers' stories is valuable in understanding the motivated actions which keep the teacher coming to work five days a week, 42 weeks a year.

Bourdieu (1991) would refer to teachers' stories as their cultural capital. They are the wealth that teachers possess in the form of their knowledge, ideas, attitudes and values. Preskill has categorised this cultural capital into five particular types of narratives:

- the narrative of social criticism
- the narrative of apprenticeship
- the narrative of reflective practice
- the narrative of journey
- the narrative of hope.

Not all narratives fit neatly into a particular category. Some narratives, such as that by Elizabeth McPherson, can be understood on different levels. So the story of Luke is about a teacher's journey of discovery into understanding the mind of a small boy and yet is also a narrative of hope where she expresses a sense of wonder at the life that is being transformed before her eyes (p. 11f)

The narrative of social criticism

The narrative of social criticism is about redressing an imbalance – this can be socio-economic, racial, gender or ability. Commonly, in Australian teacher-training programmes, pre-service teachers are encouraged to be professionally critical of education systems and practices. This is frequently done through subjects which offer an introductory understanding of education and which critically reflect on the history, practices, culture and aims of education. Preskill observes that pre-service teachers are often unaware of the role that education has played in maintaining social inequities. While they tend to focus on the importance of educating young minds and providing a safe and secure environment for intellectual growth, they are often unaware that schools are also places where all children should be valued, respected and given the opportunity to overcome disadvantage.

There are many teachers' narratives in the popular media which critique school and social practices. These narratives of social criticism focus on issues, both historical and contemporary, that prevent schools from fulfilling their mandate. *To Sir With Love* (Braithwaite, 1959) is a story about a black engineer who is forced to take a job in a rough London school. While the story chronicles Mr Thackery's journey of self-discovery, it also investigates the effects of low socio-economic status on life opportunities. This rookie teacher gradually becomes aware of how social circumstances have disadvantaged his students. This knowledge compels him eventually to undertake affirmative action to redress the situation.

The movie *Stand and Deliver* (Dir. Menendez, 1988) presents a similar scenario. Mr Escalante is a brilliant and inspirational high school mathematics teacher who motivates and encourages his low-achieving, East Los Angeles *barrio* students to overcome social stigma and disadvantage. This story focuses on the assumptions and biases held by mainstream authorities about disadvantaged children. Escalante's compassion for these students motivates them to pass the Advanced Placement Calculus Test – a feat unheard of in the history of the school.

Likewise, in her story, 'Alex wins a race', Karen Kearney (p. 37f) tells the story of Alex – a young adolescent with learning disabilities and a lack of motivation. It is her insights into Alex's interests and her actions to motivate him that open up a world of opportunities for the Year 6 student. Without her efforts to redress an imbalance, Alex would never have had the opportunity to conquer his fears and 'go for gold'. Narratives of social criticism play an important role in highlighting and supporting the principles of social justice and equity.

The narrative of apprenticeship

The narrative of apprenticeship is about teacher discipleship or mentoring. One of the earliest examples of this form of narrative is the story of how Jesus Christ trained his twelve disciples to follow in His footsteps. After a three-year apprenticeship period of studying his methods and pedagogy, these 12 men then undertook their own teaching ministry. Without their teacher's support and encouragement, these 12 men would not have gone on to change philosophical and theological thought in the Western world.

Similarly, pre-service teachers in their university-based lessons are exposed to the theories and practices of schools. While this is deemed valuable, it is also recognised that field training is essential. Throughout their training period, pre-service teachers are stationed with an experienced practising teacher in an attempt to be apprenticed into the system. While most Australian universities continue to adopt the two to three weeks per semester practicum, others have recognised the value of prolonged exposure to real teachers in real classrooms and have adopted internship programmes. These 'interns' are stationed with an experienced teacher for a complete semester and gain the invaluable experience of day-to-day life in the classroom over a complete school term.

Louanne Johnson's (1993) autobiography has elements of this form of narrative. Louanne's story is that of another 'neophyte' teacher being challenged by unruly and riotous high school students. She relates her trials and tribulations as she seeks to conquer their rebellion and fire their enthusiasm. It is partially through the nurturing, support and encouragement of co-workers that she finds the strength and motivation to continue in her efforts. Narratives of apprenticeship are valuable as they explicate the teacher's journey from novicehood to effective practitioner.

The narrative of reflective practice

The narrative of reflective practice is inherent within all teachers' stories. Teachers are, or should be, reflective. The importance of being a reflective practitioner is emphasised throughout pre-service training. Trainee teachers are required to examine and critique their practice, their thinking and their effectiveness. While this skill is nurtured and fostered in teacher training institutions, it is in the field that this skill is fully developed. The practising teacher engages in reflection throughout the school day: in how their lessons are planned, implemented and evaluated; in how they interact with the children, staff and parents; and in how effective and socially just they are. It is through this reflective practice that the teacher identifies inadequacies and improves their practice. This is particularly evident in Louanne's story. She continually reflects on her inadequate teaching practices and inability to gain the attention and focus of the class. Being aware that these students will not respond to conventional teaching and behaviour management strategies, she adopts an unconventional approach that is particularly student-centred.

The stories in this book are all narratives of reflection. Larry Taylor's story about Tom (p. 34f) is an illustration of teacher reflection in practice. Larry contemplates the strategy he used to understand the animosity that had developed between himself and his student. It is careful reflection on the child's response to the strategy and his own willingness to take a risk that enables Larry to come to a more complete understanding of their relationship. Likewise, Elizabeth McPherson's story of Luke (p. 11f) demonstrates the cognitive processes that a teacher continually engages in to understand the complexities of a child. It was the dawning realisation that fear and insecurity were driving forces in Luke's life that prompted Elizabeth to modify her attitude and behaviour towards this child.

The narrative of journey

The narrative of reflection is also evident in the narrative of journey, for without reflection, growth and change cannot occur. These narratives are autobiographical and highlight how the teacher grows and changes throughout their years of teaching. These narratives will frequently express the highs and lows, the trials and tribulations of teaching, as the teacher comes to a new understanding of their role as they travel along the path of their teaching journey.

'My Global Classroom' by Peter D'Angelo (p. 15f) is representative of this form of narrative. It speaks of his journey as a new language teacher in the suburbs of multicultural Melbourne. As we follow along in his journey, we witness his struggles to communicate with the students, and his growing revelation of his own prejudices and assumptions. His journey as a teacher became a journey of self-discovery.

While Peter's story is evidently one of journey, the narratives already mentioned also depict journeys travelled. Mr Thackery's journey of discovery in *To Sir With Love* (Braithwaite, 1959) involves learning some enduring lessons about his sense of commitment and the value of people and relationships. For Elizabeth McPherson, her journey entailed an understanding of the meaning of love and compassion.

The narrative of hope

The fifth of Preskill's narrative types is the 'narrative of hope'. This narrative accentuates optimism and imagination and a sense of wonder as foundations for good education. Pre-service teachers commonly have a sense of wonder about the teaching profession. Their idealism and exuberance is evident in their discussions and classroom activities. It is folklore that as the young recruit becomes more entrenched in the system, this idealism and wonder gives way to cynicism and pragmatism. Practising teachers who still evince a sense of optimism about their profession are sometimes seen as 'an anomaly'. This cynicism is reflected in teachers' practice and expectations for their students.

Robin Williams' role as John Keating in *Dead Poets Society* (Dir. Weir, 1989) is an example of a 'teacher anomaly'. Although he is surrounded by conservatism and ingrained practice, he embodies all that is fresh, new and exciting in teaching. He imparts his enthusiasm for learning to his students and encourages them to abandon tradition and venture out into the unknown.

Peter D'Angelo, too, evinces a narrative of hope. His story captures a sense of optimism and enthusiasm. Even after many years of teaching, his belief in the value of education as a life-changing force is evident. He notes that education is about instilling dignity and worth and from his words we can gather that he sees this as the noblest of pursuits.

To conclude

Stephen Preskill's five narrative types provide a valuable tool for analysing teachers' narratives. The stories in this book appear, at first reading, to be simple reflections of life in the classroom. However, through applying his framework, it becomes apparent that the stories deal with disparate and various aspects of a teacher's life, work and relationships (see, particularly, Chapter 6 in this book).

The particular narratives in this book have provided insight into the lives and cultures of our teachers. Whatever the narrative, be it that of social criticism, hope, journey, reflection or apprenticeship, these stories have offered a glimpse into what is important and valuable in the lives of our educators.

First and foremost, teachers are people, but it is their evident commitment to service and their ability to reflect on who they are and what they do that differentiates them. This ability to reflect ensures that teachers are and will continue to be agents of change. These stories tell of the lives that have been touched and changed. As Bill Rogers notes in his contribution, 'We can't predict where our children may end up' (p. 5). Who knows where these individuals have trod and what impact they have had on society? And while we can but wonder about Alex, Luke, Trung, Rebecca, Talia or Tom, those teachers who have touched their lives can know that in some small way, they made a difference.

Conclusion

The art of balancing: in the daily grind – a teacher's welfare

In his poem *Ulysses*, Tennyson muses on the burden of leadership: '... I mete and dole unequal laws unto a savage race, that hoard and sleep and feed and know not me ...'. He then suggests, however, that:

'... some work of noble note may yet be done.
Tho' much is taken, much abides, and tho' we are not now that strength which
In old days moved heaven and earth ...'[1]

I read this as a teacher (not, of course, that we manage and lead a 'savage race'!). We can all remember that first and early vigour, energy, enthusiasm and motivation at the start of our teaching career. As the years progress, we may sometimes feel (like Tennyson) that 'much is taken ...' and that '... we are not now that strength which in the old days moved heaven and earth ...'. 'Much is taken ...' over the days, months and years. There is the natural stress of it all, what Shakespeare's Hamlet calls 'The thousand natural shocks that flesh is heir to ...'[2]

It is the wearing down of it all. Whenever I talk with non-teachers about our profession, they invariably raise our 'short hours', our 'fantastic holidays'(!). How many times have we had to 'defend' those misconceptions? If they only knew, (although I am sure many of the parents of our more challenging students know how demanding it is spending a third of one's waking day with their children.)

Teaching is a rewarding profession – no question; it is also very demanding, taxing and naturally requires multi-tasking. The *natural* stress of relating to many

---

1. Alfred, Lord Tennyson (1842) wrote the poem *Ulysses*. This poem is, of course, about Odysseus and his journeying back to Ithaca (his kingdom) after the fall of Troy. I have taken poetic (and metaphorical) licence with the poem. Ulysses is the Latinised name for Homer's Odysseus.
2. In *Hamlet*: in the most well-known of his soliloquies, Act 3:1: 62.

children with varying needs, and to have the professional responsibility for their educational development, also occasion our *natural* concern. Most teachers have significant goodwill, generosity of spirit, commitment to each of their children *beyond* their formal role as teacher. It is always that aspect of the teacher–student relationship that children remember as reflective adults; that their teachers cared.

Teaching is a profession that can eat up the margins of our lives; there is *always* more we can do. It is also crucial – however – that we consider our personal welfare – within our role. We need to do this not out of mere self-interest but because it is necessary; it is right. Getting a *reasonable* balance between the formal demands of our role and those demands we place on ourselves as teachers. Then there are the elements we need to balance between work, home, family ... this is not easy.

In his book *The Road Less Travelled*[3], the psychiatrist Scott-Peck (1990) notes that 'Balancing is the discipline that gives us flexibility. Extraordinary flexibility is required for successful living' (p. 66).

We have to 'balance'; we have no choice – that is the very nature of our living and work. To enhance a healthier, more realistic 'balance', we need to revisit areas of personal, relational and professional needs from time to time.

- We *need* our 'holidays'. We need time for body, mind and soul to repair, to recreate. This is – in part – what is meant by *recreation*.
- We need time for personal professional reflection as well as collegial reflection on what we do as teachers. Teaching is a *busy* profession – we need to value, and make time for, personal and collegial reflection.

    In working with colleagues in colleague mentoring, we have had extremely valuable discussions based on mutual classroom 'observation' and feedback in team-teaching sessions. An opportunity for professional self-awareness in a climate of elective professional trust. How many times do we ask 'How aware am I of my *characteristic* behaviour as a teacher? *Non-judgemental* peer mentoring can enable such reflection and growth as a teacher (Rogers, 2002a).
- An interesting hypothetical question we sometimes ponder is: 'Would I like to be a student in a class where I was the teacher?' Bad day notwithstanding!
- We need to 'let off steam' from time to time, without vilifying, shafting or maliciously labelling our students. Staffroom 'off-loading' is healthy, necessary; it is a form of 'moan-bonding'. Sometimes the off-loading is enough; at other times, it needs to move towards reflection, analysis and action. One of the least helpful comments in a staffroom is 'I don't have a problem with ... (a particular student or class).' This is a deflating comment. Even if true, it hardly helps the colleague who is struggling with Jason, or 6B, or 8D. Further, it is likely to inhibit a colleague seeking necessary support. We can be quite self-recriminating as a profession (honest self-reflection and willingness to change is

---

3. *The Road Less Travelled* (1990) by M. Scott-Peck, published by Hutchinson and Co., London.

different). We have our bad days, sometimes very bad days. We do not effectively always reach every child; we reach many. We have learned not to blame – or berate – ourselves for what we cannot do.

■ We naturally whinge and complain in our profession (student behaviour, *some* parents, our workload, 'The Department' ...). There is a big difference between the 'whinge' that makes things worse, the dissenting and the divisive whingeing, and that 'whinge' that affirms, alerts, acknowledges and can lead to something *we* can do about it. I rather like the term I have heard in some schools: 'moan-bonding'. After all, the etymology of whinge is effectively the combination of whining and cringing; 'moan-bonding' sounds more positive.

■ Frustration and anger are natural; at times they are healthy and *right*. It is right, it is just to get angry at significant injustice, intolerance, abuse, bullying, racism, sexism ... As teachers, we have had to learn to communicate our anger constructively. To assert and not aggress. Sometimes, it is right to assert unambiguously in 'the emotional moment'; at other times, we may need to restrain ourselves, have cool-off time and then make our point clearly and calmly. There is a balance, even in our communication of anger. The *feeling* of anger never tells us what to *do*. The communication of anger with some clarity and justice is a learned behaviour. It is an element of will, and skill, that can be learned (p. 161–65).

■ At times we will *feel* helpless, we will *feel* a failure. There are times we will feel momentarily helpless. There is no shame in this – it, too, is normal. *Feeling* a failure does not mean we *are* a failure, it does mean we have failed *in a given instance*. Forgiving ourselves (and others) is crucial in contrast to 'mentally kicking ourselves' and indulging in recurrent self-blame (pp. 9, 120).

■ Colleague support is a significant factor in 'keeping the balance', particularly when we feel stretched, confused, unfocused, worn down by it all. The moral support of our colleagues – those in the 'same boat' – is consistently noted in the research as highly valued (Rogers, 2002a)[4]. As basic as a shared coffee, a word of reassurance, the note in the pigeon-hole, the flowers when you have been away sick, a colleague taking a difficult child to their class for 10–15 minutes to give you (and your class) a breather, through to the off-loading, moan-bonding and to those times of shared planning and problem-solving.

One primary school's in-house norm is that 'the difficult student in our school is a difficult student for all'. Contrast this with the staffroom comment, 'Do you know what *your* Jason did in the playground!?' Our colleagues can and do encourage, affirm, assure. At times, though, we will have to ask for support from our colleagues because they may not 'know'.

■ It is important to remember that there are many factors we cannot control in

---

4. I Get By With a Little Help (2002) by B. Rogers, published by A.C.E.R. Press, Melbourne.

our profession, within the children's home environment: family dysfunction; substance abuse; neglect; poor diet; structural poverty; long-term unemployment ... When we focus on what *we* can do at *our* school, the natural stress is more realistically focused. Nor can we control 'the Department' and its mandates. We can control *our response as a school* to 'the Department'; we can decide what we will do, where we can do it – *in our school, in our class, with our students.* We can manage external mandates rather than merely letting them manage us!

■   A crucial factor in 'the balance of it all' is paying some attention to our personal physical health, and the reasonably basic things we can do. Even a basic walking routine several times a week, the fruit, veggies and water will help (we all know what we should be doing *most* of the time!)

In Shakespeare's Henry VI, there is a passage that (to me) nicely sums up this 'balance' of time, work, recreation and rest:

> To carve out dials ... thereby to see the minutes – how they run. How many makes the hour full complete. How many hours bring about the day. How many days will finish up the year ...
> So many hours must I tend my flock.
> So many hours must I take my rest.
> So many hours must I contemplate.[5]

These lines could almost have been written for a teacher. We needs must balance time over 'our flock', 'our rest', even 'our contemplation'.

We do our best, then, to balance the natural stresses and demands of our profession and the normal 'wear and tear':

> 'that which we are, we are; one equal temper of heroic hearts, Made weak by time and fate, but strong in will, To strive, to seek, to find and not to yield' (Tennyson, *Ulysses*).

How many days till the end of term?

---

5. Shakespeare 3 Henry VI II. v. 24–40.

Epilogue

The nineteenth-century novelist George Eliot (Mary Ann Evans) was once asked if she was a pessimist or an optimist.

'I am neither,' came the reply, 'I am a meliorist.' (cited in Potter, 1950).

I had to look up the meaning of meliorist. In *The Oxford Reference Dictionary*, its meaning is noted as, 'A doctrine that the world may be made better by human effort.' It does not say, 'made perfect ...' – better is possible.

In re-reading these essays – and reflecting on them yet again – I suspect that this might be the settled response of the teachers here. We are 'meliorists'.

I know I am a 'meliorist' – someone who believes that the world (and our little bit of it: Jason, Dean, Bilal, Tran, Melissa, Rebecca – 4C, 8D, 10E ... our class, our school) *may be improved by persistent, practical, human effort.*

Each of these teachers has enabled their students to feel special, to feel positive and more secure about themselves and their place in their world. They have encouraged their students to see the best in themselves and have sought to enable them as learners to take conscious and thoughtful control of their learning and behaviour.

These teachers showed continuing respect and affirming for their students, even in the face of difficult, challenging, disruptive and hostile behaviours; they didn't give up, or give in. While not ignoring or 'playing down' (or to) their inappropriate and disruptive behaviour, they taught their students different and better pathways, gave new options. They gave guidance, direction, support and hope. In these teachers – at least – the young people found adults who believed in them and who helped them belong and grow.

They won't forget these teachers. Nor will their parents.

In a sense, there is no 'conclusion' to a book like this. There will always be teachers like these, here, who have shared themselves – and their teaching journey – with us. Thank God that there are teachers like this in our schools.

I hope their accounts will continue to encourage the kind of teaching, and humanity, they have shared with us.

Appendix: Nick's Individual Behaviour Management Plan

Musgrave Hill State School

Nick's goal behaviours

- Follow teacher's directions ⎫
- Work quietly on task ⎬ Each of these behaviours has been discussed and
- Keep hands and feet to self ⎭ rehearsed.
- Use the computer only when given permission

Acknowledgements for Nick's goal achievement

- Whole-class acknowledgement system (personal points/group points)
- Each smiley face = 1 stamp
- 10 stamps = 15 minutes on computer or 30 minutes in Middle Brumby

Proactive strategies

1. Breakfast programme: Mum takes scooter to classroom and Nick goes straight to the office for breakfast and his medication.
2. Family is seeking interagency support.
3. Ring Nanny with good news or to calm himself down with her.
4. Modified programme – attached. (Collegial support from Support Teacher Learning Difficulties.)
5. Learning support assistance.
6. Chaplain/Counsellor (Rock and Water programme).
7. Seasons Programme – issues from parents' divorce.
8. Use computer for writing because of fine motor issue.
9. Chill out place – in reading corner of his own choice.
10. Wear glasses.
11. PALS – Positive Approach To Life Situations Programme (Griffith University Gold Coast Programme).
12. Teach class to ignore his inappropriate behaviour (while Nick was not present).
13. Build in time with Junior Stage reading teacher from 10–10.30 a.m.
14. Allow take-up time.
15. Mother has agreed to respond to phone calls from school.

Consequences plan

Re-issue direction:

'Nick, you need to (e.g. keep your hands and feet to yourself).' Allow take-up time by moving away and doing something else for a minute.

Complies: 'Good choice, Nick. Well done.' (Reinforce with smiley face for following directions.)

Does not comply: 'Nick, you have chosen not to (e.g. keep your hands and feet to yourself). You are now on Marker 1.'

I have had this document explained to me and I agree with the contents.
Date _____

_____   _____   _____   _____

Appropriate behaviour in the classroom – positive reinforcement system.

Inappropriate behaviour – direction given – Where are you? Where do you want to be? How do you find your way back?

1 Inappropriate behaviour continues – direction and choice given.

2 Inappropriate behaviour continues – move to Reading Corner. S re-enters by saying 'I'm ready to come back now'.

3 Inappropriate behaviour continues – ring deputy principal, student to deputy principal.

4 Inappropriate behaviour continues – parent informed.

5 Total refusal to comply or aggression – removal of S to admin or removal of class and teacher using red card system. Repair and rebuild. Parent informed.

There is always a way back.

On Marker 1

'Nick, you are on Marker 1. You have the choice to (e.g. keep your hands and feet to yourself) or go to Marker 2, which is the Reading Corner for 5 minutes' (cool-off time/reflection time).

Complies: 'A responsible choice, Nick. Well done.' (Reinforce with smiley face for following directions.)

Does not comply: 'Nick, you have chosen not to (keep your hands and feet to yourself). You are showing me that you have chosen the Reading Corner.'

On Marker 2

'Nick, you need to go quietly to the Reading Corner. This is a thinking time to help you make better choices. If you cannot do that, I will need to ring Mrs Smart, and she will ring your mother.'

Complies: After Nick has settled, encourage him: 'Well done for going to the Reading Corner.' Nick sits quietly for 5 minutes. The timer will ring when the 5 minutes is up. Nick returns to his work.

Does not comply: 'Nick, you are showing me that I need to ring Mrs Smart. You need to go to the office.'

On Marker 3

Complies: Nick goes to the office.

Does not comply: Mrs Smart phoned who will advise mother of Nick's behaviour.

On Marker 4

Complies: Nick goes to the office.

Does not comply: Mother will be phoned again to collect Nick.

Re-entry

From Reading Corner:	– own choice
	– no comments made (i.e. the teacher does not start a conversation with the child …).
From Mrs Smart/Mr Marsh: after a session	– Nick needs to say, 'I'm ready to go back.'
	– Teacher to acknowledge by giving a nod.
	– No verbal comment – no judgement – no negative emotions.

Summary of consequences plan

Re-issue direction

Marker 1   Last warning

Marker 2   Time-out (5 min) in the classroom

Marker 3   Time-out in office and phone call to parent
Marker 4   Another phone call to parent and Nick collected to go home
            If necessary suspension or exclusion will be implemented.

Class Teacher	**Student**
Parent	**Parent**

Editor's postscript

When listed on a single page like this, Nick's plan and the teacher's verbal cueing looks a little 'clinical' (in a behaviourist sense). In reality, it was not like that at all. As in all the behaviour plans noted in this text (particularly Chapter 3), the teachers' inter-actions are always grounded in the positive relationships that they developed with their students. Even the use of the verb 'comply' sounds overly behaviourist(!). Again, in reality, these teachers have developed a positive, warm and caring relationship with Nick. Where they have had to discipline Nick (including time-out), they have been decisive and firm, but always encouraging.

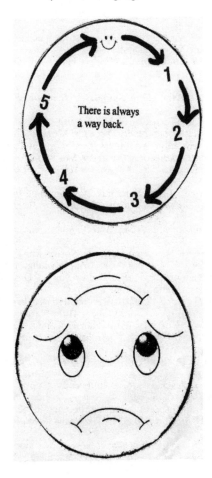

Bibliography

Adler, A. (1957) *Understanding Human Nature*. New York: Fawcett.

Aristotle (1969) *The Ethics of Aristotle* (*The Nichomachean Ethics*) (Trans. J.A.K. Thomson). London: Penguin Classics [Aristotle's other books on Ethics are the *Eudaimonian Ethics* and the *Magna Moralia*].

Aurelius, M. (1980) *The Meditations of Marcus Aurelius* (Trans. G. Long). Grolier, CT: The Harvard Classics.

Bentley, N. (1957) *How Can You Bear to be Human?* London: Penguin.

Bernard, M. (1990) *Taking the Stress Out of Teaching* Melbourne: Collins-Dove.

Bourdieu, P. (1991) *Language and Symbolic Power* (Trans. G. Raymond and M. Adamson). Cambridge: Polity Press.

Braithwaite, E.R. (1959) *To Sir With Love*. London: Bodley Head.

Breheney, C., Mackrill, V. and Grady, N. (1996) *Making Peace at Mayfield: A Whole-School Approach to Behaviour Management*. (Armadale) Melbourne: Eleanor Curtain Publishers.
> This is a book I would strongly encourage colleagues to purchase when they are addressing challenging students and classes within a whole-school approach. This is a book of hope about a school that decided to make a difference in a demanding and difficult social environment where hostility, suspicion, poor communication, conflict – even violence – was a recurrent pattern. It shows how a whole-school approach can and does work.

Brophy, J. (1983) Research on the self-fulfilling prophecy and teacher expectations. *Journal of Educational Psychology*, 75: 631–61.

Brophy, J. (1985) Teacher–student interactions. In J. Dusek (ed.), *Teacher Expectations*. Hillside, NJ: Erlbaum Press.

Brophy, J. (1986) Teacher behaviour and student achievement. In M.C. Wittrock (ed.), *Handbook of Research on Teaching*. New York: Macmillan.

Brophy, J. and Good, T.L. (1986) Teacher behaviour and student achievement. In M.C. Wittrock (ed.), *Handbook of Research on Teaching*. New York: Macmillan.

Bruner, J. (1996) *The Culture of Education*. Cambridge: Harvard University Press.

Clough, P., Pardeck, J.T. and Yuen, F. (eds) (2005) *Handbook of Emotional and Behavioural Difficulties*. London: Sage.

Cohen, S. and Shires, L.M. (1988) *Telling Stories: A Theoretical Analysis of Narrative Fiction*. London: Routledge.

Cooper, P. (1997) The reality and hyperreality of AD/HD and educational and cultural analysis. In P. Cooper and K. Ideus (eds), *Attention Deficit/Hyperactivity Disorder: Medical, Educational and Cultural Issues* (2nd revised edition). East Sutton: The Association of Workers for Children with Emotional and Behavioural Difficulties.

Coopersmith, S. (1967) *The Antecedents of Self-Esteem*. San Francisco, CA: Freeman.

Crawford, D., Bodine, R. and Hoglund, R. (1993) *The School for Quality Learning*. Champaign, IL: Research Press.

Cummings, C. (1989) *Managing to Teach*. Edmonds, WA: Teaching Inc. Publishing.

Dreikurs, R. (1968) *Psychology in the Classroom: A Manual for Teachers* (2nd edition). New York: Harper and Row.

Dreikurs, R., Grunwald, B. and Pepper, F. (1982) *Maintaining Sanity in the Classroom* (2nd edition). New York: Harper and Row.

Erickson, E. (1970) *Identity, Youth and Crisis*. London: Norton Press.

Frankyl, V. (1985) *Man's Search For Meaning*. New York: Washington Square Press.

Gillborn, D., Nixon, J. and Ruddock, J. (1993) *Dimensions of Discipline: Rethinking Practice in Secondary Schools*. London: Her Majesty's Stationery Office.

Ginott, H. (1971) *Teacher and Child: A Book for Parents and Teachers*. New York: Macmillan.

Glasser, W. (1986) *Control Theory in Classrooms*. New York: Harper and Row.

Glasser, W. (1992) *The Quality School*. New York: Harper Collins.

Good, T.L. (1995) Teacher expectations. In L.W. Anderson (ed.), *International Encyclopaedia of Teaching and Learning* (2nd edition). Tarrytown, NY: Pergamon Press.

Halonen, J.S. and Santrock, J.W. (1996) *Psychology: Contexts of Behavior*. Madison Dubuque, IA: Brown and Benchmark.

Hatch, S. (2004) Narratives: how teachers' stories connect us, support us and enable us as teachers. In B. Rogers (ed.), *How to Manage Children's Challenging Behaviour*. London: Sage Publications.

Howell, K. (1993) Eligibility and need: is there a difference in being disturbed and being disturbed? In S. Richardson and J. Izard (eds), *Student Behaviour Problems: Positive Initiatives and New Frontiers*. Hawthorn, Victoria: ACER Press.

Johnson, L. (1993) *My Posse Don't Do Homework*. New York: Saint Martin's Press.

Kermode, F. (2000) *Shakespeare's Language*. London: Penguin.

Kyriacou, C. (1986) *Effective Teaching in Schools*. Oxford: Basil Blackwell.

Kyriacou, C. (1991) *Essential Teaching Skills*. London: Basil Blackwell.

Langellier, K.M. (1989) Personal narratives: perspectives on theory and research. *Text and Performance Quarterly*, 9: 243–76.

Lindon, J. (2005) *Understanding Child Development: Linking Theory and Practice*. London: Hodder-Arnold.

McGrath, H. and Francey, S. (1993) *Friendly Kids, Friendly Classrooms*. Melbourne: Longman.

McInerney, D.M. and McInerney, V. (1998) *Educational Psychology – Constructing Learning* (2nd edition). Sydney: Prentice-Hall.

Maslow, A. (1970) *Motivation and Personality* (2nd edition). New York: Van Nostrand Reinhold.

Menendez, R. (Director) (1988) *Stand and Deliver* [Film]. USA: Warner Brothers.

Mussen, P. and Rosenzweig, M.R. (1977) *Psychology: An Introduction*. Lexington, MA: D.C. Heath and Co.

O'Brien, T. (1998) *Promoting Positive Behaviour*. London: David Fulton Publishers.

Preskill, S. (1998) Narratives of teaching and the quest for the second self. *Journal of Teacher Education*, 49(5): 344–57.

Potter, S. (1950) *Our Language*. London: Pelican Books.

Rickard, J. (1994) *Relaxation for Children*. Melbourne: ACER Press.

Robertson, J. (1996) *Effective Classroom Control: Understanding Teacher–pupil Relationships* (3rd edition). London: Hodder and Stoughton.

Rogers, B. (1992) *Supporting Teachers in the Workplace*. Milton, Queensland: Jacaranda Press [In the UK (1996) Managing Teacher Stress, London: Pitman].

Rogers, B. (1994) *Behaviour Recovery: A Whole-school Program for Mainstream Schools*. Melbourne: Australian Council for Educational Research. *The revised edition (2003) addresses EBD behaviours and programmes for addressing challenging and EBD behaviours in mainstream and special school settings. This edition includes many* photocopiable masters *to enable teachers to draw up plans for a range of distracting and disruptive behaviours from calling out and rolling on the mat to badly handled anger.* [In the UK (2004) London: Paul Chapman Publishing.]

Rogers, B. (1996) *Managing Teacher Stress*. London: Pitman.

Rogers, B. (1998) *You Know the Fair Rule and Much More: Strategies for Making the Hard Job of Discipline and Behaviour Management in Schools Easier*. Melbourne: Australian Council for Educational Research. (In the U.K. London: Sage Publications).

Rogers, B. (2002a) *I Get By With a Little Help: Colleague Support in Schools*. Melbourne: Australian Council for Educational Research.

Rogers, B. (ed.) (2002b) *Teacher Leadership and Behaviour Management*. London: Paul Chapman Publishing.

Rogers, B. (2003) *Behaviour Recovery: Practical Programs for Challenging Behaviour*. London: Paul Chapman Publishing. (In Australia – Melbourne: Australian Council for Educational Research).

Rogers, B. (ed.) (2004) *How To Manage Children's Challenging Behaviour*. London: Sage Publications.

Rogers, B. (2006a) *Cracking the Hard Class*. London: Sage Publications. (In Australia – Sydney: Scholastic Books).

Rogers, B. (2006b) *Classroom Behaviour: A Practical Guide to Effective Teaching, Behaviour Management and Colleague Support*. London: Sage.

Rogers, B. and McPherson, E. (2008) *Behaviour Management with Young Children: Crucial Steps with Children 3–7 Years*. London: Sage.

Rogers, C.R. (1959) A theory of therapy, personality and interpersonal relationships as developed in the client-centred framework. In S. Koch (ed.), *Psychology: A Study of a Science. Vol. 3*. New York: McGraw-Hill.

Rosenthal, R. (1973) The Pygmalion Effect lives. *Psychology Today*, September: 56–63.

Rosenthal, R. and Jacobson, L.F. (1967) Teacher expectations for the disadvantaged. *Readings from Scientific American*. San Francisco, CA: W.F. Freeman and Co.

Rosenthal, R. and Jacobson, L. (1986) *Pygmalion in the Classroom*. New York: Holt Rinehart and Winston.

Rutter, M., Maughan, B., Mortimer, P. and Ouston, J. (1979) *Fifteen Thousand Hours*. London: Open Books.

Scott-Peck, M. (1990) *The Road Less Travelled*. London: Arrow Books.

Seligman, M. (1970) On the generality of the laws of learning. *Psychological Review*, 77: 406–18.

Seligman, M. (1975) *Helplessness: On Depression, Development and Death*. San Francisco, CA: W.H. Freeman Press.

Seligman, M. (1991) *Learned Optimism*. Sydney: Random House.

Shaw, G.B. (1913, 1965) *Pygmalion*. London: Penguin Books.

Sprinthall, R.C. and Sprinthall, N.A. (1974) *Educational Psychology: A Developmental Approach*. Wesley, MA: Addison.

Sunday Express (2008) Parents who bully teachers, by Hilary Douglas, 14 September, p. 47.

Wall, D. (2000) The art of the narrative. *Southern Accents*, 23(6): 90–4.

Weir, P. (Director) (1989) *Dead Poets Society* [Film]. USA: Touchstone Pictures.

Wragg, J. (1989) *Talk Sense to Yourself: A Program for Children and Adolescents*. Melbourne: Australian Council for Educational Research.

Author index

Subject index

Added to a page number 'n' indicates notes.